THE GARDEN AND THE FIRE

THE GARDEN AND THE FIRE

HEAVEN AND HELL IN ISLAMIC CULTURE

Nerina Rustomji

COLUMBIA UNIVERSITY PRESS

NEW YORK

Columbia University Press

Publishers Since 1893

New York   Chichester, West Sussex

Copyright © 2009 Columbia University Press

All rights reserved

Library of Congress Cataloging-in-Publication Data

Rustomji, Nerina.

The garden and the fire : heaven and hell in Islamic culture / Nerina Rustomji.

p.   cm.

Includes bibliographical references and index.

ISBN 978-0-231-14084-3 (cloth : alk. paper) — ISBN 978-0-231-51183-4 (ebook)

1. Eschatology, Islamic.   2. Paradise (Islam)   3. Hell—Islam.

4. Philosophy, Islamic.   I. Title.

BP166.8.R87   2008

297.2'3—dc22   2008029681

Columbia University Press books are printed on permanent and durable acid-free paper.

This book is printed on paper with recycled content.

Printed in the United States of America

c 10 9 8 7 6 5 4 3 2 1

for my parents
Aban Hodiwala Rustomji
Purvez Shiavax Rustomji

in memory of evenings
in Quetta gardens

❖ ❖ ❖

CONTENTS

Epilogue
158

LIST OF ILLUSTRATIONS

ACKNOWLEDGMENTS

I HAVE ACCUMULATED many debts while researching and writing this book. A group of scholars, including David Armitage, Dick Bulliet, Kristen Gillespie, Geraldine Heng, Syed Akbar Hyder, Ayesha Jalal, Neil Kamil, Jean Ma, Abd al-Razzaq Moaz, Laura Neitzel, Cindy Postma, Alan Segal, and Denise Spellberg exemplify intellectual support and generosity. They have read drafts at various stages of the project and offered insightful suggestions. Dick Bulliet, Kristen Gillespie, Karen Pinto, Abd al-Razzaq Moaz, Denise Spellberg, and Aban Rustomji provided useful citations. Kristen Gillespie, with wit and vigor, read through the entire manuscript. My anonymous reviewers offered constructive commentary and criticism.

Over the years, I have benefited from the guidance of three mentors. Denise Spellberg helped me discover my interest in traditions of heaven and hell when I was an undergraduate, and her unwavering support over the years has been indispensable to the writing of the book. Since graduate school, Ayesha Jalal has encouraged me to explore the phenomenology of the Islamic otherworld, and her questions and queries have always challenged me to rethink the implications of my arguments. My advisor Dick Bulliet, who has been involved at every stage of the project, helped me expand the scope of my research and refine my argument. At all points of research and writing, I have relished his encouragement, humor, and creativity.

Research for this project has been made possible through Columbia

University's President's Fellowship, Bard College's Research Fund, the American Historical Association's Bernadotte E. Schmitt Grant, St. John's University's Summer Stipend, and the helpful staff at the Bibliothèque Nationale, Bodleian Library, British Library, Cambridge University Library, Columbia University Library, Freer Gallery, Institut Français de Damas, John Rylands Library, New York Public Library, and Royal Asiatic Society Collection. Debra Kolah at Rice University provided much-needed assistance at the final stages of manuscript production.

At Columbia University Press, I would like to thank my editor Wendy Lochner, Christine Mortlock, and Roy Thomas. Wendy Lochner's steadfast support and understanding have been indispensable to the production of the book.

Finally, I would like to express appreciation for my family. To my parents, Aban and Purvez Rustomji, I owe such gratitude that it is inexpressible. My brother Arish's wisdom and humor provide my nourishment. My husband Shehriyar has been my rock who has read numerous drafts, endured my writing at the most inconvenient of times, and helped make our home a happy place to live and work. My son Azad arrived during the final phase of the book, yet his presence has helped me reach new realizations.

The book is written for my parents as a tribute to their sense that life is meant to be lived fully. Some of the best moments of our lives have been spent sitting and enjoying the companionship of family and friends in my grandparents' gardens on lazy summer evenings in Quetta. This book has been inspired by those evenings, which offered the most simple and domestic of earthly paradises.

INTRODUCTION

ARCO POLO once related a fantastic story about a mysterious leader called the Old Man of the Mountain who fooled his adherents into believing that Paradise could be experienced on earth. The story goes that the Old Man built lush palaces encrusted with jewels and surrounded by gardens graced with fountains of honey, milk, wine, and water. The architecture of the palace compound was astoundingly immense, with each level topped by an even more beautiful garden. At the highest level, the Old Man of the Mountain and his devotees reveled in the finest environment and enjoyed sumptuous food. Female companions adorned in gold and silk attended to every desire, and the Old Man of the Mountain provided drugs. Surrounded by pleasure, the adherents believed that the inner complex of the fortress was Paradise itself. It was there within the palace that the Old Man of the Mountain trained his devotees to kill and dispatched them to eliminate his enemies. He promised that once they completed their missions he would permit them to reenter the complex of supreme bliss. Muslims later designated these devotees as *hashishiyya*, or "those who take hashish." Through a subsequent Italian mispronunciation of the name, the killers entered European lore as the "Assassins."[1]

While the story is based on the life of Hasan-i Sabbah, the leader of an offshoot branch of Ismaiʻili Shiʻa who took control of a northern Iranian mountain fortress in 1090, it is undoubtedly legendary. Nonetheless, the possibility that heaven could exist on earth both fascinated and threatened medieval Christian and Muslim writers.[2] In Marco Polo's story, the devotees are deluded into believing that they were already in Paradise. Such a deception would have been easy to comprehend, given that the Old Man of the Mountain's misleading Paradise mirrors the normative Islamic one.

In Islam, heaven and hell are afterworlds where believers and unbelievers can live full, dynamic afterlives. If converting to Islam is a contract with God, then the reward for righteous behavior is the pleasure of heaven and the punishment for wayward behavior is the pain of the hell. Heaven, or *al-janna*, translates to "the Garden," while Hell, or *al-nar*, is "the Fire." Muslims spoke and wrote about the Garden and the Fire as places of existence; and like most places, they were filled with things. In the Garden, there are gardens, rivers, fountains, golden thrones, silk couches, fine food, pure wine, abundant fruit, luxurious carpets, glorious music, eternal virgins, angels, prophets from the Hebrew Bible, and the presence of the God. Rivers of wine, milk, honey, and water flow through heaven where bricks are made of gold and silver, mortar is composed of musk, pebbles consist of pearls and rubies, and soil is pure saffron. In the Fire, there are fetid waters, blazing sparks, a tree with the heads of demons, and enough pus and decay to contaminate the world in a single drop. These depictions originate in the Qur'an, which Muslims believe to be the literal word of God.

This book presents the development of the Garden and the Fire from an early doctrinal innovation introduced in the seventh century to a highly formalized ideal of perfection that the afterworld represented beginning in the twelfth century. By tracing the ways that Muslims have related their lived, earthly lives to the yet to be experienced afterlife, the book focuses on how Muslims imagined their afterworlds over the centuries and how those imaginings often had complicated, multivalent relationships with earthly realities. While unvisited during most lifetimes, the afterworld provided a comparison to this world. Through reflections about the future world, Muslims articulated both the realities that informed their earthly lives and their expectations of the otherworldly conditions that would provide them utter respite in the Garden or intensified toil in the Fire. I argue that the complex relationship between world and afterworld in Islamic history found expression through invocations of material objects and realities of the afterlife. From the seventh century, when the afterlife was introduced as a central doctrine of the new faith, to the twelfth century, when writers of eschatological manuals employed earlier canonized traditions to create fully formed narratives, the afterlife was presented as a world with material conditions that were informed by earthly experiences or expectations. As the image of the afterworld crystallized into metaphors beginning in the twelfth century, the afterlife was more often invoked to describe the ideals of the earthly world as illustrated in the case of the Old

Man of the Mountain and his deceitful Paradise. While the Garden and the Fire began as a potent doctrine with the power to reform religious behavior and complex spaces with intricate relationships with the earthly world, they also transformed into representations of perfection and injustice. Muslims understood heaven and hell through a distinct material culture, and that culture eventually gave shape to an aesthetic vocabulary that could describe realities that exceeded the capacity to articulate the very best and worst of earthly life.

In order to trace the ways that the Garden and the Fire within Sunni Islam transformed over time, this book spans several centuries over seven chapters. The book begins in the seventh century with the advent of the prophet Muhammad's revelations and continues its analysis until the thirteenth century, when the descriptions of the Garden and the Fire adhered to a set narrative form. The book also introduces some of the ways that Muslims used images to represent the Garden on earth from the seventh to the nineteenth centuries. Some of the images are artistic representations of the afterworld, while other sites became reinterpreted and imbued with eschatological significance over time.

Chapter 1, "The Garden, the Fire, and Islamic Origins," questions the governing assumption in Islamic narratives that faith in the afterlife was automatic. By studying Ibn Ishaq's *Sira Rasul Allah,* an eighth-century chronicle of Muhammad's life, it situates Muslims' developing faith in the afterlife in the persecution by and battle with their enemies, the Meccans. Chapter 2, "Visions of the Afterworld," continues the examination of the *Sira Rasul Allah* alongside prophetic traditions (hadiths) and argues that Muhammad's visions during an eclipse and his journey to the heavens reinforced the promise of an afterworld. The chapter suggests that Muhammad's special access to the afterworld encouraged a culture of envisioning the Garden, since certain Muslims began to dream of scenes of the Garden within their earthly lives. After tracing the concept of both the afterlife and afterworld in early Islamic narratives, the book turns to chapter 3, "Material Culture and an Islamic Ethic," which demonstrates how faith in the Garden and the Fire helped formulate an Islamic code of ethics that was linked to the idea of eschatological consequences and the practice of rejecting certain material objects, such as silk and silver vessels. By employing prophetic traditions, the chapter also explores why the majority in hell will be women and how the possibility of intercession links the prophet Muhammad with the behavior of his community.

Chapters 4 and 5 draw on Qur'anic verses and prophetic traditions in order to explore the contours of the afterworld. Chapter 4, "Otherworldly

Landscapes and Earthly Realities," studies the topography and geography of the afterworld through objects, such as fountains, rivers, trees, perfumes, precious metals and stones, animals, and fire. It suggests that descriptions of the Garden and the Fire in the Qur'an were tied to the material realities of the Hijaz region of Arabia; however, traditions expanded Qur'anic descriptions until they acquired other symbolic meanings. Chapter 5, "Humanity, Servants, and Companions," examines the social life of the afterworld by focusing on the transformation of human bodies and the conception of households. It pays particular attention to the tension between replicating family structures and fulfilling individual desires. It also analyzes the retinue of the Garden, which includes servant boys (*wildan* and *ghilman*) and pure female companions (houris) and argues that while they are beings, they, too, were considered material objects of the Garden.

In chapter 6, "Individualized Gardens and Expanding Fires," the book presents later eschatological manuals from the ninth to the thirteenth centuries in order to demonstrate how theologians developed narratives that could be used to reinforce fear of eventual judgment. The chapter also demonstrates how the Garden was seen to be a realm of individual pleasure, which did not include familial companionship, while the Fire expanded in scale so that it was filled with a greater number of demons and forms of punishment. By the twelfth century, both the Garden and the Fire evinced a definite function and architecture. After presenting the developed images of the Garden and the Fire through eschatological manuals, the book explores in the seventh and final chapter, "Legacy of Gardens," the ways that the image of the Garden and the Fire shaped artistic forms. The chapter also considers epistemological concerns about how not to be deceived when trying to perceive the unseen world and surveys some ways that believers could have imagined the Garden through mosque mosaics, illustrated manuscripts, and landscape architecture. One note: the book examines the development of the afterworld for the majority of Muslims, who are Sunni, through an analysis of Arabic and Persian religious texts and images. While the work does not focus on Shi'a, Sufi, and poetic texts, it does make reference to them in relevant chapters.

HEAVEN AND HELL: A COMPARISON

Islamic eschatology provides an after*world*, while Christian eschatology focuses on an after*life*. While some Eastern Christian texts incorporate metaphors of a physical world, Christian texts in general present the quality of future lives through relationships with humans, angels, and the divine. By contrast, Muslims enjoy an afterlife within the parameters of a physically described afterworld. The connotation of "The Garden" and "The Fire" involves spaces or objects more than states of being. The closest approximation that a Christian work ever reaches to the Islamic afterworld is Dante's *Divine Comedy*. Teodolinda Barolini suggests that Dante encourages readers to accept that he is telling the truth when he claims to have visited these places.[3] Ironically, Miguel Asin presents a theory that Dante based his vision of Paradise on a philosophical manual discussing the prophet Muhammad's Ascension and Night Journey to the heavens (*al-isra' wa-l-mi'raj*), when, Muslims believe, the angel Gabriel led Muhammad through the levels of hell and heaven.[4] Even the textual culmination of Christian vision of heaven and hell as places may have been intrinsically shaped by Islamic conceptions of the afterworld.

Beyond the distinction between an afterlife and an afterworld, the Islamic concepts of the Garden and the Fire intimate a closer connection with the material world than the English terms "heaven" and "hell." In the *Oxford English Dictionary*, "heaven" is defined as an expanse by which the sun, moon, and stars can be seen, indicating the notion of the sky above, which is in opposition to the earth below. Heaven is also the region in space where the heavenly bodies move, and so the term is linked with cosmography and astrology. In this sense, heaven is the place for divine beings. Heaven, then, opposes earth in a physical, cosmological, and ontological sense. It is above the earth and the realm of the planets and other celestial objects. It stands apart from the matter and purpose of the earth. Quite simply, heaven is not earth, and it is not for humans. It is the domain of God, God's providence, or the deities of the various pantheons. It is for this reason that heaven stands apart from the location and timeframe of human experience.

"Hell" is more closely identified as a physical site that acts as an abode. It is the place of departed spirits and the infernal regions or "lower world," regarded as a place of existence after death, the grave, or Hades. Since it is part of this world, hell shares attributes with the earthly world. Its identification as the lower world is a metaphor for the grave. In this sense, "hell" appears in the Bible of 1611 as a translation of the Hebrew *sheol*. It also appears as a translation of "grave," "pit," the Greek "Hades," and the Hebrew "Gehenna." The opposition of heaven and earth, then, is one of direction and of substance. Heaven is up there and filled with ether. Hell is down below and filled with the emptiness found below the dirt.

In its earliest conception, all souls rested in the realm of hell because it was the abode of the souls. It is only at a later stage that hell transformed from its neutral locale to one that is charged with a sense of torment, condemned spirits, and punishment for the wicked.[5] In medieval Christian theology, the righteous experienced the glory of Christ in the heavens, while those who did not prove themselves extraordinary were assigned to the lower realms that continued the grit of earthly life: filled with dirt, a certain emptiness, and identification with mortality. Hell is a continuation of life on earth, but heaven is a different state altogether. In heaven, one gains the immortal life like God; in hell, one earns the everlasting taint of mortality. Heaven acts as a transformed state, not an actual locale.

Unlike the terms "heaven" and "hell," *al-janna* and *al-nar* operate in different semantic fields. They are simultaneously places and things. One can walk into the Garden or the Fire. There are also several traditions in which the Garden and the Fire are animated beings. They act as beasts or at least form a classification of God's creatures. Yet, when the Garden and the Fire are promised, it is their spatial dimensions that are invoked. A preacher is once to have said: "O people of eternity and perpetuity. You were not created to be destroyed; you were created only for eternal existence. You will merely be transferred from one house to another, from the womb to the world, from this world to the grave, from the grave to the Judgment, from the Judgment to eternal existence in either the Garden or the Fire."[6] The idea of location is emphasized in the journey from womb to grave to Judgment and eventually to Garden or Fire. Humans transfer through one state of existence to another, and these states are marked by their differing locales and timeframes.

While *al-janna* and *al-nar* are the main terms used to designate the Islamic afterworld, the Qur'an employs others as well, such as *al-samawat*, "the heavens," and *al-akhira*, "the hereafter." Certain texts conflate *al-janna* with *al-firdaws*, often translated as "Paradise" and represented as the highest level of the Garden. Aside from *al-nar*, other terms are also translated as "hell." They include *hawiya* (abyss), *jahim* (hellfire), *sa'ir* (fire), *jahannam* (hell), *laza* (flame), *saqar* (blaze) and *hutama* (furnace).[7] By the twelfth century, each of the terms designated a different gate of the Fire. While the use of *al-janna* and *al-firdaws* tends to be distinct, the invocation of *al-nar* at some points and *al-jahannam* at others remains unclear. English equivalents for the terms will be used, and all variations in terminology will be noted throughout the book.

METHODOLOGY

The history of the Garden and the Fire is one of how Muslims related their lives to the world of the unseen. Muslims understood the seen by often invoking the unseen; and conversely, came to terms with the unseen with the help of the seen. The relationship between the world that was made manifest was inextricably linked to the invisible world that was not tangible, yet shaped life. While daily life may have been rooted in mundane experiences and practices, its foundation was not solely earth-based. The Garden and the Fire provide potent illustrations, since faith in the afterlife shaped aspects of daily practices, and earthly life was understood through the prism of life to come.

The challenge of studying the relationship between earthly life and the afterworld lies in understanding a state or place in time that has yet to occur. For this reason, a history of the afterlife necessarily involves examining human expectations, fears, longings, and imaginings. Furthermore, the non-event-driven Garden and Fire are so ubiquitous within Islamic texts that they do more than provide details of the life to come; they inform a sensibility. Nearly every sura, or section, in the Qur'an invokes the Garden and the Fire, and many theological and literary works employ metaphors about the Garden. References to the afterlife are so pervasive that the concept loses visibility as an article of faith.

How to write a narrative of an article of faith that is so central that it often disappears within texts? The answer rests in understanding what can be achieved when trying to link earthly experience with otherworldly sensibilities. The history of heaven and hell in Islam, with a particular focus on material culture, is neither a history of imagination, nor a history of mentalities, nor a genealogy. A history of imagination focuses on the active agency of humans; yet, for believers, the afterlife may be imagined, but it is not a figment of their imagination. A history of mentalities assumes that subconscious drives inform cultures; but it is a believer's conscious longings to know the future that directs historical discourse. A history of genealogy may show origins of recorded doctrine, but it detracts from lived, historical experience. Muslims had faith in the Garden and the Fire without necessary knowledge of the Zoroastrian tradition of religious Judgment or Judaic or Ethiopian philological roots in Arabic.

Instead of seeking origins of a doctrine or specific agents who gave shape to the way the doctrine was defined and disseminated, this book analyzes descriptions and their contexts within texts in order to demonstrate that faith in the afterlife has a history. The historical development from article of faith to realm of imaging to refined metaphor depends on Muslims' expanding interest in material culture. Whether understood as metaphorical or literal, the afterworld was discussed through its objects. The "Islamic culture" in the title of the work, then, refers less to the religious culture invoked by texts than to the landscape, objects, and social realities that informed the Islamic afterworld. For this reason, the book reads texts in order to evaluate how they describe the afterworld instead of assessing sources for their veracity.

The texts used in this book each pose historiographic challenges. The Qur'an is ambiguous about certain issues such as female companions. Furthermore, it took about three centuries to record, systematize, and fully vocalize revelations. Ibn Ishaq's (d. 767) *Sira Rasul Allah* presents a chronology of Muhammad and his community in Mecca and Medina, but was recorded at least a century and a half after the death of the prophet in 632. Its current rescission, edited by Ibn Hisham (d. 828 or 823), dates from nearly three centuries after the death of the prophet. Traditions of the prophet Muhammad, or hadiths, offer rich material about the afterlife, but they present canonical material that tell us more about what the religious learned (*'ulama*) wanted to record in terms of chains of transmission (*isnad*) and content (*matn*). For example, the canonical Sunni hadith collections that the book draws upon, date from the eighth to the ninth centuries, but they do not indicate whether, when, or where the traditions circulated.[8] Instead, the compilers of hadiths were more concerned with the status of the traditions and developed a system to classify them (mainly based on their *isnads*) as sound (*sahih*) or weak (*gharib*). It is also possible that some hadiths were exaggerated and perhaps in some cases fabricated.

The field of Islamic history responds to the challenges that the sources present in different ways. One school of thought accepts generally the narrative provided by Muslim tradition: that Muhammad was a man who lived in the town of Mecca in the seventh century, and who received a series of revelations, believed by Muslims to be the word of Allah (literally, "the God"). He delivered these revelations to the people of Mecca who worshipped local Arabian gods and goddesses. Historians of this school, thus, do not deny the imprint of later time periods on the sources; however, they accept the narrative of Islamic origins as legitimate. Another more skeptical school of thought has a discomfort with the later sources and has developed various approaches that do not assume that oral transmission was a legitimate carrier of tradition. Some works cast doubt about the nature of the Qur'an, the narrative projected in the *Sira Rasul Allah*, and the validity of hadiths. Historians of this school have undermined the accepted Islamic narrative and intimate that the actual origins of Islam may derive from a different region, a later century, or perhaps by Jews or Christians.

In many respects, these two approaches battle over narrative authenticity. While determining whether a narrative is historically sound is a valid enterprise, it is not the aim of this book for two reasons. First, the book is not concerned with the questions of origins (as will be discussed in chapter 1) because trying to find an origin for faith in heaven and hell leads us away from human experience and into a world of abstract intellection. Instead, the book is more concerned with finding how the afterworld as a concept developed within the parameters of a narrative that Muslims believed to have been true over the centuries. Second, because the textual traditions about the afterworld are an extension of human imaginings, they do not require the same scrutiny that other topics require. For example, hadiths about legal matters that have been fabricated pose more problems for jurists and theologians than traditions about the afterlife. Indeed, chapter 6 analyzes a critique of preachers that suggests that certain narrative license was seen as acceptable when it came to traditions about the Garden and the Fire as long as the traditions encouraged religious reform. Sifting through traditions to see if hadiths were exaggerated when some exaggeration was tolerated is moot. The chief purpose of the traditions of the afterworld was to affect listeners and to satiate their curiosity about the world to come.

While the approach of the book is tailored for its subject matter, there have been a few eschatological studies that use other frameworks. These works shed light on the entire continuum from dying to being judged. The social development of rites involving death, burial, and the body is examined in Leor Halevi's *Muhammad's Grave: Death Rites and the Making of Islamic Society*. An intellectual history of eschatological events from death to the Last Judgment based on several classical Sunni manuals and contemporary works is provided by Jane Idleman Smith and Yvonne Yazbeck Haddad's *Islamic Understanding of the Afterlife*. The temporal, spiritual, and spatial significance of *barzakh*, the intermediate state between life and death, is discussed in Ragnar Eklund's *Life Between Death and Resurrection According to Islam*. Additionally, apocalyptic traditions within early and contemporary Islam are addressed in David Cook's *Studies in Muslim Apocalyptic* and *Contemporary Muslim Apocalyptic Literature*.

Aside from journal articles and essays in the exhibit catalogue *Images of Paradise in Islamic Art*, there are three works that focus on the afterworld. Soubi el-Saleh's *La vie future selon le Coran* (The Afterlife According to the Qur'an) catalogues texts that mention the Garden and the Fire and eventually describes and determines the parameters of their discourse. Shemuel Tamari's *Iconotextual Studies in the Muslim Vision of Paradise* uses a distinct methodology to examine Judeo-Muslim eschatological motifs. Ibrahim Mahmoud's *Jughrafiyat al-maladhdhat al-jins fi al-janna* (Geography of Pleasures: Sex in Paradise) employs several methodological frameworks, including Jacques Lacan's psychoanalytic theory, to read the afterlife with particular focus on the senses. The present work benefits from these studies; however, it makes a different contribution in topic and method. It demonstrates how Muslims, through reflections, discussions, and constructions, actively shaped and constructed their afterworlds. By employing material culture as a mode of historical inquiry, the work reveals for the first time that imaginings about the afterworld culminated in a distinct religious aesthetic that has shaped Islamic culture.

THE GARDEN AND THE FIRE

{ 1 }

THE GARDEN, THE FIRE,
AND ISLAMIC ORIGINS

N O PERIOD in Islamic history elicits such careful examination and divergent interpretation as prophet Muhammad's life in Mecca and Medina. There are other eras that figure prominently, of course, but the life of the prophet holds a special lure. Not only does studying Muhammad's career allow for appreciation of the central figure in Islamic history, but focusing on his life in Mecca and Medina also offers the main way of assessing the nature of the new faith and the behavior of its followers. The allure of focusing on the history of Mecca and Medina is the opportunity not just to scrutinize the earliest texts, but also to interrogate the very narrative of Islamic origins.

The quest for origins offers the ultimate romance in academic study, but in the case of Islam, a focus on origins is also a basic element for understanding the configuration of Islamic societies. If there is an Islamic narrative, then its beginning is seen by Muslims to be formed in the seventh-century Hijaz region of Arabia when living in the community of believers (*umma*) meant being guided by revelations from God and shaped by Muhammad's personal example. As a result, this first Islamic society provides a paradigm for the ideal community that Muslims interpret and reinterpret until the present day. When Muslims searched and continue to search for examples of righteous behavior, they turn to Muhammad and his companions. When Muslims needed and continue to need a societal model to guide them through change and transformation, they turn to the trials in Mecca and Medina.

Like any search for origins, the quest for Islamic origins presents its own challenges. There is a problem with texts: the earliest are written over a century and a half after Muhammad's death, and the only version we have is one edited two hundred years after his demise. There is a problem with verification: we have only texts written by scholars who reflect their own sense of Muslim identity and shape their own present within Islamic chronicles. Most of all, there is the problem of the concept of "origin" itself, which promises to locate the very moment of beginning and, even more daunting, an explanation for that moment. It is not surprising, then, that the quest for origins is seen as dangerous territory for careful, academic study. In particular, the focus on the origins of Islam is even more challenging if one does not incorporate the terms of Islamic faith: after all, how can one *historically* explain the first revelation from God to Muhammad via the angel Gabriel? All of its challenges notwithstanding, the focus of this chapter is on the role of the Garden and the Fire in the Islamic narrative of origin. In the narrative, Muhammad received revelations in 610 (all dates are CE) from God to deliver a message to his people about the need for faith, the primacy of monotheism, and the inevitability of judgment. Judgment entailed eternal reward and punishment in two respective realms in the world to pass after the end of given time. These realms are the Garden and the Fire.

In the Qur'an and early historical texts, the Garden and the Fire are at the center of the narrative of origin. The Islamic narrative presents the Garden and the Fire as a doctrinal innovation that distinguishes the new faith. Yet, the narrative is also predicated upon the assumption that upon hearing Qur'anic revelations, newly converted Muslims automatically accepted the explanation that they would have to answer for themselves at the end of time. The idea that Muslims accepted the guiding orientation of these new worlds fits into a larger story of faith; however, it contributes to the misleading sense that faith in the Islamic afterlife was axiomatic. That the acceptance of the Islamic narrative necessitates an acceptance that belief in the afterlife was inevitable illustrates just how closely interwoven the afterlife and the Islamic narrative of origins actually are. This chapter will tease apart these two strands and show how the promise of the Garden and the Fire functioned and developed within the earliest Islamic text purporting to chronicle the time period of Muhammad in Mecca and Medina.

What was the precise nature of Muhammad's message about the afterlife? How did listeners understand the Qur'anic assertion of judgment? What did they make of the various promises and punishments? And how did they come to believe in the existence of a world never experienced? While we know that Muhammad's detractors resisted his message, we cannot accept without examination that the faithful were unquestioning upon hearing about the Garden and the Fire. Faith in the afterlife has a history, and it has been unexplored. The question, then, is how did early Muslims come to believe in the afterlife? Ibn Ishaq's (d. 761/2 or 767) *Sira Rasul Allah* reflects the ways in which the people of Mecca and Medina learned about, believed or disbelieved in, and battled over the reality of the Last Judgment. Instead of a vision of automatic acceptance of the after-world, the *Sira Rasul Allah* presents a discourse where Muslim faith in the Garden and the Fire developed over time and through Meccan opposition to Muhammad and Muslims. The Garden was not just an abstract promise made to believers, but also an end for which they worked and fought.

PRE-ISLAMIC ESCHATOLOGICAL TRADITIONS IN ARABIA

There is little evidence that the Arabs in pre-Islamic Arabia believed in an afterlife with a distinct place and time. Unfortunately, what little is known about Central Arabian religion comes from Islamic sources that stress monotheism's superiority over idol worship in an effort to demonstrate the difference between the two systems.[1] Stories about pre-Islamic beliefs suggest a pantheistic system where each tribe worshipped stones, trees, or goddesses.[2] The pilgrimage to and the circumambulation of the Ka'ba, which contained objects of veneration, testify to the same form of worship. *Kuh-han,* or soothsayers, were said to receive divinely inspired poetry from the gods or from *jinn,* beings of the desert understood to be composed of vapor and flame.[3] The belief in deities and *jinn* suggests the belief in an unseen world. Yet, that world did not necessarily exist outside the realm of time. Instead, life occurred on one plane of existence. Each person had a fixed time or *ajal.* What happened after one's *ajal* was reached is unclear.[4]

There may have been some notion of transformation after death, but that transformation did not necessarily entail an afterlife or an afterworld. It has been suggested that hadiths that liken souls to birds may be based on the pre-Islamic belief that the soul becomes like an owlish apparition that hovers over the grave and head of the deceased person.[5] Another way to investigate pre-Islamic beliefs is to look at the myth of the prophet Salih of the tribe of Thamud and the she-camel whose piercing screech brought about the end of their world. As narrated in the Qur'an as an example of one of God's chosen groups gone astray, the people of Thamud were prosperous, but they had become corrupt, so God sent them the prophet Salih. They identified him as a mere mortal and asked that he give them some indication of his divine mission. God then sent a she-camel as a test. The she-camel required water rights every other day, and neither the tribe nor its animals could use water then. The Thamud soon broke the injunction, and they hamstrung and slew the she-camel. Three days later a great scream destroyed them.

In one version of the myth, the scream came with a crash, and a large she-camel emerged from the mountain. Her shrieks brought such pain that people bled from their ears; their skin turned yellow, then red, and finally black. Realizing that their fate was sealed, they prepared themselves for death and awaited their punishment. Then came the final scream. Afterward all was silent. Fire rained down for seven days until everything was ash. On the eighth day, the sky cleared, and Salih and his few adherents carried their belongings and journeyed to Palestine.[6] The story is also analogous to Muhammad's plight. The motif of the scream in the Qur'an functions as a warning to Muhammad's detractors that unimaginable pain is pending if they do not follow Allah's messenger just as the Thamud did not follow Salih. Qur'anic verses present analogies between the story of the Thamud and other peoples who "went astray" from rightly guided messengers, such as Lot or Abraham or Noah.

In this story, the scream indicates the beginning of eschatological time. However, while the concept of pain is apparent, there is little indication of a realm or time beyond the scream. The cataclysmic end is brought about not because of the world's end, but because the Thamud did not respect the she-camel. The end of the tribe, then, is not the end of time; rather, it is the punishment for disobeying divine commandments. Individual judgment is not apparent; instead, there is only a collective fate for the tribe.

When publicly proclaiming the revelations he received, Muhammad had difficulty convincing the people of Mecca and Medina that the Last Judgment was impending. There are numerous revelations in the Qur'an that assert the reality of the Judgment and the consequence for those who do not have faith. Similarly, as recorded in hadiths and the *Sira Rasul Allah*, Muhammad attempted to persuade people that their lives had a future; and their future lives were in peril if they did not heed the calling of Allah. The concept of the judgment played a central role in the early history of Islam.

What is so innovative about the Last Judgment? As in the case of the Thamud, collective judgment reflected the tribal ethic of solidarity. A judgment for each individual separated him or her from social and familial contexts. Performing pilgrimage and circumambulating the Ka'ba with its interior idols was deemed unacceptable. What Muhammad presented as a good life was to live by the precepts of "those who submit" to Allah and solely Allah. Other gods and tribal affiliations were irrelevant. Yet, the judgment itself was not limited solely to Muslims; indeed, the judgment was also levied against those who have no belief at all. The Fire affected even those who did not subscribe to the faith.

Other than Muhammad's visions, the revelations he delivered, and his words that were to become hadiths, there was no proof of an unseen world that lay *outside* time and space. The belief in *jinn* was evident; however, the *jinn* were believed to exist within the spatial parameters of the earthly world.[7] A future realm of existence in both time and space, then, was an innovation. That there was a world beyond this one whose options depended on how one lived life in this world did not accord with the common understanding of a life span.

Both the *Sira* and the Qur'an record the difficulty Meccans faced in trying to understand the afterlife. The following pages will analyze their incomprehension in greater detail. The extension of judgment beyond time and space was the most trying concept to comprehend. The concept of the afterlife not only challenged individual conceptions of life, it also challenged assumptions of earthly tribal solidarity. By contrast, in the afterlife, judgment allowed an individual a new life unencumbered by tribal affiliation; yet, once within the Garden, an individual could experience ultimate solidarity by uniting with ancestors and progeny. One essentially experienced one's life in the next world, but the framework of life was transformed in terms of time and space.

DEBATING THE DOCTRINE OF THE AFTERLIFE

The *Sira Rasul Allah* reflects that the Garden and the Fire were used as metonymies for the new faith. The text introduces the two realms as what marks Islam as distinct from other systems of faith before it actually uses the terms "Muslim" or "Islam." The Garden and the Fire provided a doctrine that focused the attention of both Muhammad's adherents and detractors. Both alluded to the afterlife in moments of strife: Muhammad's early companions employed it as inspiration; his detractors used it to illustrate the absurdity of Muhammad's message. At different points in Muhammad's life, belief in the afterlife took on different meanings. In Mecca, it provided consolation to new converts who faced persecution. Sometimes the terms *al-janna* and *al-nar* are specifically employed; other times there is reference to particular items found in the Garden and the Fire.

The near-iconic power of the Garden and the Fire as a marker of Islam can be best illustrated by the passages in the *Sira* that chronicle Islam's place in the world by foretelling the appearance of Muhammad. In one anecdote, Ibn Ishaq reports a Jewish man discussing an upcoming prophet and foretelling the rise of Islam:

> Salih b. Ibrahim b. 'Abdul al-Rahman b. 'Auf from Mahmud b. Labid, brother of B. 'Abdu al-Ashhal, from Salama b. Salama b. Waqsh (Salama was present at Badr) said: "We had a Jewish neighbor among Bani 'Abdu al-Ashhal, who came out to us one day from his house. (At that time I was the youngest person in my house, wearing a small robe and lying in the courtyard.) He spoke of the resurrection [*al-qiyama wa-l-ba'th*], the reckoning [*al-hisab*], the scales [*al-mizan*], the Garden [*al-janna*], and the Fire [*al-nar*]. When he spoke of these things to the polytheists who thought there could be no rising after death, they said to him, 'Good gracious man! Do you think that such things could be that men can be raised from the dead to a place where there is a Garden [*al-janna*] and a Fire [*al-nar*] in which they will be recompensed for their deeds?' 'Yes,' he said, 'and by Him whom men swear by, he would wish that he might be in the largest oven in his house rather than in that Fire [*al-nar al-'azim*]: that they would heat it and thrust him into it and plaster it over if he could get out from that fire on the following day.' When they asked for a sign that this would be, he said, pointing with his hand to Mecca and the Yaman, 'A prophet will be sent from the direction of this land.' When they asked when he would appear, he looked at me, the youngest person, and said: 'This boy, if he lives his natural term, will see him,' and by God, a night and a day did not pass before God sent Muhammad his apostle and he was living among us. We believed in him, but he denied him, in his wickedness and envy. When we asked, 'Aren't you the man who said these things?' he said 'certainly, but this is not the man.'"[8]

In this passage, the Jew functions as someone who is privileged with divine knowledge not only because of his ability to see the future, but also because the *Sira Rasul Allah* portrays Jews as legitimate authorities of divine wisdom (although in this case, the man recants his own vision). When the man speaks, it is to signal apocalyptic time when there will be the Resurrection, the Reckoning, and humans' lives will be weighed by the cosmic Scales. Each one of these events forms a part of eschatological time, which the passage reflects is surprising to the listeners. It is within this framework that the Garden and the Fire is first introduced. In a kind of doctrinal refrain, the Jewish neighbor is questioned about the possibility of an afterlife to which he responds about the heat or the greatest part of the Fire. In the passage, then, it is the Fire that is privileged as a marker of Islamic denial: if one does not accept the future (as the Jewish man does not by the end of the anecdote), then one may face it. The Garden, by contrast, is not highlighted at all.

Even more interesting is what is not mentioned about this new faith. The Jewish neighbor neither mentions the concept of *tawhid* (unity) that marks forms of Islamic theology, nor monotheism that would reinforce the narrative against polytheism, nor the name of the Islamic God "Allah," nor what will become the social legislation of Islamic faith. Instead he introduces the future faith by the most fantastic attribute of them all: life beyond this life and cosmic reward and punishment. His audience's amazement at events after life confirms the novelty that eschatological time provides in the Islamic narrative. In terms of the significance of the anecdote, one can argue that by the time it was committed to writing and even edited by Ibn Hisham (d. 828 or 833) in the early ninth century, the eschatological terminology was well known and projected into the narrative as a mechanism of foretelling the future. Or we can read the passage literally and allow that a Jewish man before Muhammad's time would mention the significant words *al-janna* and *al-nar*. The result does not affect the observation that the afterlife became a way to designate Islam as a system of belief. In the earliest textual moments, the new faith is identified through the concept of the afterlife.

Meccan contestation of the validity of an afterlife is more pronounced in later anecdotes that focus on Muhammad's call and preaching in Mecca. In a section entitled "Negotiations between the Apostle and the Leaders of the Quraysh and an Explanation of the Sura of the Cave," the tensions between Muhammad and Meccan leaders are apparent, and the doctrine of the afterlife as a point of contention plays a part in the articulation of difference.

Ibn Ishaq relates that after Islam began to spread to Muhammad's tribe of Quraysh, leading members of each clan met after sunset outside the Ka'ba and decided to send for and negotiate with Muhammad. They charged Muhammad with treating his tribe in a peculiar way and tried to placate what they perceived were his desires. If he wanted money, they would make him the richest; if he wanted honor, they would make him a governor or prince (*amir*); if he sought sovereignty, they would make him king; if a spirit had possessed him, they would find a cure. Ibn Ishaq reports Muhammad's response:

"I have no such intention. I demand not your money, nor honor from you, nor sovereignty over you, but God had sent me to you as a messenger, and revealed a book to me, and commanded me to become an announcer and warner for you. I brought you messages of my Lord and given you good advice. If you took the message of my Lord, then you would have a portion in this world [al-dunya] and the hereafter [al-akhira]; if you rejected it, I can only patiently await the issue until God decided between me and you," or words to that effect.[9]

Ibn Ishaq ends with "or words to that effect," in order to indicate to readers that the wordings may not be exact. In this passage, we see the framework of what would soon constitute Islamic belief. Sections before this incident in the *Sira* mention individual conversion, but no section articulates Muhammad's message. In this anecdote, Muhammad offers a synopsis—which is still not identified as a religion called "Islam"—and adds his counsel. The advice is ultimately one that involves the promise or threat of a life beyond. What is offered is success in this world and the next. The rewards for accepting Muhammad's message are framed temporally so that the benefit extends in this earthly existence to the hereafter.

The Qurayshi leaders were not interested in the idea of apportioned reward, and instead, they responded by making demands to determine whether Muhammad's message was divine. Additionally, Muhammad's warning was not adequate. For them, the granting of reward is proof of prophecy:

You know that no people are more short of land and water, and live a harder life than we, so ask your Lord, who has sent you, to remove for us these mountains which shut us in, and to straighten out our country for us, and to open up in it rivers like those of Syria and Iraq, and to resurrect for us Qusayy b. Kilab, for he was a true shaikh, so that we may ask him whether what you say is true or false. If they say you are speaking the truth, and you do what we have asked you, we will believe in you, and we shall know what your position with God is, and that he has actually sent you as an apostle as you say.[10]

Here the leaders ask for relief from their present state, and they invoke their ancestor who was renowned for his wisdom. Their wish list also indicates a temporal difference with Muhammad's statement. He spoke about the future beyond the material world, while they ask for the present. It is this temporal shift that the Qurayshi leaders were unable to recognize.

The inability to see the import of Muhammad's message at this stage soon transformed into the desire to ridicule him for suggesting that landscape, for example, can ultimately be changed. When Muhammad does not grant their wishes, he sends Qurayshi leaders the message that his God expects allegiance, and whatever reward may be granted will be enjoyed after death. Such a spiritual contract between God and man does not appear attractive for those who have yet to be convinced that there is a future life.

The Qurayshi leaders then ask Muhammad for what they consider a natural alternative to granting their wishes. They indicate that he should ask his God something for himself in order to give some sort of sign: "Ask God to send an angel with him to confirm what he said and to contradict them; to make him gardens and castles, and treasures of gold and silver to satisfy his obvious wants." The leaders ask for these sumptuous items for him because he stood on the streets like them and earned a living, and this, they felt, did not mark him from common men who had no message to deliver. They finally suggest that his God punish them immediately: "Then let the heavens be dropped on us in pieces."[11]

Within the Islamic narrative, the position of the Meccan resistance to Muhammad's message remains ironic for what Meccan leaders ask from Muhammad mirrors what the elect will gain in the Garden. Their request for "gardens and castles, and treasures of gold and silver" are items that believers receive as elaborated through revelation. The function of this inversion brings into high relief the lack of sagacity of Meccan leaders. Given the promises of the material items in the Qur'an and the hadiths, the Meccan leaders' statement demonstrates their inability to accept what is presented to them.

For the leaders, the goods would indicate that Muhammad was not a simple worker, but someone of spiritual stature. Their requests demonstrate how strange Muhammad's position must have been to them. He neither conjured miracles nor delivered divine rewards on request. Incredibly, he worked just as they did. As Salih was for the Thamud, Muhammad was too mundane for their prophetic expectations. Their frustration is finally reached when they challenge him to let the heavens drop on them. A statement of such drama acts as a type of taunt: if they believed his God could destroy them, they would not likely utter the challenge so simply.

In terms of the goods mentioned, the leaders' demands evince the types of material realities unavailable in the Hijaz. While Mecca was a town of trade, it was not a metropolis of gardens and castles, and it was not a mining center for gold and silver. What the leaders demand, then, is unavailable in a Meccan setting; and hence, it would be seen as a divine gift. (The same could not be said for a setting in Jerusalem and Damascus where there were gardens and castles and sufficient trade for precious metals.) A similar argument may be made for another anecdote in which Abu Jahl mentions that Muhammad claims that people will be raised to "gardens like those of the Jordan."[12] Both these statements evince a world removed from gardens, palaces, and precious metals. While all sorts of textual corruptions must be entertained for the anecdotes, the framework of the leader's wishes reflects a material reality that resembles the conditions of Mecca, rather than greater Syria or Iraq.

The material dimension of the leaders' requests is further reiterated in the next exchange after Muhammad responds that he was a mere messenger and claims that he cannot provide the miraculous events that the leaders seek. In return, 'Abdullah b. Umayya chastises Muhammad for not delivering any of the things for which they asked. In a prefiguring of Muhammad's Night Journey and Ascension to the heavens, 'Abdullah b. Umayya claimed that he would not believe Muhammad even if he climbed a ladder to the sky and four angels came testifying that he was speaking the truth. A few pages later Ibn Ishaq records his fully articulated stance: "We will not believe in thee until fountains burst forth from us from the earth, or you have a garden of dates and grapes and make the rivers within it burst forth copiously, or make the heavens fall upon us in fragments as you assert, or bring God and the angels as a surety, or you get a house of gold, or mount up to heaven, we will not believe in thy ascent until you bring down to us a book which we can read."[13] Muhammad does not make any of these come true. Yet, according to Islamic beliefs, each one of the events eventually comes or will come to pass. The images of the fountains, gardens of copious fruit irrigated by underground rivers, domiciles of precious metals, and the vision of angels and possible presence of God are all rewards of the Garden that will be discussed in chapter 4. The last item of the book is the Qur'an, in which these otherworldly promises are described.

In the passages, the desires of the leaders foretell the blessings and goods of the Garden; yet, their wishful thinking also indicates the reality of their material conditions. What Muhammad promises in the next world is respite from a harsh desert land and palaces of silver and gold with resplendent gardens with rivers flowing beneath. Yet, the leaders' understanding is literal. Instead of recognizing that submission to God will gain these goods in the future life, they focus on the present world. Their comprehension is limited because they are negotiating for the goods in the wrong world. Instead of fulfilling the terms of the bargain for the rewards of the next world, they demand the rewards in this world in order to determine the quality of their faith.

Meccan incomprehension of eschatological time did not signify lack of awareness of what was promised in the afterlife. Ibn Ishaq records significant details about the afterlife when describing the actions of those who oppose Muhammad. It is in these narratives that we learn of further Meccan intimidation and specific items of the Fire. 'Amr ibn Hisham vehemently denied the idea that something lay beyond this life; hence his sobriquet Abu Jahl, "father of folly." He appears to be one of the Qurayshi leaders who recognized how threatening Muhammad's eschatological message was to Meccan social life. In Ibn Ishaq's text, Abu Jahl's threats not only inspired divine intervention in the form of angels and revelation to protect Muhammad, but they also offer the best clues for how Meccans received the premise that eventual judgment awaited each human.

It is also in Abu Jahl's recorded diatribes that we receive the first specific textual allusions of attributes of the Fire. For example, Abu Jahl speaks out against the nineteen punishing angels mentioned in the Qur'an: "Muhammad pretends that God's troops who will punish you in the Fire and imprison you there, are nineteen only, while you have a large population. Can it be that every hundred of you is unequal to one man of them." In response to his challenge, Muhammad received a revelation. Ibn Ishaq continues: "God then revealed, 'We have made the guardians of hell angels, and We have made the number of them a trial to those who disbelieve.'"[14] The passage is remarkable not only because the Meccan opposition is part of consolidating knowledge about the afterlife, but because the instigation on the part of Abu Jahl resulted in revelation from God.

The connection among Abu Jahl, revelation, and the attributes of the afterworld are further developed when Abu Jahl responded to a revelation about the feared tree of al-Zaqqum, located in the Fire, whose bitter fruit are like demonic heads hanging from its branches: "O Quraysh, do you know what the tree of al-Zaqqum with which Muhammad would scare you is?" When they said that they did not he said: "It is Yathrib dates buttered. By Allah, if we get hold of them we will gulp them down in one!"[15] Another revelation was soon brought down, and Ibn Ishaq—or, more likely, Ibn Hisham—reports the verse and corresponding commentary: "'Verily the tree of al-Zaqqum is the food of the sinner like molten brass seething in their bellies like boiling water,' i.e. it is not as he said. God revealed concerning it, 'and the tree which is cursed in the Qur'an; and we will frighten them, but it increases them in naught save great wickedness.'"[16]

In both cases, revelations are sent down to rebut Abu Jahl's insinuations.

The debate in both the *Sira* and the Qur'an, then, involve Allah's response to Abu Jahl's taunts for the battle for Meccan allegiance. In both cases, Abu Jahl chose to address the unrealistic material claims of the afterlife. He questions how only nineteen can overpower hundreds of men. He suggests that the fruits of the tree of al-Zaqqum are in fact dates from Yathrib, the original name of Medina. Ironically, one of the meanings of *zaqqum* is "buttered dates," so his suggestion was part of a verbal play. Nonetheless, while his statements draw on the material goods of the afterlife, they also reveal an assumption that the goods will be exact replicas of the goods on earth. His statements belie a limited understanding of a reformed sense of time and space.

Most significant for thinking about the narrative of origins, Abu Jahl not only was cognizant of the details of the Fire, but his charges imply that so were others in Mecca. For the tree of al-Zaqqum to be discussed publicly suggests that it was recognized. What Abu Jahl intended by mentioning the specifics of the afterlife was not to provide an exposition of its topography, but to elucidate the ridiculous nature of Muhammad's revelations and the legitimacy of the new faith. Whereas the joys of the Garden are met with ridicule, it is the terror of the Fire that merits public debate and Abu Jahl's denunciation.

Yet, contestation about the afterlife was not limited to debate. The battle of words also led to physical intimidation of Muslims at the hands of the Meccans. Ibn Ishaq presents traditions where Muslims faced harsh treatment by Meccans who were either threatened by the new religious movement or felt it was prudent to punish their fellow Meccans for falling into Muhammad's traps. Often the terms of the punishment were linked with the promise of the afterlife.

In one such story, the tribe Banu Makhzum took three early converts, 'Ammar b. Yasir and his parents, out of their homes and exposed them to the extraordinary heat of the Meccan day. Ibn Ishaq continues, "The Apostle passed by them and said, so I have heard 'Patience, O family of Yasir! Your meeting will be the Garden.' They killed his mother, for she refused to abandon Islam."[17] Thus, the Garden is a promise not in an abstract sense, but as reward for current trials. The promise that Muhammad utters entails that the family meet in the next world under better conditions.

Another case illustrates a non-Muslim's understanding and eventual manipulation of the promise of the Garden. Khabbab b. al-Aratt was a Muslim smith who made swords. He sold some swords to a certain al-'As b. Wa'il. When Khabbab b. al-Aratt went to collect the money he owed, al-'As b. Wa'il was to have said: "'Does not Muhammad, your companion whose religion you follow, allege that in the Garden there is all the gold and silver and clothes and servants that his people can desire?' 'Certainly,' said Khabbab. 'Then give me till the day of resurrection until I return to that house and pay your debt there; for by God, you and your companion will be no more influential with God than I, and have no greater share in it.'"[18] It is clear from this passage that later texts such as the *Sira* record people's knowing about the particular promises of the Garden, inasmuch as al-'As b. Wa'il refers to gold, silver, clothes, and servants. He alludes to this debt in the future all the while mocking Khabbab b. al-Aratt's actual status of belief. In this case, Khabbab b. al-Aratt does not receive his worldly due since he subscribes to a faith that has even greater otherworldly dues.

What is remarkable is that the anecdote operates on two levels as a type of joke about the afterlife. First, al-'As b. Wa'il suggests that he is not obligated to pay his dues on the basis of the future life; second, embedded within his promise is another promise that he can cheat as much as he wants in his life until he is held responsible in the next world. Yet, al-'As b. Wa'il's humor also illustrates his inability to recognize that alongside the promise of the Garden is the inevitable punishment for irreligious behavior.

The *Sira* also records other stories that show Meccan mockery of Muslims based on the belief of the afterlife. For instance, a certain Ubayy took an old bone, crumbled it into pieces and asked Muhammad if God could revivify it. The action suggests that Muhammad's opposition not only came to understand what Muhammad was proposing, but also referred to his promises when trying to discredit Muhammad's claims. In the case of Ubayy, after crumbling the bone in his hand, he blew the pieces in the apostle's face. After his assertion of allegiance to the doctrine, the apostle answered: "God will raise it and you, after you have become like this. Then God will send you to the Fire."[19] These moments of discord also produced moments of drama, as seen in the case of 'Ammar's family suffering in the heat, with his mother finally succumbing to death.

Meccan opposition did not provoke every moment. In the case of 'Uthman, Muhammad's friend and eventually the third caliph, some Muslims defended their belief fiercely. According to the account, a poet was to have read: "Everything but God is vain / And everything lovely must inevitably cease." 'Uthman, who replied true to the first line, cried at the second: "You lie, the joys of the Garden will never cease" after the second life. He started a brawl that resulted in his black eye.[20] This tale suggests that believers viewed the Garden as a realm of unceasing reward.

The *Sira* also records that Muslims and non-Muslims understood Muhammad's message that one underwent a certain moral and spiritual regimen in this life in order to gain the ultimate bliss in the next. In the story of al-'Aqaba, the leaders from the tribes al-Khazraj and al-Aws in Medina promised loyalty to Muhammad and asked what they would get in return. Muhammad promises them the Garden.[21] They converted after al-'Abbas b. 'Ubada b. Nadla al-Ansari reasoned, "O men of Khazraj, do you realize to what you are committing yourselves in pledging your support to this man? It is to war against all and sundry. If you think that if you lose your property and your nobles are killed you will give him up, then do so now, for it would bring you shame in this world and the next (if you did so later); but if you think that you will be loyal to your undertaking if you lose your property and your nobles are killed, then take him, for by God it will profit you in this world and the next."[22] The cosmic contract that dictates that you offer all in this world for the promise of the next is precisely what Muhammad's adversaries contested. Previously, they must have sacrificed to certain gods in order to gain the blessings they sought in life. Those acts, centered on the Ka'ba, were for blessing in this life. The innovation of Muhammad's message was that blessings needed to extend to the time beyond this life's expectations. No longer was it adequate to worry about the state of one's life on earth; now the concern had shifted to the eternal life beyond death. In this sense, Allah for all time, and by extension Muhammad during earthly time, remained the arbiter of sanctioned behavior until Judgment Day.

It has been accepted in scholarly circles that Islam posed a threat to the social and economic well being of Meccans. Socially, Islam broke the traditional tribal structure and replaced it with a religious community headed by Muhammad. Economically, by cleansing the Ka'ba of its gods and idols, the new Muslim community threatened trade that occurred during pilgrimage. Yet, religiously, Islam also posed the threat of the Fire whether one was Muslim or not. It also proposed a reward for those who submitted to the will of God. The placement in either the Garden or the Fire affected everyone in Mecca. The stories related in the *Sira* suggest that a cornerstone of the Islamic narrative is that Muslims strove for Meccans to understand their eschatological doctrine, and Meccans employed it to ridicule and sometimes intimidate and threaten Muslim inhabitants.

"PARADISE IS UNDER THE SHADE OF SWORDS"

In the quest for defense against the Meccans, Muslims immigrated to Medina and then sought to win Mecca. Muhammad and his companions fought three significant battles: the Battle of Badr (624), the Battle of Uhud

(625), and the Battle of the Ditch (627). The *Sira* reflects that in Medina the belief in the afterlife drummed up theological and military strength. If in Mecca the afterlife distinguished newly converted Muslims from their fellow Meccans who did not accept eschatological time, it is in Mecca that the rewards of belief in an afterlife were fully realized. The reward was not just consolation for military losses, but also justification for Muslim defense and victory. Yet, the consolation provided by the afterlife was not fully shared; however, the afterlife became the dominant belief with which Muslims agreed or disagreed. Within the context of warfare is the first mention of the houris, and the idea that martyrdom wins a place in the highest heaven where a Muslim can stand in the presence of Allah.[23]

Muhammad instigated the Battle of Badr when he decided to attack a Meccan caravan that was said to consist of a thousand camels carrying fifty thousand dinars of goods.[24] His troops numbered more than three hundred men, some of whom may have been from the members of the Medinan tribes al-Khazraj and al-Aws. After hearing about the impending raid, Abu Jahl assembled approximately 950 men in order to protect the caravan. The two parties met at the wells near Badr. In blocking the wells, Muhammad forced a confrontation. The Muslims were terrified of the large numbers of Meccans. Even though vastly outnumbered, the Muslims soon won the battle. Within Islamic narratives, the Muslim victory was later interpreted as a testament to their strength and to the truth of their cause. A revelation in the Qur'an explicitly refers to how God helped Meccans during the battle: "Allah helped you at Badr, when ye were a contemptible little force; Then fear Allah; thus May ye show gratitude" (3.123).

The *Sira* records odes about Muslim courage. In one of them, 'Ubayda b. al-Harith, whose foot was eventually cut off after being struck in battle, later recounted the bravery that he, Muhammad's uncle Hamza, and Muhammad's cousin 'Ali exhibited:

A battle will tell the Meccans about us:
It will make distant men give heed,
When 'Utba died and Shayba after him,
And 'Utba's eldest son had no cause to be pleased with it.
You may cut off his leg, yet I am a Muslim
I hope in exchange for life near to Allah
With houris fashioned like the most beautiful statues
With the highest Garden for those who mount there.
I have bought it with the life of which I have tasted the best
And which I have tried until I lost even my next of kin

The Merciful honored me with his favor
With the garments of Islam to cover my faults
I did not shirk from fighting them
The day that men called on their peers to fight them,
So that we came out to the herald
We met them like lions, brandishing our spears
We fought the rebellious for God's sake
We three did not move from our position
Till their fate came upon them.[25]

In the poem, 'Utba's amputated leg is exchanged for his future life. The next life is located within the highest Garden, characterized by its proximity to God and houris who are like beautiful artworks. Within this description is an implicit hierarchy where 'Utba's actions gain the very best of rewards, as opposed to a possibly lower level of reward in the Garden. This much-awaited fate is framed as a type of commercial transaction: He "bought" the highest heaven with the sacrifice of his limb. 'Utba's narration of the event highlights not only that he braved the battle for glory, truth, and reward, but that his losses and subsequent gains take the form of things. He loses a leg; he gains houris. He loses his life; he gains a better life. He states that he wins these things through his Muslim devotion, but he can still benefit from the compassion of God to cloak his faults. The focal point within this proof of faith and bravery in battle is his loss of earthly limb and gain of otherworldly beneficence and beauty.

Yet, the distinction between earthly world and otherworld do not always remain sharp within the *Sira*. In another account, the houris are mentioned as occupying the battle space as ethereal nurses who tend to the sick and deceased: "'Abdullah b. Abu Najih told me that he was told that, when a martyr is slain, his two wives from the dark-eyed houris pet him, wiping the dust off his face, saying all the while, 'May God put dust on the face of the man who put dust on your face, and slay him who slew you!'"[26] The houris, then, have a special place on the battlefield, acting not only as an indication of the promised life that will soon arrive,[27] but also as a precursor to that life within the earthly moments of dying.

In another instance, Muhammad sees houris. He turned away from a fighter who recently died. When questioned why he turned toward and then away from the man, Muhammad replies that he was with his "two wives from the dark-eyed houris" and averts his gaze out of respect.[28] The houris' function may have been akin to wives in the actual battles; however, given their otherworldly origin, their visibility is curious. The appearance of the houri suggests that death is a type of intermediate state where attributes of the Garden can be experienced within earthly time. Here the Garden is not just the extension of eschatological time, but it also acts as a frame for meaning within earthly time. After all, the houri does not appear in any mundane moment or natural death. Instead, houris are visible on earth only with the spilled blood of battle.

While such an image may have provided motivation to fight other battles or consolation for the death itself, there were also Muslim voices of grief and eventual disbelief of the promise of the Garden. Hatib b. Umayya b. Rafi''s son Yazid was grievously wounded at the Battle of Uhud. As he was dying, he was brought to his family's settlement. His family gathered around, and people said to Yazid's father, "Good news of the Garden, O son of Hatib." The transmitter Asim adds, "Now Hatib was an old man who had lived long in the heathen period and his hypocrisy appeared then, for he said, 'What good news do you give him? Of a Garden of rue? By God, you have robbed this man of his life by your deception (and brought great sorrow of me.)'"[29] The disbelief of Hatib is fully vocalized within the frame of his hypocrisy. When we lift the outer justification of Hatib's complaint, his words suggest that the Garden not only did not provide consolation for his son, but was also a way to console those who faced unbearable loss. What is invalidated within Hatib's lament is the logic that there will be a better place called the Garden. Instead, he talks of a garden not of ultimate beauty, but of rue, which is used to anoint bodies. For Hatib, the Garden is a hoax designed only to compound his loss. What is clear from the narration about battles is the extent to which the Garden was invoked. Because the battle of Uhud was a militarily draw between the Meccans and Medinans, its costs were high in terms of lives, and it demoralized believers. In fact, the Qur'an addresses sorrow about their losses and fear that Allah no longer favored the Muslim community. In Medina, it is the Muslims who contest the meaning of the Garden; for Yazid's kin, the Garden acts as reward. Only his father cried out what was obvious to the pre-Islamic sensibility of death in battle: his son is lost to him and to the world.

Yet, Hatib's lament is not the only development that arises out of the losses at the Battle of Uhud. The battle also inspired traditions regarding martyrdom.[30] Like the passage about the houris on the battlefield, some traditions involve collapsing eschatological time. For example, one man died saying, "By the Lord of al-Nadr, the Garden! I am smelling its aroma from before the Mountain of Uhud."[31] Here the man experiences the Garden through the sense of smell as he dies.

More common are passages involving consolation. Sometimes the consolation is for family members. Such is the case when Muhammad reassures a mother that there are gardens in *al-janna*, and her son is in the highest Paradise (*firdaws*).[32] Her son's loss, then, is ranked high within the large hierarchy of dying. Also striking is when Muhammad reassured Muslims of their place in the Garden as opposed to the place of their enemies: "Narrated al-Mughira bin Shu'ba: Our Prophet told us about the message of our Lord that ' . . . whoever amongst us is killed will go to the Garden.'" 'Umar asked the prophet, is it not true that our men who are killed will go to the Garden and theirs will go to the Fire?' The Prophet said 'yes.'"[33] Here the consolation is not only determined by reward for self, but also punishment for others. The placement of Muslims in the Garden and their enemies in the Fire reinforced the faith of the fighters as they proceed to battle. Interestingly, the mention of both realms also further delineated and created cleavages between Muslim and non-Muslim. The function of the afterlife as a defining dogma helped Muslims to define their fellow Meccans as enemies as well as past peoples (like the Thamud) gone astray.

Yet, sacrifice in battle did not always result in a promise of the Garden. Correct behavior still played a large role in determining whether the fighter was granted a place in the Garden. In Imam Malik's *al-Muwatta'*, attendees of the funeral proclaim the Garden as destination; yet, Muhammad indicates that merely dying for the cause of God does not guarantee entry into the Garden:

Yahya related to me from Malik from Thawr ibn Zayd al-Dili from Abu al-Ghayth Salim, the *mawla* of ibn Muti' that Abu Hurayra said, "We went out with the Messenger of Allah, may Allah bless him and grant him peace, in the year of Khaybar. We did not capture any gold or silver except for personal effects, clothes, and household goods. Rifa'a ibn Ziyad gave a black slave boy called Mid'am to the Messenger of Allah, may Allah bless him and grant him peace. The Messenger of Allah, may Allah bless him and grant him peace, made for Wadi al-Qura. After he arrived there, Mid'am was struck and killed by a stray arrow while unsaddling the camel of the Messenger of Allah, may Allah bless him and grant him peace. The people said, 'Good luck to him! The Garden!' The Messenger of Allah said, 'No! By He is whose hand my self is! The cloak which he took from the spoils on the Day of Khaybar before they were distributed will blaze with fire on him.' When the people heard that, a man brought a sandalstrap—or two sandalstraps—to the Messenger of Allah, may Allah bless him and grant him peace. The Messenger of Allah, May Allah bless him and grant him peace, said, 'A sandalstrap or two sandalstraps of fire!'"[34]

Here Mid'am's stealing of a cloak before distribution leads to his placement in the Fire. Assisting in battle was invalid; his punishment would eventually be meted out due to his immoral behavior of stealing. Mid'am's fate suggests that even though "Paradise lies under the shade of swords,"[35] not everyone benefits from the cosmological exchange of life in this world for elevated life in the next world.

Such a caveat did not invalidate the use of the Garden as a motivational device. In another passage, Ibn Ishaq discusses the preparation for the Battle of the Ditch. The Muslims were outnumbered vastly and in order to protect themselves, they dug a trench around Medina for defense. Muhammad built morale during the task: "He drew a trench about Medina and worked at it himself encouraging the Muslims with the hope of reward in the Garden."[36] Here we are presented the image of Muhammad encouraging Muslims with the idea that they will be awarded a place in the Garden.

Other passages suggest that the motivation of the Garden was offered as a more concrete promise. In Malik's *al-Muwatta'* there is a hadith that illustrates what a fighter may have been assured when leaving for battle: "Yahya related to me from Malik from Abu al-Zinad from al-'Araj from Abu Hurayra that the Messenger of Allah, may Allah bless him and grant him peace, said, 'Allah guarantees either the Garden or a safe return to his home with whatever he has obtained of reward or booty for the one who does jihad in His way, if it is solely jihad and trust in His promise that brings him out of this house.'"[37] Here the options are set out clearly. The fighter will either receive the Garden or return to his home with appropriate booty given that his efforts of jihad or struggle are for God and God alone. In this instance, there is no mention of righteous behavior invalidating the reward. Instead, what is highlighted is the material aspect of reward: the glories of the Garden or glories in the form of war booty.

Within the framework of the Islamic narration of origin, Islam became the religion of the Garden. In Mecca, it was assured and doctrinally battled. In Medina, it was tested as Muslims gave their lives or lost their family members in service to God through battle. Discussions that Muhammad had with Muslims about the afterlife in Medina were far different from debates he had with the Quraysh in Mecca. In Mecca, the Garden began as an abstract concept to be experienced later in life. With growing Meccan pressure and persecution, the Garden became less abstract. By the time of the community of Medina, the Garden was the fate for those who prepared for battle. While not everyone accepted the promise of the Garden, from the standpoint of Islamic origins, the Garden began to offer ultimate refuge and pleasure from worldly pain, and the Fire was designated for those who caused it.

The sessions of discourse or battle in Ibn Ishaq's *Sira* demonstrate how the concept of dying and being judged in Islamic doctrine threatened Meccans and provided most Muslims with consolation. In a dramatic moment in Mecca between Muhammad and Abu Jahl, the eschatological import of Muhammad's message is highlighted: "Yazid b. Ziyad on the authority of Muhammad b. Ka'b al-Qurazi told me that when they were all outside his door Abu Jahl said to them: 'Muhammad alleges that if you follow him you will be kings of the Arabs and the Persians. Then after death you will be raised to gardens like those of the Jordan. But if you do not follow him you will be slaughtered, and when you are raised from the dead you will be burned in the Fire.' The apostle came out to them with a handful of dust saying: 'I do say that. You are one of them.'"[38] Abu Jahl sums up succinctly the import of Muhammad's message: If you follow his message, then you will be victorious and resurrected into glorious gardens; if you are against his message, you will be killed and resurrected only to be punished eternally in Fire.

As a point of doctrine and an answer to Muslims' questions about the moments after death, the idea of the afterlife was one of the easiest ways to mark what was both central and innovative about the new faith. In terms of explicit mention, there are few other topics within the early texts that elicit such concern and questions. Tenets such as the substance of faith and almsgiving constitute other widely discussed topics. If we count implicit references, however, the afterlife is not merely a doctrine, but a way in which Muslims came to identify themselves and recognize their place in the world.

[2]

VISIONS OF THE AFTERWORLD

M UHAMMAD'S MESSAGE not only promised humanity an after-life, but it also detailed an afterworld. While the notions of an afterlife and afterworld are often conflated, they occupy different conceptual spaces. The afterlife signifies life after death and transforms earthly experience into merely one stage in the greater progression of life, death, judgment, resurrection, and final judgment. The promise of eternal existence further frames earthly time as a preamble to a fuller life. The more glorious life is in a world whose parameters are ultimately mysterious. Within this eschatological spectrum, humanity experiences death and judgment and then ultimate pain and reward. Beyond that is the unknown and ineffable, which by nature defies description.

By contrast, the afterworld provides a setting. Accompanied by an afterworld, the afterlife is transformed from an abstract state to a detailed vision about life in cosmological time. The afterworld is not just the eschatological space where one happens to live after life; instead, it is a place that operates according to a distinct logic. The logic of an afterworld does not always provide a coherent or even fully comprehensible vision of life after death. Often, the idea of an afterworld raises more questions than provides answers. However, afterworlds are typically unambiguous about one idea: life after death is not a nebulous state accessed only by the soul or the mind. Instead, an afterworld offers the structure of a world, the rhythm of daily life, and the complexity of interaction experienced in the earthly world.

Eschatological dramas in Islamic narratives promise a future afterlife *and* detail an *existent* afterworld. Within the narratives, conventional understanding of time and space is suspended: one may experience the afterlife after this earthly life, but certain people are able to experience the afterworld within earthly time. Strangely, the afterlife is part of the future, but the afterworld is a place that can be brought near during apocalyptic time: "One Day We will ask Hell (al-jahannam), 'Art thou filled to the full?' It will say, 'Are there any more to come? And the Garden will be brought nigh to the Righteous—no more a thing distant'" (50.30–31).

The realization of the afterworld is one of the central motifs of the Islamic narrative. With the promise of judgment and a future life came a vision of a future world. In revelations in the Qur'an and passages from the *Sira*, humanity is not just offered a new life after the mundane one. Instead, the new life will be situated in a realm that may resemble aspects of earthly life, but far exceeds its pains and pleasures. The Islamic afterworld is the ultimate expression of the eschatological possibility that the Qur'an and hadiths proposed: one's future life will be led in a distinct future world. By offering a setting to represent eschatological warning and promise, the afterworld became a realm for realizing the power of the new faith.

Muhammad's experience with the afterworld developed the proof of an otherworldly place. Not only did Muhammad promise a future life, but he also claimed to see and visit the future world through visions, dreams, and the Night Journey and Ascension (al-isra' wa-l-mi'raj) to the heavens. While the descriptions during these moments were conflated eventually in Islamic textual tradition, they were not generally contested. Instead, there was significant debate about the nature of his claim: did he literally or metaphorically visit the afterworld? Muhammad's visions of the afterworld, then, are significant because they articulated prophetic access to the unseen world. However, Muhammad was not the only person who saw the afterworld. Through dreams and visions, some of his companions also claimed to have had otherworldly experiences.

How did Muhammad's claims to be in contact with the future world affect Islamic eschatology? What are the implications for Islamic eschatology that he was able to experience future space and time on earth and during his lifetime? What is the significance of his companions' (who did not enjoy prophetic status) access to the future world? Ibn Ishaq's *Sira* and al-Bukhari and Muslim's collections of hadith suggest that Muhammad's visions of the afterworld provided ultimate proof of the afterlife and created a culture of seeing the Garden through dreams and visions. This visual culture allowed Muslims to see the earthly world through an eschatological lens and to identify their companions' places in the Garden and their enemies' punishments in the Fire. Both Muhammad's experiences and his companions' dreams created a hierarchy among early companions. For the elect there was a prevalent culture of seeing the afterworld while still remaining in the present world. These visual moments allowed Muslims to perceive that they could see the promise of better things to come and contributed to what would become the common understanding of the afterworld's topography.

SEEING THE AFTERWORLD

Hadith collections report a number of traditions when Muhammad began to pray upon seeing a solar eclipse and saw the fruits of the Garden and the punishments of the Fire. This moment, identified in the hadith as "the eclipse prayer," allowed Muhammad to access the afterworld while in a waking state. While there are several variations of the eclipse prayer in al-Malik's *al-Muwatta'* and al-Bukhari and Muslim's *Sahih*, the narrative is fairly standard. There was a solar eclipse. As a response, Muhammad led people in prayer. During his prayer, he reached out for something with his hand. When asked about the meaning of his action, he responded that he was reaching for a bunch of grapes from the Garden. Afterward, he identified the types of sinners he saw in the Fire. Several of the traditions record him as discussing women as sinners or naming specific people.

Imam Malik's first version offers a fairly standard account:

Yahya related to me from Malik from Zayd ibn Aslam from 'Ata ibn Yasar that 'Abdullah ibn 'Abbas said, "There was an eclipse of the sun and the Messenger of Allah, may Allah bless him and grant him peace, prayed, and the people prayed with him. He stood for a long time, nearly as long as (it takes to recite) Sura *al-Baqara*, and then went into *ruku'* for a long time. Then he rose and stood for a long time, though less than the first time. Then he went into *ruku'* for a long time, though less than the first time. Then he went down into *ruku'* for a long time, though less than the first time. Then he went down into *sajda*, and by the time he had finished the sun had appeared. Then he said, 'The sun and the moon are two of Allah's signs. They do not eclipse for anyone's death nor for anyone's life. When you see an eclipse, remember Allah.' They said, 'Messenger of Allah, we saw you reach out for something while you were standing here and then we saw you withdraw.' He said, 'I saw the Garden and I reached out for a bunch of grapes from it, and if I had taken it you would have been able to eat from it for as long as this world lasted. Then I saw the Fire—and I have never seen anything more hideous than what I saw today—and I saw that most of its people were women.' They said, 'Why, Messenger of Allah?' He said, 'Because of their ungratefulness to Allah?' He said, 'They are ungrateful to their husbands and they are ungrateful for good behavior [toward them]. Even if you were to behave well towards one of them for a whole lifetime and then she were to see you do something [that she did not like] she would say that she had never seen anything good from you.'"[1]

Most of the variations involve the precise order of the prayers. In terms of the events, the solar eclipse provided natural drama. Upon seeing the eclipse Muhammad stood for a long period of time. In the tradition, the time is compared to the length it takes to recite the sura *al-Baqara*, which is the longest sura in the Qur'an. Only after his observation did Muhammad complete the prayer and indicate that the meaning of the eclipse is tied to the power of God.

Muhammad's vision of the Garden and the Fire is striking because of its immediacy. Muhammad saw the otherworld, and what he saw was so lucid that he reached out to touch his vision. In particular, the Garden was represented by the image of the bunch of grapes. Through his efforts to reach for the grapes, Muhammad in effect made contact with the Garden. It is unclear if his inability to bring back the fruit was a choice or a reality; however, his explanation suggests that he was able to gauge its otherworldly value of abundance. The ampleness of the grapes suggests the infinity of the riches of the Garden. By his ability to see the afterworld, Muhammad emphasizes his privileged position as a prophet to see and understand what his believers could only learn from him.[2]

During his eclipse vision, Muhammad was also able to assess the Fire. In this variation, instead of naming specific types of sinners, Muhammad focuses on women as a population of the Fire. This portion of the tradition reinforces other hadith about the role of women in the Fire. While the question of why women form the majority of the Fire will be fully addressed in the next chapter, here it is significant to note how hell is represented in Muhammad's limited vision in the eclipse prayer. Just at the grapes acted as a metonymy of the Garden, women became a major category of sinner for their ungratefulness to God or their husbands.

Women were not the only ones who were part of Muhammad's vision. One of the traditions in Muslim's collection alludes to the sin of idolatry:

'A'isha, the wife of the Apostle of Allah (may peace be upon him), reported, "There was an eclipse of the sun during the lifetime of the Messenger of Allah (may peace be upon him). So, the Messenger of Allah (may peace be upon him) made a long recital (of the Qur'an) and then pronounced takbir and then observed a long *ruku'*. He then raised his head and said: Allah listened to him who praised Him: our Lord, praise is due to Thee. He then stood up and made a long recital, which was less than the first recital. He pronounced *takbir* and observed a long *ruku'*; and it was less than the first one. He again said: 'Allah listened to him who praised Him; our Lord, praise is due to Thee.' (Abu Tahir, one of the narrators) made no mention of: 'He then prostrated himself.' He did like this in the second *rak'a*, till he completed four *ruku'* and four prostrations and the sun became bright before he departed. He then stood up and addressed people, after lauding Allah as He deserved, and then said: 'The sun and the moon are two signs among the signs of Allah. These do not eclipse either on the death of anyone or on his birth. So when you see them, hasten to prayer.' He also said this: 'Observe prayer till Allah dispels the anxiety (of this extraordinary phenomenon) from you.' The Messenger of Allah (may peace be upon him) said: 'I saw in my place everything, which you have been promised. I even saw myself desiring to pluck a bunch (of grapes) from the Garden (and it was at that time) when you saw me moving forward. And I saw the Fire and some of its parts crushing the others, when you saw me moving back; and I saw it in Ibn Luhayy and he was the person who made the she-camels loiter about.'" In the hadith transmitted by Abu Tahir the words are: "He hastened to prayer," and he made no mention of what follows.[3]

In this tradition, Muhammad also reaches out for the grapes. Additionally, he notes the active nature of the Fire crushing itself and reacts by moving back from the flames. In the Fire, Muhammad sees 'Amr Ibn Luhayy, who Arabs believed was the first to turn to idolatry after Isma'il established his religious practice in Arabia.

The use of the eclipse prayer to identify specific sinners is furthered in another tradition under the section of the "Mention of the Torment of the Grave in Eclipse Prayer." A Jewess came to Muhammad's wife 'A'isha to ask about the final hour, and 'A'isha questions Muhammad if there will be torment in the grave. The hadith continues with the formulation of the eclipse followed by Muhammad praying. He is then believed to have said that the trial in the grave is like the turmoil brought about by al-Dajjal, the one-eyed being that is commonly understood as the antichrist.[4] In this tradition, Muhammad seems to grasp a bunch of grapes. At that point, the Fire was brought to him, and in it he saw a woman of the tribe of Israel tormented because she tied a cat and did not give it food or free it to eat. He also saw Ibn Luhayy, "who was dragging his intestines in the Fire."[5]

While this tradition continues other themes such as the grasping of the grapes and the appearance of Ibn Luhayy, it also introduces another element of damnation for women. In the hadith, the woman is condemned to the Fire because of her cruelty of starving a cat.

In another hadith, thieves and the miserly are specifically targeted: "I saw the owner of the curved staff who dragged his intestines in the Fire, and he used to steal (the belongings) of the pilgrims with his curved staff, but if he was unaware of that, he would take that away. I also saw in it the owner of a cat whom she had tied till the cat died of starvation. The Garden was brought to me, and it was on that occasion that you saw me moving forward till I stood at my place of worship. I stretched my hands as I wanted to catch hold of its fruits so that you may see them. Then I thought of not doing it. Nothing that you have been promised was there that I did not see in this prayer of mine."[6] By announcing both the sinners and the ample fruits of the Garden, Muhammad provides an assurance about the promises made to humanity regarding the inevitability of judgment and the placement in the Garden and the Fire. His vision during the eclipse prayer not only provided an opportunity to send messages of reform by focusing on sinners, but it also verified the existence of the afterworld that would be experienced at the end of time. The final statement reinforces the verification, where Muhammad states that he saw everything that was promised in the Qur'an.

VISITING THE AFTERWORLD

If the eclipse prayer supplied natural drama, then the Night Journey and Ascension acted as the cosmological drama in the narrative of Muhammad's life because of the claim that he visited the heavens and saw the fires of hell. Like the eclipse prayer, the Night Journey and Ascension provided Muhammad a glimpse of the goods found in the Garden and an identification of sinful behaviors and their corresponding punishments. Unlike the eclipse prayer where the afterworld was brought to Muhammad, during the Night Journey and Ascension Muhammad claimed to have visited the afterworld. By his visit, Muhammad not only established his significance as a prophet who was in direct contact with the unseen world, but he also bolstered the immediacy about the afterworld. If during the eclipse prayer the afterworld was within his reach, then during the Night Journey and Ascension he provided the ultimate proof of the afterworld because he visited and spatially experienced its contours.

Within Islamic narratives, the Night Journey and Ascension have a near-iconic quality. From medieval book arts to contemporary decorations of Afghan trucks, the image of Muhammad riding Buraq through the night sky is the most popular depiction of Muhammad. It serves as a model for earthly pilgrimage for those en route to Islamic pilgrimage sites, and it also represents the spiritual ascent of the soul in forms of Islamic mysticism. The journey is sanctified not just because Muhammad visited the heavenly realms, but also because his visit accorded Muhammad a special status that could only be achieved through miracle.

It is generally accepted that the journey is alluded to in Qur'an 17.1: "Praise be to God who took his servant by night for a journey from the sacred place of worship to the far distant place of worship, whose surroundings We have blessed, in order to show him Our signs." This verse is tenuous because it does not explicitly refer to the event and does not use the term *mi'raj*; nonetheless, post-Qur'anic narratives have interpreted it as referring to a physical journey by Muhammad.[7] In the narratives, Muhammad was awoken one night by the angel Gabriel who placed Muhammad on the fantastic steed Buraq and took him to Jerusalem where Muhammad acted as the leader of prayer for Moses, Jesus, and Abraham. After the prayer, Muhammad ascended a fine ladder where he first saw the Fire and subsequently fainted. Afterward, he visited each of the levels of heaven, which is guarded by a different biblical prophet.

While the above account forms a dominant narrative, there are many versions of the Night Journey and Ascension. Part of the reason is that the journey became the most popular motif for poetry, mystical writings, and miniature painting; like all powerful narratives, it expanded in detail and scope. The varieties in the stories before the tenth century, however, are due to a more significant matter. While the narrative today is presented as a cohesive whole, it is, in fact, several narrative strands that were brought together to form a two-part journey.[8] Indeed, even Ibn Ishaq separates the Ascension from the Night Journey. What we are likely reading then are a series of stories whose different strands are woven together. When they get woven and how to account for their variety are separate studies in themselves. Storytellers may have used the verse to meet the demands for more miraculous stories regarding Muhammad.[9]

No matter the attribution of the Night Journey and Ascension, it is clear that the cosmology of levels of heaven provided a space for Islamic tradition to assert itself among other religions, and Muhammad's manner of ascension placed him at the top of the prophetic hierarchy.[10] More profoundly, the Night Journey and Ascension provided an image for the "deep-seated need for the marvelous" where the future world was not just a reward for the righteous, but also a "spectacle" that offered happiness.[11] Whether believed or not, Muhammad's vision of the afterworld provided a topography that became attributed to the afterlife.

The earliest recording of Muhammad's visions of the heavens and the Fire is Ibn Ishaq's *Sira*. In his account, Ibn Ishaq took several variations he had heard from several sources, often companions of the prophet, and wove them to make a single narrative. While Ibn Ishaq was careful to provide attribution for strands, he remarkably quoted some transmissions from unidentified transmitters. His prose is quite tenuous, and it is for that reason that it is worth examining each section. Also, while Ibn Ishaq refers to the Fire as *al-nar*, the heavenly realms are not designated as the Garden, but as the heavens (*al-samawat*). While the terminology is different, the structure of these seven heavens reinforces the Qur'anic image of the paradise.

NIGHT JOURNEY

Ibn Hisham begins the account by naming Ibn Ishaq as a principal transmitter. "Ziyad b. 'Abdullah al-Bakka'i from Muhammad b. Ishaq told me the following: Then the apostle was carried by night from the mosque at Mecca to the Masjid al-Aqsa, which is the temple of Aelia, when Islam had spread in Mecca among the Quraysh and all the tribes."[12] It is clear that this experience took place earlier, during Muhammad's prophetic career. Generally the date is understood as being before 622. "Masjid al-Aqsa," or "The Farthest Mosque," refers to Jerusalem, which the Romans called Aelia.[13]

Ibn Ishaq then introduces his transmitters and describes the way that he collated the account:

> The following account reached me from 'Abdullah b. Mas'ud and Abu Sa'id al-Khudri, and 'A'isha the prophet's wife, and Mu'awiya b. Abu Sufyan, and al-Hasan b. Abu al Hasan al-Basri, and Ibn Shihab al-Zuhri and Qatada and other traditionalists, and Umm Hani daughter of Abu Talib. It is pieced together in the story that follows, each one contributing something of what he was told about what happened when he was taken on the night journey. The matter of the place of the journey and what it said about it is a searching test and a matter of God's power and authority wherein is a lesson for the intelligent; and guidance and mercy and strengthening to those who believe. It was certainly an act of God by which He took him by night in that what He pleased to show him His signs which He willed him to see

so that he witnesses His mighty sovereignty and power by which He does what He wills to do.[14]

Ibn Ishaq implicitly admits that the story contains inconsistent fragments. In the passage, Ibn Ishaq notes the controversy about the Masjid al-Aqsa's location and the manner in which Muhammad reached it. He indicates neither a preference for literal nor metaphorical interpretation; however, it becomes clear through his reporting that he harbors doubts about the tradition. The following traditions in this section may be grouped under three different categories: Muhammad's journey to the heavens, the incredulity of the Meccans, and Muhammad's describing the prophets.

For the first tradition, Ibn Ishaq records 'Abdullah b. Mas'ud who described Buraq as "the animal whose every stride carried it as far as its eye could reach on which the prophets before him used to ride,"[15] and says that he was brought to Muhammad. In later texts, Buraq is described in a variety of animal composites: generally a horse with wings and sometimes with a peacock's head. Along with Gabriel, Muhammad saw "the wonders between heaven and earth until he came to Jerusalem's temple. There he found Abraham the friend of God, Moses, and Jesus assembled, and he prayed with them."[16] Then Muhammad was brought three vessels containing milk, wine, and water respectively. He heard a voice saying that if he took the water, he and his people would drown; if he took the wine, he and his people would go astray; but if he took the milk, he would be rightly guided. After choosing the milk, other prophets approved Muhammad's choice and noted that he was rightly guided.

In al-Hasan's account, while Muhammad was sleeping, Gabriel awoke him three times. The third time Gabriel led Muhammad out of the mosque door and "there was a white animal, half mule, half donkey, with wings on its sides with which it propelled its feet, putting down each forefoot at the limit of its sight and he mounted me on it."[17] Ibn Ishaq then refers to a story that Buraq shied away from Muhammad. After Gabriel rebuked him, he sweated with shame and allowed Muhammad to mount him. Returning to al-Hasan's version, Ibn Ishaq reports that they went to the temple at Jerusalem. "There he found Abraham, Moses, and Jesus among a company of prophets. The apostle acted as their imam in prayer."[18] After being given the bowls, Muhammad once again chose milk and was deemed rightly guided.

In all the variations in this section, the journey is introduced with Buraq the fantastic animal. Then Muhammad met other biblical prophets in a sort of prophetic brotherhood between the Arabs, Jews and Christians. In praying with them, he exhibited his role as prophet, and in al-Hasan's version his acting as the leader of the prayer, or *imam*, asserted his superiority over Abraham, Moses, and Jesus. In this sense, this part of the story establishes the primacy of Islam over other religions of the book; however, it still allows association of them. Muhammad is the last to join this prophetic brotherhood. By welcoming him, they signify their recognizing of the truth of Muhammad's message that there is one God, and that Muhammad himself is his final messenger.

In the second section, Ibn Ishaq records the reactions of the Meccans to Muhammad's claim of his journey to Jerusalem and back in one night. He was met with the charge that his account was absurd. Ibn Ishaq records, according to al-Hasan, that it was then that "many Muslims gave up their faith."[19] Some approached Abu Bakr, and he asserted that if God could send down revelation, then anything could be possible. After meeting Muhammad and asking him if he indeed went, Abu Bakr asked him to describe Jerusalem in order to demonstrate Muhammad's claim, since the prophet had never traveled to Jerusalem. Abu Bakr then claimed that Muhammad was truly the apostle of God; Muhammad at that point calls him *al-siddiq*, the testifier to truth.

Ibn Ishaq records another tradition that attests to the Ascension as being a test of faith by God: "Al-Hasan continued: God sent down concerning those who left Islam for this reason: 'We made the vision which we showed thee only for a test to men and the accursed tree in the Qur'an. We put them in fear, but it only adds to their heinous error. Such is al-Hasan's stories with additions from Qatada.'"[20] It is clear, then, that some found the story outrageous and subsequently apostatized. What seems to be in doubt is not the actual sequence of the narrative or the fantastic nature of Buraq and the meeting of the prophets; instead, what is contested is whether Muhammad actually went to *al-ard al-muqaddasa* (the Holy Land) and returned in one night. Why would this be such an abomination? As seen earlier, Muhammad's vision during the eclipse prayer did not elicit such hostility. In this instance, some people in his community felt as though they were being tricked. For this reason, the otherworldly journey became the ultimate test of faith.

In the next three paragraphs, Ibn Ishaq structures his viewpoint and adds commentary, which is rare in the *Sira*:

> One of Abu Bakr's family told me that 'A'isha the prophet's wife used to say: "The apostle body remained where it was but God removed his spirit by night."

Ya'qub b. 'Utba b. al-Mughira b. al-Aknas told me that Mu'awiya b. Abu Sufyan when he was asked about the apostle's night journey said, "It was a true vision from God." What these two latter said does not contradict what al-Hasan said, seeing that God Himself said, "We made the vision which we showed thee only for a test to men"; nor does it contradict what God said in the story of Abraham when he said to his son, "O my son, verily I saw in a dream that I must sacrifice thee" and he acted accordingly. Thus, as I see it, revelation from God comes to the prophets waking and sleeping.

I have heard the apostle used to say, "My eyes sleep while my heart is awake." Only God knows how revelation came and he saw what he saw. But whether he was asleep or awake, it was all true and actually happened.[21]

Ibn Ishaq suggests that Muhammad went in some form and probably through spirit, but the importance is not to doubt, but to believe that whatever happened (and here Ibn Ishaq seems to have diplomatically given up on the historical search) did so by the will of God.

Through this story we see an interesting tension in the early Muslim community. As long as Muhammad received revelation or saw visions of heaven during the eclipse prayer, he was deemed legitimate. By raising his prophetic stake by actually claiming to go and see the afterworld, his words were seen as incredulous. His community could easily accept his visions as long as he described the pleasures of the Garden that his believers would receive and the torments of Fire that non-Muslims would be granted. However, once he crossed the temporal and spatial threshold by journeying to a far city by night and claiming to visit the next realm, some found his claim incredible.

Furthermore, as opposed to his earlier statements, through the Ascension and Night Journey, Muhammad sees pleasures and pains: the Garden becomes a place of reward where there are gradations and types of punishments. The afterworld has stratifications in the same way that this world does. It is no longer sufficient to be a good Muslim to reach the Garden; one had to be an exemplary one to reach its highest level.

Ibn Ishaq ends this section with a tradition describing what Abraham, Moses, and Jesus looked like and then records a tradition from Umm Hani, Muhammad's cousin Hind, who claimed that he went on his Night Journey when he was staying with her and then proves that he did actually travel there. This account is discordant with others considering that Umm Hani insisted that he left from her house. Ending with this account that contradicts the previously cited ones casts doubts about Ibn Ishaq's intended interpretation.

ASCENSION

In the Ascension narratives, Muhammad ascends a fine ladder to the heavens and sees specific punishments. Ibn Ishaq suggests that the actual Ascension took place after a visit to Jerusalem. Whether it took place directly after or sometime later is unclear. Also unclear is the position from which Muhammad ascends. Does he ascend from the meeting with the prophets or from another place? The questions do not detract from the power of the narration that follows. Considering the importance of the *mi'raj* story for the accounts that describe the heavens, the traditions will be given in their entirety:

> One whom I have no reason to doubt told me on the authority of Abu Sa'id al-Khudri: I heard the apostle say, "After the completion of my business in Jerusalem a ladder was brought to me finer than any I have ever seen. It was that to which the dying man looks when death approaches. My companion mounted it with me until we came to one of the gates of heaven [*al-sama'*] called the Gate of the Watchers. An angel called Isma'il was in charge of it, and under his command were twelve thousand angels each of them having twelve thousand angels under his command." As he told this story the apostle used to say, "and none knows the armies of God but He." When Gabriel brought me in, Isma'il asked who I was, and when he was told that I was Muhammad he asked if I had been given a mission, and on being assured of this he wished me well.[22]

Peculiarly, Ibn Ishaq does not name from whom he receives this tradition. In the following episode, he does not even give a name, instead using the generic "traditionist" in the *isnad*:

> A traditionist who had got it from one who had heard it from the apostle told me that the latter said: "All the angels who met me when I entered the lowest heaven [*al-sama' al-dunya*] smiled in welcome and wished me well except one who said the same things but did not smile or show that joyful expression which the other had. And when I asked Gabriel the reason he told me that if he had ever smiled on anyone before or would smile on anyone hereafter he would have smiled on me; but he does not smile because he is Malik, the keeper of Fire [*al-nar*]. I said to Gabriel, he holding the position with regard to God which he has described to you "obeyed there, trustworthy," "will you not order him to show me the Fire [*al-nar*]?" And he said, "Certainly! O Malik, show Muhammad the Fire

[al-nar]." Thereupon he removed its covering and the flames blazed high into the air until I thought that they would consume everything. So I asked Gabriel to order him to send them back to their place which he did. I can only compare the effect of their withdrawal to the falling of a shadow, until when the flames retreated whence they had come, Malik placed their cover on them.[23]

In this unidentified tradition, Muhammad is greeted by all the angels and yet does not receive smiles from Malik the keeper of hell. After requesting Gabriel to command Malik to show the Fire, Muhammad is overwhelmed by its intensity. With his allusion to the fires as falling shadows, Muhammad paints an image that is almost anthropomorphic.

It is here that Muhammad experiences the intensity of the Fire, an attribute that becomes important in other hadith: "In this tradition Abu Saʿid al-Khudri said that the apostle said: 'When I entered the lowest heaven [al-samaʾ al-dunya], I saw a man sitting there with the spirits of men passing before him. To one he would speak well and rejoice in him saying: "A good spirit from a good body" and of another he would say "Aff!" and frown, saying: "An evil spirit from an evil body." In answer to my question Gabriel told me that this was our father Adam reviewing the spirits of his offspring; the spirit of a believer excited his pleasure, and the spirit of an unbeliever excited his disgust so that he said the words just quoted.'"[24]

Adam's reviewing humanity and exclaiming at their ugliness or beauty is an interesting scene since he is considered to be the father of them all. Here there is no mention of previously seeing Adam when Muhammad prayed with him, which reinforces the idea of combined narratives. Muhammad then sees other punished peoples:

> Then I saw men with lips like camels; in their hands were pieces of fire like stones that they used to thrust into their mouths and they could come out of their posteriors. I was told that there were those who sinfully devoured the wealth of orphans.
>
> Then I saw men in the way of the family of Pharaoh, with such bellies as I have never seen; there were passing over them as it were camels maddened by thirst when they were cast into hell [al-nar], treading them down, they being unable to move out of the way. These were the usurers.
>
> Then I saw men with good fat meat before them side by side with lean stinking meat, eating of the latter and leaving the former. These are those who forsake the women that God has permitted and go after those he has forbidden.

Then I saw women hanging by their breasts. These were those who had fathered bastards on their husbands.

Ja'far b. 'Amr told me from al-Qasim b. Muhammad that the apostle said: Great is God's anger against a woman who brings a bastard into her family. He deprives the true son of their portion and learns the secrets of the *harim*.[25]

Here the sinners that Muhammad sees in the lowest heaven are a motley lot. The punishments themselves are not organized or ranked in the way that they are in other eschatological texts. For example, the Sassanian Zoroastrian text *Arda Wirag Namag* tells the story of a priest who in an induced state visits heaven and sees the sinners in hell categorized by the severity of their sin. In Dante's *Divine Comedy*, each level of hell contains a different rank of sinner. Muhammad's view of sinners is far more random: he notes significant sins, but does not create a hierarchy among them. The location of these sinners is also interesting. Apparently, they are still in the lowest heaven (*sama' al-dunya*) whose significance is somewhat dubious.

To continue the tradition of Sa'id al-Khudri:

Then I was taken up to the second heaven and there were the two maternal cousins Jesus, Son of Mary, and John, son of Zakariah. Then to the third heaven there was a man whose face was at the moon at the full. This was my brother Joseph, son of Jacob. Then to the fourth heaven and there was a man called Idris. "And we have exalted him to a lofty place." Then to the fifth heaven and there was a man with white hair and a long beard, never have I seen a more handsome man than he. This was the beloved among his people Aaron son of 'Imran. Then to the sixth heaven, and there was a dark man with a hooked nose like the Shanu'a. This was my brother Moses, son of 'Imran. Then to the seventh heaven and there was a man sitting on a throne at the gate of the immortal mansion. Every day seventy thousand angels went in not to come back until the resurrection day. Never have I seen a man more like myself. This was my father Abraham. Then he took me into the Garden and there I saw a girl with dark red lips and I asked her to whom she belonged, for she pleased me much when I saw her, and she told me "Zayd b. Haritha. The apostle gave Zayd the good news about her."[26]

In this section Muhammad meets the other prophets, each of whom attends to a different level of the Garden. Their order indicates a cosmological hierarchy for prophets. On the lowest level, Adam, Malik, and

Isma'il reside. In the next level are the biblical prophets. Jesus is coupled with John, most likely reinforcing the Qur'anic polemic that Jesus is human, not divine. After Jesus are Joseph, Idris (who may refer to Enoch), Aaron, and Moses. At the top is the person to whom Muhammad likens himself: Abraham, the father of the Arabs.

Muhammad also sees a girl waiting for Zayd b. Haritha, his adoptive son who married one of Muhammad's cousins whom Muhammad married after Zayd divorced her. The girl promised to Zayd is not referred as to a wife or a houri, so the nature of her being is unclear. Perhaps she is thought of as a slave. Afterward, Muhammad reaches Allah in *al-janna*, the term that is used for the higher heaven. It is there that he receives the injunction to pray and, with Moses' help, negotiates five prayers a day as opposed to Allah's original command of fifty.

The account of the Night Journey and Ascension is curious, and it raises more questions than possible answers. Initially, the use of terminology is striking. There are no competing terms for hell since *al-nar* is used to both describe the fire within hell as well as the place of the Fire. By contrast, the term for the Garden is the heavens (*sama'* or *samawat*). *Al-janna* is the highest realm within the heavens, while *sama' al-dunya* is the realm closet to the earth. The terminology belies a more complicated sense of cosmological structure. What is the significance of *sama' al-dunya* where Adam reviews humanity? Is this level in heaven, hell, or an in-between realm that is closest to earthly attributes?[27] Furthermore, how does the guardian al-Malik's *al-nar* fit within the cosmological structure since Muhammad ascends to see *al-nar*, yet *al-nar* is not necessarily depicted above earth?

The complex structure extends to the ordering of prophets. While it is clear that the ordering indicates a hierarchy, what that hierarchy signifies is quite opaque. Abraham is clearly the favored prophet with his seat closest to God, and his significance is bolstered by the idea that he most resembles Muhammad. Jesus and John are coupled together because doing so (as is evident in Qur'anic verses) emphasizes Jesus' humanity as opposed to Christian claims of his divine nature. But the ordering of Joseph, Idris, and Moses is not entirely evident.

Finally, just as the sinners are presented in a piecemeal fashion so are the rewards. For example, the awarding of Zayd b. Haritha's girl is striking because she is described as a very alluring object with red lips. We can read greater significance into the material by focusing on Zayd's close relation with Muhammad, but that does not fully explain why only Zayd is viewed in his future life.

The topography, beings, and objects found in this story will be analyzed in chapters 4 and 5. Here, the historical value of the Night Journey and Ascension is apparent. Ibn Ishaq offers no commentary or discussion of how these traditions were received. Instead, he quotes unnamed characters. No matter what actually happened, the intense debate about the journey was not restricted to theological circles. At the heart of the Night Journey and the Ascension is Muhammad's claim that he visited the heavens. Unlike everyone else who would have to strive to be good Muslims and only then be allowed in the Garden, Muhammad was able to visit the heavens while alive. His assertion intensified the debate of whether the Garden and the Fire existed in space and time. For the believing Muslim, his visit proved that the afterworld existed as a place. For those who cast doubts on the possibility of the afterlife, his visit became another claim to be invalidated.

ENVISIONING THE AFTERWORLD

Muhammad's visions of the afterworld were not limited to dramatic moments like the eclipse prayer and Night Journey and Ascension. Like revelations, his visions also occurred in more mundane, waking states. The claim of accessing the afterworld may have been a more constant way that Muhammad assured his believers of the wisdom of submission to God. Seeing, visiting, and dreaming of the afterworld became ways that Muhammad was able to provide a preview of the world to come. Part of the preview also acted as an affirmation for believers. For example, once Muhammad lectured about eschatological events and as his listeners wept, he revealed that "the Garden and the Fire were displayed in front of me on this wall just now and I have never seen a better thing (than the former) and a worse thing (than the latter)."[28]

Aside from visions during waking moments, Muhammad also gained knowledge of the afterworld through dreams. In one instance, Muhammad sees his companions and their places: "Narrated Jabir ibn Abdullah: the Prophet said, 'I saw myself in a dream entering paradise and behold I saw al-Rumaysa, Abu Talha's wife. I heard footsteps. I asked, 'Who is it?' Somebody said, 'It is Bilal.' Then I saw a palace and a lady sitting in its courtyard. I asked, 'For whom is this palace?' 'Umar and his jealousy.'"[29] In another extended dream, Muhammad relates a story much like the Ascension and Night Journey narrative. He is taken by two men and sees various sinners such as one who is hefting a large rock, another who is near an iron hook, and yet another who is consuming stones. He then visits the green expanse of the Garden.[30]

Muhammad's visions and dreams not only offered more paradisiacal details for believers and reassured them of the pleasures of the Garden and the pain of the Fire, but they also signaled the importance of certain companions. These companions acted as models of individual behavior, and the recording of their acts and intentions form their own corpus of literature in hadith manuals. In these hadiths, Muhammad either wishes for or sees his companions' places in the Garden. Eventually, a narrative form emerged that identified the companions whose virtues gain them a place in the Garden. These works, known as *fada'il ashab al-nabi* and *manaqib al-ansar* (virtues of the companions of the prophet and merits of the helpers), employed companions' biographies in order to offer ethical teachings about Islam. Within these lessons, specific companions were identified as the people of the Garden.[31]

In the hadith collections, Muhammad signals Abu Bakr, Bilal, 'Umar, and 'Uthman as distinguished. Abu Bakr, Muhammad's friend, father-in-law, and successor, was mentioned earlier as *al-siddiq*[32] or "the faithful" for believing the veracity of the Night Journey and Ascension as actual event. In terms of his exemplary behavior, hadiths record that Muhammad wished that Abu Bakr be called from all the gates of heaven.[33] At one point, Muhammad also claimed that he heard in the Garden the steps of Bilal, Abu Bakr's freed slave and also the caller of prayer for the community in Medina.[34] 'Umar and 'Uthman, respectively the second and third caliphs, also enter the Garden.[35] In a dream, Muhammad saw 'Umar's palace.[36] The series of hadiths refers to 'Umar's palace and his jealousy (*ghayra*). The same word is used for Allah in the sense that Allah does not want believers to worship any other deity.

Male companions are not the only ones whom Muhammad sees in the Garden. Muhammad's first wife Khadija is awarded a special place there. She will have a place called Qasab, which will be adorned with precious stones and pearls.[37] Muhammad and Khadija learned of her palace from Gabriel. Presumably, her placement was because of her preeminent status in Islamic narrative and her steadfast companionship during the prophet's most difficult trials. Hadith collections regard her award as one gained through labor on earth. One day, she was bringing Muhammad some soup while he was in Gabriel's presence. Gabriel instructed Muhammad that he should tell Khadija that she has a palace in the Garden where there will be no noise and fatigue.[38] Khadija's special abode in the Garden marks her as the most honorable women of all the prophet's companions.

While some of Muhammad's companions are already envisioned to be in the afterworld, others are seen to be in the Fire. For example, Muhammad admits that his father was in the Fire. In one hadith, a man asks about the fate of his own father. Muhammad replied that the man's father was in the Fire. When the man turned away, Muhammad called out to him: "Verily my father and your father are in the Fire."[39] Muhammad only intercedes for his non-Muslim uncle Abu Talib, who protected him from the persecution of the Quraysh, by bringing him from the lowest to the shallowest part of the Fire: "'Abdullah b. al-Harith reported: I heard 'Abbas say: I said: Messenger of Allah, verily Abu Talib defended you and helped you; would it be beneficial for him? He (the Holy Prophet) said: 'Yes, I found him in the lowest part of the Fire and I brought him to the shallowest part.'"[40] Other hadiths note that even though Abu Talib has two shoes in the Fire, his brains will boil, the lightest of punishments in the Fire.[41] In this hadith, the vision of the afterworld is realized through the placement of Muhammad's beloved uncle. If his uncle who supported and protected Muhammad, but never converted, is awarded such a gruesome fate, then others who made a similar choice will also be placed in more severe levels of the Fire. Here Muhammad's comment not only damns those who did not accept his message, but it also signals a temporal barrier between those who could accept the message and those who could not. Even his closet family and supporters are not exempt from the Fire.

Yet, Muhammad was not the only Muslim who had visions of the afterworld. In one remarkable hadith, companions also had visions of the future world. Al-Bukhari states that men used to dream during the prophet's lifetime. In some ways, these dreams may have been encouraged. In Ibn 'Umar's dream, angels bless those who pray, and hell (here the term *jahannam* as opposed to *al-nar* was used) is described as a well with side posts on which each angel carries an iron mace, and people hang upside down from iron chains. These people, not surprisingly, were the men from the Quraysh.

The dreams about the afterworld suggest that for some Muslims, eschatological space became a realm of the imagination. Instead of merely focusing on revelation or asking Muhammad questions about the afterworld, Muslims could also envision their own forms of pleasures and punishments. The afterworld, then, did not just offer an architectural frame for the dogma of the afterlife. Instead, it became a place that was filled with its own things and peopled by particular inhabitants. Muslims could learn about the afterworld in two ways. They could die, wake up a few seconds before final death to talk about the nature of death, and then die finally again. Most common, dreams are the way that believers learn about the next world.[42]

Within this realm of imagination was also the possibility for reform. For example, Ibn 'Umar dreamed that a silk cloth took him to whichever part of *al-janna* he desired; in his dream, he asked an angel to take him to the Fire and so the angel took him and abandoned him there. When the dream was related to Muhammad, he replied that Ibn 'Umar was a good man and wished that he would offer night prayers. From then on, Ibn 'Umar offered his prayers.[43] Ibn 'Umar's vision of the afterworld, then, also served the purpose of instilling spiritual discipline within his earthly life.

The descriptions of the Garden were not just abstract promises made to Muslims; they were also ways in which certain companions claimed importance over others. The blissful landscape of the Garden, the purified state of bodies and homes, and the life filled with servants and companions were discussed and awarded to those who provided righteous models of behavior for both their contemporary companions and for generations of Muslims to come. Certain companions had dreams that allowed them to participate and also verify the blissful life that Muhammad was offering. Dreaming of the afterlife may have allowed Muslims to taste personally the fruits of their labor on earth. Even in the earliest stages, it also acted as a way that the community could reform Muslims.

The culture of envisioning the Garden, then, was initiated by Muhammad's prophetic experiences. His connection with the afterworld encouraged others to develop their own images of the unseen world. No matter through revelation, discussion, lectures, or dreams, the promise of the Garden for Muslims and the threat of the Fire for their Meccan enemies, who were often clan members, developed the early Islamic community's sense of self and position in the world. While belief in the afterlife may or may not have been easily accepted, the strife that Muslims faced intensified their faith and provided them inspiration and consolation. It was to the afterworld they turned to explain their losses and to goad them to further victory. Muhammad's experiences of seeing the afterlife further enhanced the promises granted in revelation. By the time that Muslims dreamed on their own, the asserted reality of the Garden and the Fire had become not only one of the distinguishing traits of the new faith, but also one of its most potent weapons.

[3]

MATERIAL CULTURE
AND AN ISLAMIC ETHIC

L IFE IN the Garden and the Fire necessarily follows life on earth. Yet,
because the Garden and the Fire act as metonymies for reward and
punishment, they do not exist solely as distant realms. Within the
Qur'an and hadiths, they also provide a guiding force in a believer's life.
Given that statements of whether the behavior will warrant a place in the
Garden or the Fire often accompany injunctions or prohibitions, eschatological realities could have been felt within the temporal parameters of
believers' lives. Thus, while the Garden and the Fire act as ends, they are
also the very means to those ends. As ends, they represent the final spatial
realm of a believer's life: one dies to be resurrected in order to live eternal
life in either the Garden or the Fire. As means, they provide guidance: by
following the behavior of the people of the Garden, one achieves a blissful
eternal life; by following the action of the people of the Fire, one ensures
eternal suffering.

The temporal link between the world and the afterworld begins at the
onset of death. When a person dies, his or her soul is in the intermediate
state (*barzakh*).[1] Some Sunni manuals suggest that forty days before a
person is to die, a leaf falls from a tree, and an angel records the deed and
informs Death. Death is sometimes seen as an independent entity, but
more often is personified in the terrifying angel 'Izra'il. Aside from facing
'Izra'il, death itself is an anguishing process. On the day of death, four
angels force the deceased to relinquish provisions, drink, breath, and the
term of life. A scribe then records the deceased's life. Often souls will be
tested. For example, in one tradition Satan takes the form of relatives,

offers cool drink, and suggests that all will be well when the individual renounces Muhammad and his religion in favor of Judaism, since it produced the messiah.[2] Whether adjudicated a righteous believer or not, the soul faces torment owing to the terrorizing process of being in the grave itself. Graves are said to contain snakes, scorpions, and worms. Everyone suffers, but the unbeliever faces punishment.[3] In some manuals, the individual's soul is said to slip from the body, and Gabriel shows the soul the place it will be accorded after the torment of the grave and the Last Judgment. At some point, the soul reunites with the body in the grave, but how and when this occurs is unclear. After death, two angels, Munkar and Nakir, interrogate the soul. They sit by the grave and question the believer's loyalties to Islam by asking the believer to identify his or her Lord, prophet, and correct religion.[4] The two angels predominate in the eschatological narrative; yet, they are not named in the Qur'an and canonical hadith collections.

The actual resurrection takes place at the appointed hour (sa'a). Bodies will be reunited with their spirits. The angel Israfil blows his trumpet, once to herald the beginning of the resurrection, a second time to announce its end.[5] The possibility of intercession (shafa'a) is promised as humanity prepares for the end of time-driven events. Natural disasters and disintegration of morality foreshadow both the coming of the antichrist (al-Dajjal) and Gog and Magog (Yajuj and Majuj), twin monsters said to prefigure the savior. The savior (mahdi) will follow and battle with al-Dajjal. Then follows the Resurrection (qiyama) and the Gathering (hashr). The body will then form beginning with the coccyx, and a naked, shivering, terrified humanity will gather together. Souls will then be assigned to their proper abodes. Finally, it is the time to cross the bridge (Sirat) to verify the soul's status. If the soul is deemed a righteous one heading to al-janna, the bridge is easy to cross because it widens. If the soul is damned, as we have seen, then the bridge will narrow until it is as thin as the edge of a blade, and the person will eventually fall into the blazing fire beneath. Certain collections involve another moment: a beautiful maiden greets a righteous soul, and an ugly hag meets a damned soul.[6] After the final placement of the soul, there appears the possibility of intercession. Only after this general sequence do believers enter the Garden or the Fire.

Through a thematic linking of world and afterworld, invocations of the Garden and the Fire also exerted influence even before the realms are fully experienced at the end of time. The connection between life and afterlife forms an inherent eschatological polemic found in the Qur'an and instructions about daily behavior in various hadiths. There was a prevailing Islamic ethic regarding the promise or threat of the afterlife that may have affected the beliefs and behaviors of Muslims during their earthly lives. The ethic itself reflected that life and the afterlife were linked in the early Islamic community through material objects that were appreciated in this world, but meant to be enjoyed in the next. These sumptuary objects, such as silver vessels and silk garments, linked the limitations of the earthly world and the glories of the afterworld. They also formed an early sensibility about how Muslims were supposed to behave in relation to non-Muslims. The early ethical framework sought to define what was distinctly Muslim both in terms of afterlife and in terms of daily behavior. Yet, the ethical framework was not universal. In fact, hadiths suggest that there was a different understanding of what constituted acceptable behavior for male and female Muslims.

LINKING LIFE AND AFTERLIFE IN THE QUR'AN

One of the prominent themes in the Qur'an is the announcing of the impending doom of the Last Judgment. Verses address those who are condemned to the Fire, as in the case of Abu Lahab mentioned in chapter 1. Verses also contain implicit references and explicit statements about *al-janna* and *al-nar*. For example, the Garden appears with a variety of set phrases such as "rivers that flow underneath." Statements about the Last Judgment and the Garden lead to the same idea: an Islamic life is a prelude to the reality of the Garden. In verses admonishing female infanticide, the Fire is wielded. For those who believe in the power and unity of god, the Garden is promised. For those who act against sin, there is the hereafter of bliss, and those who have been rewarded with the Fire cry out to those who have been rewarded with the Garden.

Aside from the myriad of allusions to the Garden and the Fire, the Qur'an presents itself as an eschatological warning that God is the creator and those who do not follow his wishes will not understand the nature of their punishment until it is too late. The aim of the verses is for humanity to see what will follow their perception of existence so they will be able to comprehend the meaning of their lives in the fullest cosmological picture. In order to depict these cosmological realities, Qur'anic verses are didactic in nature. They focus both on the temporal linkages between life and afterlife through discussions of the resurrection, warnings to humanity, and tales of past peoples who have been punished or annihilated. In many ways, the warnings given to humanity are couched in the most dramatic terms. For example, the opening of the sura *Qaf* presents a dialogue framed by

God's voice in response to unbelievers' incredulous attitudes about the possibility of resurrection:

1. Qaf. By the Glorious Qur'an (Thou art Allah's Messenger) 2. But they wonder that there has come to them a warner from among themselves. So the unbelievers say: "This is a wonderful thing!" 3. "What! When we die and become dust (shall we live again?), that is a (sort of) return (far from our understanding)." 4. We already know how much of them the earth takes away. With us is a record guarding (the full account). 5. But they deny the truth when it comes to them: so they are in a confused state.

The Qur'an is named as an authority of Allah's message, and Muhammad is named as the "warner" (*al-mundhir*). The unbelievers marvel at the idea that life continues after death. Meanwhile, in verse 4–5, Allah uses the nominative plural "We" and asserts that while the body is taken, the life still can be judged. Implicit in the statement is that the recording of the life includes piety and veneration directed to Allah. Verses then introduce what believers ought to understand in order to dispel their confusion:

6. Do they not look at the sky above them? How We have made it and adorned it and there are no flaws in it? 7. And the earth We have spread it out and set thereon mountains standing firm, and produced therein every kind of beautiful growth in pairs. 8. To be observed and commemorated by every devotee turning (to Allah). 9. And we send down from the sky Rain charged with blessing and we produce therewith Gardens and Grain for harvests. 10. And tall (and stately) palm trees, with shoots of fruit stalks, piled one over another. 11. As sustenance for (Allah's) servants. And we give (new) life therewith to land that is dead: thus will be the resurrection.

The message supports the idea of the Resurrection: just as plants are "resurrected" from the earth, so too will bodies rise from their graves.

Aside from asserting the validity of the Resurrection through the focus on creation, verses also present the narratives of past peoples who have disregarded the truth of Resurrection: "Before them was denied (the Hereafter) by the People. Of Noah, the Companions of the Rass, the Thamud. the 'Ad, Pharaoh, the Brethren of Lut, the Companions of the Wood and the people of Tubba'; each one (of them) rejected the messengers, and My warning was duly fulfilled (in them)" (50.12–14). The verses highlight that just as the Meccans disregarded Muhammad's message, these groups disregarded the warning of their own prophets. Their denying is expressed through the word *kadhdhaba*, which has connotations of lying. Other suras fully develop the stories of these past peoples, and their fates are incorporated in the Qur'an as a warning about the consequences of not heeding the message of the current messenger, Muhammad.

Aside from focusing on the Resurrection, sometimes verses also make the explicit linkage between the creation of the earthly world and the afterworld. For example, the sura *al-Tur* narrates the undoing of God's worldly creation and the structuring of God's otherworldly creation. The sura begins by invoking the eternal truth contained within the created world:

> *1. By the Mount (of Revelation) 2. By the decree inscribed 3. In a scroll unfolded 4. By the much frequented Fane 5. By the canopy raised high 6. and by the ocean filled with swell 7. Verily, the Doom of thy Lord will indeed come to pass 8. There is none can avert it 9. On the Day when the firmament will be in dreadful commotion 10. and the mountains will fly hither and thither 11. then woe that day to those that treat (truth) as falsehood 12. that play (and paddle) in shallow trifles. 13. that day shall they be thrust down to the Fire of Hell irresistibly 14. "This" it will be said, "is the fire—which ye were wont to deny! 15. Is this then a fake, or is it ye that do not see? 16. Burn ye therein; The same is it to you whether ye bear it with patience or not; ye but receive the recompense of your (own) deeds."*

At the end of time, Allah takes apart his creation. The firmament will shatter, and the mountains fall apart. Those who did not recognize the truth during their lives will finally taste the truth through pain. They will be cast into the Fire that they refused to acknowledge. The events are inevitable just as punishment inevitably awaits unbelievers. The believers, however, are promised a far different future. Instead of pain, they will experience the true nature of bliss:

> *17. as to the righteous they will be in Gardens and in Happiness 18. Enjoying the Bliss which their Lord hath bestowed on them, and their Lord shall deliver them from the Penalty of the Fire. 19. (To them will be said) "Eat and drink ye with profit and health because of your (good) deeds." 20. They will recline (with ease) on Thrones (of dignity) arranged in ranks; And we shall join them to Companions, with beautiful Big and lustrous eyes. 21. And those who believe and whose families follow them in faith—to them shall we join their families; Nor shall we deprive them (of the fruit) of aught of their works: (Yet) is each individual in pledge for his deeds. 22. And we shall bestow on them, of fruit and meat, anything they shall desire. 23. They shall there*

exchange One with another, a (loving) cup free of frivolity free of all taint of ill. 24. Round about them will serve (devoted) to them, youths (handsome) as Pearls well-guarded. 23. They will advance to each other, engaging in mutual enquiry. 26. They will say: "Aforetime, We were not without fear for the sake of our people. 27. But Allah has been good to us and has delivered us from the penalty of the scorching wind. 28. Truly we did call unto him from of old; Truly it is He, the Beneficent, the Merciful!"

The bliss then is not only being saved from the Fire and the scorching wind, referred to in the previous sura, but also enjoying certain pleasures. The elevated status would include lounging on thrones, which are elsewhere mentioned as covered with silk cushions and placed on silk carpets, and being joined with houris marked by their large eyes. Chapter 1 noted the role of houris as nurses for the wounded in battle. Their sensual nature will be further analyzed in chapters 5 and 6.

The scene offered by the above verses paints a perpetual banquet of bliss. Believers will be joined with their families. One can meet ancestors and descendants. Part of the enjoyment includes eating fruit and meat and other things that are desired. This includes wine that will not make anyone ill, presumably with drunkenness. Handsome youths, described as "pearls well-guarded," form a retinue who serve food and drink. Each person, upon greeting others, will mention the former fear of Allah, and how Allah has finally rewarded them. The recognition that they are saved comes from the fact that they did not face Allah's punishment, not that they enjoy the pleasures of Garden life. It is the alleviation of the fear of the Fire as opposed to the rewards of the Garden for which they are truly grateful.

The linkage of earthly creation and otherworldly creation not only highlights the continuum of life within its natural elements of flora, but it also demonstrates the continuum of social dynamics. Yet, part of the linkage between life and afterlife is to show the superlative nature of the afterlife in terms of material objects. While many suras explore objects in the afterworld, two in particular, al-Rahman and al-Waqi'a, present a rich vision of how the life to come is linked to behavior during earthly time. The aim of the following paragraphs is to introduce the suras' visions of the afterlife, which will be analyzed in chapters 4 and 5.

Al-Rahman, "The Merciful," refers to one of the names of God. The title also governs the sura's content: each component of the verse exemplifies the power and gracious mercy of Allah.[7] The sura maintains symmetry in form and content through the use of dualities and with the refrain, "Which of the favors of your Lord will ye deny?" The sura begins with the manifold creations of Allah that extend from sun and moon, herbs and trees, and the firmament to flora, man, and jinn that support a balanced world "in order that ye may not transgress (due) balance" (55.8). Before the creation of man begins the refrain "which of the favors of your Lord will ye deny?" This refrain follows the mention of every creation that include bodies of waters out of which come small pearls or coral (55.21).[8]

The creations of Allah are extended to the other world, and the sura turns to the Last Judgment. *Jinn* and men will not be able to pass through the "zones of the heavens and the earth" without Allah's permission (54.33). Their punishment is described:

> 35. On you will be sent (O ye evil ones twain!) A flame of fire (to burn) and a smoke (to choke): No defense will ye have: 36. When the sky is rent asunder, and it becomes red like ointment: 38. Then which of the favors of your Lord will ye deny? 39. On that day no question will be asked of man or jinn as to his sin, 40. Then which of the favours of your Lord will ye deny? (For) the sinners will be known by their marks: and they will be seized by their fore-locks and their feet. 42. Then which of the favors of your Lord will ye deny? 43. This is the Hell which the sinners deny. 444. In its midst and in the midst of boiling hot water will they wander round! 45. Then which of the favors of your Lord will ye deny?

Interestingly, the punishment is mentioned for both sinners and *jinn*. The refrain emphasizes the actual sin, which is to deny the favors that Allah has granted. It is due to the denial that the unbelievers are placed in the Fire.

Finally, the sura turns to a vision of the Garden. Reiterating the theme of pairs, there will be two gardens that contain trees and springs in order to empathize perfection and completion. Fruit will even cluster in pairs.

> 46. But for such as fear the time when they will stand before (the Judgment seat of) their Lord there will be two Gardens. 47. Then which of the favours of your Lord will ye deny? 48. Containing all kinds (of trees and delights)— 49. then which of the favours of your Lord will ye deny? 50. In them (Each) will be two springs flowing free. 51. Therein which of the favours of your Lord will ye deny? 52. In them will be fruits of every kind, two and two. 53. Then which of the favors of your lord will ye deny?

The section turns to the surroundings of the Garden and objects such as carpets, brocades, pomegranates, and dates:

54. They will recline on carpets whose inner linings will be of rich brocade: the fruit of the gardens will be near (and easy of reach). 55. Then which of the favors of your Lord will ye deny? 56. In them will be (maidens) chaste, restraining their glances, whom no man or jinn before them has touched. 57. Then which of the favors of your Lord will ye deny? 58. Like unto rubies and coral. 59. Then which of the favors of your Lord will ye deny? 60. Is there any Reward for Good—other than Good? 61. Then which of the favors of your Lord will ye deny? 62. And besides these two, there are two other Gardens. 63. Then which of the favors of your Lord will ye deny? 64. Dark green in color (from plentiful watering). 65. Then which of the favors of your lord will ye deny? 66. In them (each) will be two springs pouring forth water in continuous abundance: 67. Then which of the favors of your Lord will ye deny? 68. In them will be fruits and dates and pomegranates. 69. Then which of the favors of your Lord will ye deny? 70. In them will be fair companions, good beautiful 71. Then which of the favors of your Lord will ye deny? 72. Companions restrained (as to their glances), in (goodly) pavilions. 73. Then which of the favors of your Lord will ye deny? 74. Whom no man or Jinn before them has touched. 75. Then which of the favors of your Lord will ye deny? 76. Reclining on green cushions and rich carpets of beauty. 77. Then which of the favors of your Lord will ye deny? 76. Blessed be the name of they Lord full of Majesty, bounty and honor.

The carpets will be of rich brocade, and believers will be able to reach and savor the fruit that abound around them. In their restrained beauty, houris will be untouched by men or *jinn*. Gardens will be filled with plenty of water. It will be a place of springs, dates, and sumptuous fruits such as pomegranate. Life will be bountiful in the beautiful canopy of the Garden, and believers will rest eternally on its green cushions and rich carpets.

The following sura, *Al-Waqi'a*, translated as "the Reality," summarizes the eschatological argument presented found in the Qur'an: what awaits both Muslims and unbelievers is linked to the existence of things that began before time. Creation, destruction, and life in the hereafter all follow each other. What is inevitable is the end of the world, but also the life beyond it that can only be experienced in the polarities of absolute bliss or torment. The sura's structure follows the division of humanity into the three groups: the foremost in faith, the companions of the right hand, and companions of the left hand. The sura begins with apocalyptic events and the sorting of humanity into three classes: "the companions of the right hand," "the companions of the left hand," and "foremost (in faith) who will be the foremost in the hereafter." Presumably, the foremost of faith consist of the elect of the companions of the right hand since their rewards are similarly described. The elect inhabit the Gardens of Bliss (*al-jannat al-na'im*) where they enjoy the rewards of their good lives (56.13):

> 15. (They will be) on Thrones encrusted (with gold and precious stones), 16. Reclining on them, facing each other. 17. Round about them will (serve) youths of perpetual (freshness) 18. With goblets, (shining) beakers and cups (filled) out of clear-flowing fountains. 19. No after-ache will they receive therefrom, nor will they suffer intoxication. 20. and with fruits any that they may select; 21. And the flesh of fowls, any that they may desire. 22. And (there will be) companions with beautiful big and lustrous eyes. 23. like unto pearls well-guarded. 24. a reward for the deeds or their past (Life). 25. No frivolity, will they hear therein, nor any taint of ill— 26. Only the saying "Peace! Peace!"

In the Garden, people recline on jewel-encrusted thrones and drink from beautiful beakers and cups. Presumably these delicious drinks have the ability to bring joy without the sin of overindulgence. These will not intoxicate; instead, they will bring forth balanced pleasure, alluded to in the first section of *al-Rahman*. Just as the drinks will please but not intoxicate, the companions will enjoy the benefits of life without its disadvantages; for example, there will be no illness. As reward, the elect will be served by houris described as "pearls well guarded." The companions of the right hand will enjoy similar pleasures as the foremost of faith; yet, their surroundings will not be so gilded.

> 28. they will be among lote trees without thorns, 29. Among talh trees with flowers (or fruits—piled one above another— 30. in shade long-extended. 31. By water flowing constantly. 32. And fruit in abundance. 33. Whose season is not limited, nor (supply) forbidden. 34. And on Thrones (of Dignity) raised high. 35. We have created (their companions) of special creation. 36. And made them virgin pure (and undefiled) 37. Beloved (by nature) equal in age 38. For the companions of the right hand.

Here the companions enjoy the garden landscape filled with lotus and *talh* trees surrounded by flowing water and abundant fruit. Although they sit on thrones like the foremost of faith, these thrones are not bejeweled or surrounded by carpets. Similarly, the companions of the right hand instead of being served by houris have companions pure and equal in age.

The companions of the left hand confront a far different future. What they enjoyed in earthly lives will be withheld from them in their future lives (56.45). They will be surrounded by blasts of fire, boiling water, and black smoke (56.42). For doubting that they will be resurrected to account for their deeds (56.47), they will face punishment. Verses list these pains and then question the companions of the left hand about the creation of the world:

> 52. "ye will surely taste of the tree of Zaqqum. 53. Then will ye fill your insides therewith. 54. And drink boiling water on top of it: 55. Indeed ye shall drink like diseased camels raging with thirst!" 56. Such will be their entertainment on the day of requital! 57. It is we who have created you: why do ye not testify to this truth? 58. Do ye then see?—The (human seed) that ye throw out— 59. Is it ye who create it, or are we the creators? 60. We have decreed Death to be your common lot, and we are not to be frustrated 61. From changing your forms and creating you (again) in (forms) that ye know now. 62. And ye certainly know already the first form of creation: why then do you not celebrate his praises?

The verses continue to name the creations that the companions ignore such as the seeds in the ground that grow, the water that comes from the clouds, and the kindled fire.

The sura follows by summarizing the choices with which humanity is faced. The verses call upon humanity to witness the setting of the stars, the revelation of the Qur'an, and the inevitability of death that exempts no one from future account (56.86). For those who accept these inevitable realities, they will enjoy "rest and satisfaction" in the Garden of Bliss (al-jannat al-na'im) (56.89). Those who "treat truth as falsehood" (56.92) will be met with boiling water and burning hellfire (56.93).

When the trumpet is blown and life ceases to exist, earth "is moved, and its mountains . . . are crushed to powder at one stroke" (69.14). As seen in the sura al-Waqi'a, on that day, humanity will be divided into the foremost of faith, the companions on the left, and the companions on the right. The distinction between those who deserve the Garden and those who deserve the Fire will be determined by the acceptance of God's power and creation during their lives. For those who reject the message of God, the gates of the Garden will not open until a camel can pass through the eye of a needle (7.40). What confirms the reality of the Last Judgment is to the extent that those who are damned are finally confronted by the fact that they had no faith in their lives; and the people of the Garden are forbidden to help those in need of succor from the Fire from which they will never escape (7.48–50). While their infinite futures are so differently marked, it is their finite past that was responsible for their eschatological placement.

The message of the Garden and the Fire is not only to set humanity on the right path, but also to warn them of coming trials. Humanity is offered a choice, and that choice has eschatological consequences. For the righteous is the promise of the Garden with its carpets, brocades, and houris, and for those who turn away from the truth of Allah, there is nothing but the pain of the Fire. In this sense, the eschatological narrative in the Qur'an is not just temporally determined. Instead, the Qur'an also provides a view of the afterworld that is similar to the earthly world, but structured on different spatial and temporal parameters. With the focus on the things found within the afterworld, the Qur'an posits not just an alternative to earthly life, but also a *material* alternative to the limitations of the world.

AN ISLAMIC ETHIC

The connection between behavior on earth and reward and punishment in the afterlife is so explicit that many descriptions of the Garden and the Fire are accompanied with explanations of which action leads to one realm or the other, and many traditions about daily life are followed by how the action will result in the calculus of entering the Garden or the Fire. Through the glimpses of the life in the Garden and the Fire, there emerges a code of behavior that constitutes a type of Islamic ethics. This Islamic ethic, which offers guidelines of how to have faith and behave like a Muslim, is presented as a choice given to humanity. Behavior enjoined upon believers on earth had an inverse relationship with behaviors to be enjoyed in the next world: what was shunned in this world is entertained in the next. The same was true for the appreciation of objects. What was enjoyed outside the lines of moderation in this world was the cause of the punishment in the Fire. What was abstained from or unavailable in this world was gifted as a reward for righteous behavior in the Garden. Theoretically, everyone had the same opportunity to be a good Muslim, and those who did not avail themselves of the compassion of Allah were to be awarded a life in The Fire.

In hadiths, the Garden and the Fire are constantly invoked when discussing the rules of Muslim behavior. For example, special prayers are formed to implore Allah to save believers from the Fire.[9] Punishment for wrongdoing was often specified by sin. Those who avoided paying tithe or *zakat* would have their wealth transform into a "white-headed serpent with a sac of venom in each cheek which will seek him out until it has him in its power, saying, 'I am the wealth that you had hidden away.'"[10] During his Night Journey and Ascension, Muhammad saw a usurer whose punishment was to drown in a river because a stone was thrown into his mouth to weigh him down. Any spending of money in an inappropriate way is seen as unfavorable on Judgment Day.[11] Keeping one's oath is another obligation that if broken warrants the Fire. Swearing on a false oath near the prophet's *minbar* (pulpit) earns a special seat in the Fire.[12] Even stealing a toothpick will gain a place in the Fire.[13] While the Fire was employed to compel religious obligations, the Garden appears more frequently in hadiths in order to enjoin ethical behavior. Keeping oaths and not lying will open the doors of the Garden. Truthfulness leads to right action, and right action leads to the Garden.[14] The purpose is not only to be righteous, but also to be mindful of the effects of bad speech and behavior.

At times the Garden and the Fire are used as symbols of antithetical behavior. If a person tells the truth, he or she will gain the Garden. By contrast, a person who utters words of no importance falls into the fires of *jahannam*, while one who watches his words will land in the Garden.[15] For example, someone who falsely alleges paternity is sure to be placed in the Fire.[16] These injunctions against wrongful speech focus on one of the potential areas of humanity's corruption. The other involves man's desire for sex outside the confines of marriage. In one hadith, Muhammad links the two areas of corruption together: "Whomever Allah protects from the evil of two things will enter the Garden. They are what is between his jaws and that is between his legs, what is between his jaws and what is between his legs."[17] Misrepresenting oneself in speech leads to Fire. So does unchecked sexual appetite.

PROBLEM OF ADORNMENT

Hadith collections present a series of narratives that encourage Muslims to protect themselves against adornment in dress and in the household. Good Muslims cannot enjoy material luxuries on earth if they are focused on the veneration of Allah. If they surround themselves with unnecessary luxury, then they forfeit the greater luxuries in the Garden. The major area of adornment that is prohibited for Muslims is dress made of fabrics such as silk. In one hadith, the prophet was given a silk robe (*farruj*) as a gift. He initially prayed in it, but then took it off, claiming that it was not the dress of Allah-fearing pious people.[18] Another hadith shows how the refusal to wear silk robes helped Muslims define themselves in relation to non-Muslims:

Yahya related to me from Malik from Nafi' from 'Abdallah ibn 'Umar that 'Abdullah saw a silk robe at the door of the mosque. He said, "Messenger of Allah, would you buy this robe and wear it on *jum'a* [Friday] when envoys come to you?" The Messenger of Allah, may Allah bless him and grant him peace, said, "No one wears this but a person who has no portion in the Next World." Then the Messenger of Allah, may Allah bless him and grant him peace, was brought some robes of the same material and gave one of them to 'Umar ibn al-Khattab. 'Umar said, "Messenger of Allah, do you clothe me in it when you said what you said about the robe of 'Utarid?" The Messenger of Allah, may Allah bless him and grant him peace, said, "I did not give it to you to wear." 'Umar gave it to a brother of his in Mecca who was still an idolator.[19]

The prophet's response mirrors Qur'anic verses that suggest that one buys with this world the pleasures of the next. By not buying these robes on earth, a believer will be offered a more glorious version of the robe in the next life.[20] In the second part of the hadith, the prophet receives a similar robe and hands it to 'Umar ibn al-Khattab, his companion and one of his eventual successors. After discussing whether it is appropriate to wear the robe, 'Umar gives it to his non-Muslim brother.[21] His brother's acceptance of the gift is possible, since his future does not have to be safeguarded against luxury. He is already doomed to the Fire.

While 'Umar's religiosity is seen as exemplary, other traditions characterize 'Ali, another companion whose succession eventually leads to the Shi'a split in the Islamic community, as having been swayed by luxury. In one tradition, Muhammad gives 'Ali a silk garment, and 'Ali wears it. The prophet gets angry so 'Ali tears it to pieces and then distributes it to women.[22] This hadith suggests a Sunni bias because it portrays 'Ali's as slightly misguided due to his luxury-seeking tendencies. Beyond the figure of 'Ali, the motif of giving the silk to the women for head coverings signifies the same concept of giving the silk to lesser humans, such as those who are not Muslim. In this narrative, women are not expected to have the same level of piety when it comes to adornment; consequently, they are represented as inferior to those who do—namely men.

Prohibitions on dress do not only involve types of cloth, but also how they should be worn. The length of a man's lower garment is one case in point: "Yahya related to me from Malik from al-'Ala' ibn 'Abd al-Rahman that his father said, 'I asked Abu Sa'id al-Khudri about the lower garment. He said that he would inform me with knowledge and that he had heard the Messenger of Allah, may Allah bless him and grant him peace, say,

'The lower garment of the believer should reach to the middle of his calves. There is no harm in what is between that and the ankles. What is lower than that is in the Fire, what is lower than that is in the Fire. On the Day of Rising, Allah will not look at a person who trails his lower garment out of arrogance.'"[23]

Women play an intermediate role between the two positions. For example, many hadiths on dress are found in the section on "dress and the women's quarters." As evinced by the tradition where 'Ali gives the silk to women, dress and the appreciation of clothes is seen to be the realm of women's pleasures. Linked to the dress is an inherent notion of sexuality that surfaces with the way that women adorn themselves: "Yahya related to me from Malik from Muslim ibn Abi Maryam from Abu Salih that Abu Hurayra said, 'Women who are naked even though they are wearing clothes, go astray and make others go astray, and they will not enter the Garden, nor will they experience its fragrance, and its fragrance can be experienced from as far as the distance traveled in five hundred years.'"[24]

The pleasures of wearing clothes, and especially the silken ones, are then seen as an extension of sexuality in which women act as enticement. Hadiths regard women as sexual objects or lures and men as sexually desiring; yet, it is women who can be easily tainted as luxury-seeking Muslims because of their feminine nature. Women cannot be ethical to the same standard as men because of their inclination to enjoy sumptuous material objects.

Sumptuary items related to foods also should be shunned, among them silk and trailing garments. Silver vessels were identified as the ware of idolatry: it is the Zoroastrian who was linked with the use of silver vessels. In one hadith, a certain Hudhayfa throws back the vessel, saying that there was to be neither enjoyment of silk or silk brocade (*dibaj*), nor eating from silver and gold vessels because "such things are for the unbelievers in this worldly life and for us in the hereafter."[25] Silver and gold rings are also forbidden.[26] Another hadith in Imam Malik's *al-Muwatta'* makes the connection between the silver vessel and the fate of the unbeliever far more direct: "A person who drinks from a silver vessel brings the fire of *jahannam* into his belly."[27] Using the vessel will literally ingest *jahannam*. In the same way, another tradition found in Muslim's collection has the prophet advising against enjoying sumptuary objects: "'Abd al-Rahman b. Abu Layla reported that Hudhaifa asked for water and a Magian gave him water in a silver vessel, whereupon he said, I heard Allah's Messenger (Peace be Upon Him) as saying: do not wear silk or brocade and do not drink in vessels of gold and silver, and do not eat in the dishes made of them for these are for them in the world."[28] In these hadiths, items such as silk and brocade are reserved for non-Muslims in this world, suggesting they are for Muslims in the next world. Even certain foods play a part in the ascetic regime. 'Umar, renowned in Sunni texts for his piety, swears not to consume ghee or clarified butter: "Yahya related to me from Malik from Yahya ibn Sa'id that 'Umar al-Khattab was eating bread with ghee. He summoned one of the desert people and he began to eat and mop up the grease in the dish with a morsel of bread. 'Umar said, 'It is as if you were poor.' He said, 'By Allah, I have not eaten ghee nor have I seen food with it since such-and-such a time!' 'Umar declared, 'I shall not eat clarified butter until people are given life again like they were first given life (i.e. on the Day of Rising).'"[29] The refusal to eat ghee and not to wear silk or enjoy the presence of silver and gold is not just an ascetic impulse within Islamic ethics. As evinced from other hadiths, Muslims were not expected to forgo all pleasures in this world, but they are expected to distance themselves from those pleasures that competed with the affection and reverence for God. Disregarding the objects and not displaying vanity showed awareness of the greater pleasures in the next life.

These objects are unacceptable for Muslims, but acceptable for non-Muslims. To gorge on the feast on earth is to have no faith that the true feast awaits. What makes the other feast the more delicious one is not only because it is a reward, but also because sense of perception will be renewed and reformed. These two polarized fields—Muslim and non-Muslim—have their own ethic. The Muslim abstains from luxuries in this life in order to afford luxuries in the future; the non-Muslim relishes luxuries in life precisely because he or she does not comply with the terms of Islamic ethics.

The injunctions against silk, brocade, and silver vessels evince an ethic that identifies itself as not Persian. While it is true that brocades and metals were available in a Byzantine-controlled Syria, the finest of fabrics and items made of precious metals were renowned products of Sassanian Iran. In fact, the word for silk that appears in the Qur'an as a promise for the believers in the Garden is the borrowed Persian term *harir*, as opposed to the Arabic word *khazz*, which was technically a mix between silk and wool, but understood to be silk.[30] What may inform the injunctions against luxury, then, may be an anti-Persian aesthetic that threatened a more moderate aesthetic within Islamic ethics. That stance against Persian goods is also used to define Muslim behavior in relation to presumably luxury-seeking Zoroastrians. It is possible that the proliferation of these hadiths come from a later time period when Arab raiding forces had occupied the Sassanian capital, Ctesiphon (ca. 637) and gained access to the Iranian plateau through the capture of the city Nihavand (642). Yet, the fact that there are similar traditions in early collections such as al-Malik's *al-Muwatta'* suggests that both the argument for an earlier or later provenance for the hadiths is possible.

What is intriguing is that Muhammad was known to wear a signet ring and to have a favorite red cloak. The case against silk, brocade, and precious metals, then, signified a battle that was larger than an individual's desire to dress. The sensibility of what Muslims as a community were supposed to wear and enjoy emerged in a commercial environment where Muslims were not supposed to be the high-end earthly consumers; instead, they were encouraged to be modest in this world so they could gain those goods, in an even more superior form, in the next world.

WOMEN IN HELL

The difference between the believer and unbeliever is significant and explicit when it comes to traditions about the afterlife. Other significant distinctions are far more implicit. In particular, the categories of male and female are another form of stratification within traditions about the Garden and the Fire. The most visible way to locate this gendered distinction is within the texts that describe the rewards of believing men: men of the Garden are awarded *houris* for their good behavior on earth. There is no indication that women are awarded houris or a corresponding being. For this reason, some have suggested that Islamic paradise is a realm that caters to men's pleasures. Other significant traditions suggest that women will form the majority in hell.

Hadiths that claim that most of the people in hell are women do not always associate their placement with any specific sin. The most basic form is the prophet claiming that he saw more women in the Fire than in the Garden, presumably during the Night Journey and Ascension or eclipse prayer:

> Usama b. Zayd reported that Allah's Messenger said: I stood at the door of the Garden and I found that the overwhelming majority of those who entered therein was that of poor persons and wealthy persons were detained. . . . The denizens of the Fire were commanded to get into hell, and I stood upon the door of Fire and the majority among them who entered there was that of women.[31]

In this hadith, the poor form a large portion of the Garden, while the rich are detained. It is unclear as to how long they are detained or to what extent being detained necessitates that they be in the realm of Fire. The corrupting factor is not just possessing things that were enjoyed in the wrong form (impure) in the wrong realm (on earth). By the second clause, it becomes clear that the hadith is making basic ontological distinctions between rich and poor, those who have enjoyed pleasures in this life, and those who have been deprived of them. Within this framework, the hadith damns the category of women who provide another ontological standard. Furthermore, that standard is reinforced by the vision of the majority of hell being women. The hadith suggests that women are seen to be in the lower realms; they are found to be lacking faith, according to normative Islamic standards.

In two other versions, the reasons why women predominate in the Fire are due to their ungrateful relationships with their spouses:

> Narrated Ibn 'Abbas, The Prophet said, "I was shown the Fire and that the majority of its dwellers were women who were ungrateful." It was asked, "Do they disbelieve in Allah?" (or are they ungrateful to Allah?) He replied, "They are ungrateful for the favors and the good (charitable deeds) done to them. If you have always been good (benevolent) to one of them and then she sees something in you (not of her liking), she will say, 'I have never received any good from you.'"[32]

The justification for punishment is not that women are ungrateful to Allah, which could constitute a lack of faith; rather, they are ungrateful to their husbands. Another hadith clarifies these infelicities:

> It is narrated on the authority of 'Abdullah b. 'Umar that the Messenger of Allah observed: "O womenfolk, you should give charity and ask much forgiveness for I saw you in bulk amongst the dwellers of the Fire." A wise lady among them said: "Why is it, Messenger of Allah, that our folk are the bulk of the Fire?" Upon this the Holy Prophet observed: "You curse too much and are ungrateful to your spouses. I have seen none lacking in common sense and failing in religion but (at the same time) robbing the wisdom of the wise, besides you." Upon this the woman remarked: "What is wrong with our common sense and with religion?" He the Holy Prophet observed: "Your lack of common sense can be well judged from the fact that the evidence of two women is equal to one man, that is a proof of the lack of common sense, and you spend some nights (and days) in which you do not offer prayer and in the month of Ramadan (during the days) you do not observe fast, that is a failing in religion." This hadith has been narrated on the authority of Abu Tahir with this chain of transmitters.[33]

The prophet counsels that women should be charitable and ask forgiveness, thus locating the reason that they are placed in hell. Once again, the theme of women's relationships to their husbands plays a major role in determining whether they enter the Garden or the Fire. It is unclear if women's religious failure is due to a separate entity or a manifestation of their lack of common sense. Yet, they are also damned because they rob the wise of wisdom. In this sense, some traditions count as one of the signs of the last hour that men will listen to their wives over their mothers. Presumably, the status of women depends on their role in the family. It is in the role of a wife that a woman has inappropriate power over righteous men, but it is in the role of a mother that she is respected. What reinforces the sense that women are not charitable is a series of hadiths where a woman is doomed to hell because she allowed a cat to starve rather than untying and feeding it.[34] While the hadiths are about a particular woman, they reinforce a sense that women are ungrateful (*kufr*) for the blessings that are provided for them, whether from God or their husbands.

The hadiths about women's earthly behavior and otherworldly placement suggest that women's ethical standing involves a more complicated judgment by normative Islamic standards: women ought strive to be good Muslims and to be rewarded a life in the Garden; yet, they are predisposed to the behavior that is similar to an unbeliever's. When it comes to expressing appreciation for aesthetic objects, this tendency of women is somewhat accepted; however, it is unclear if there is a future punishment involved. What it does indicate is that contained within the traditions is a sense that women's ethical behavior can never be the same as men's. Instead, women's differing status is made clear by the few allowances—such as enjoying silk—and the many injunctions to be grateful, charitable wives. In this sense, Islamic tradition intimates that women have the same opportunity to enter the Garden, but have more obstacles to overcome than men. Women are to be grateful not only to God, but also to their husbands. Within this hierarchy of the family is also a different opportunity that also signals their earthly placement apart from men: women may enjoy the adornments of the non-Muslim in ways that Muslim males cannot.

SHAHADA VERSUS BEHAVIOR

Faith in the *shahada*, the statement that "there is no god but Allah and Muhammad is the Messenger of God," is a prerequisite of faith and has come to be identified as one of the pillars of Islam. Yet, is faith in the *shahada* sufficient criterion for entering the Garden? Some hadiths record that belief in the *shahada* results in placement in the Garden, while others suggest that it is only righteous or ethical deeds that will insure the entry into the Garden. How are the two positions of faith and deeds to be reconciled? Is the afterlife something you actively work towards during your life? Is it something that is rewarded for good deeds and thus orients the way in which you see the continuum between this life and the next? Or is placement in the Garden bestowed solely by Allah's will?

The famous female mystic Rabi'a al-'Adawiyya (713–801) proclaimed that she wished that the Garden and the Fire did not exist because they were becoming objects of people's desires and replacing the sole and necessary preoccupation with Allah. The Qur'an is clear in its orientation that the Garden is only for the pious, and that piety is based on their sole devotion and recognition of Allah as the sole deity. Even those verses that refer to actions such as lying are related to the lie of asserting and denying the truth of Allah. While the Qur'an presents a unified vision of the relationship between faith and the Garden, hadiths tend to be more varied.

People asked Muhammad not only about the Garden, but how to reach it. Some traditions begin with statements such as "Tell me such a deed as will make me enter the Garden."[35] Certain hadiths also assert that particular actions can elicit the right type of outcome. These range from the common meritorious act of offering *zakat*[36] to the more unusual endeavors, such as "Paradise is granted to followers who launch the first naval expedition."[37] The opposite is true as well. Actions can also prohibit entry in the Garden. For example, you will not enter if you wrong your neighbor.[38]

While communal appreciation constitutes an important part of the process of recognizing if someone will win the Garden, the true test is one that is self-imposed. It is faith that will guarantee a place in the Garden. In one hadith, Muhammad claimed that if you believe in the *shahada*, you will enter the Garden. At that point, someone asked even if a person committed illegal sexual intercourse, and Muhammad replied in the affirmative.[39] Yet, the *shahada* is not the only standard by which a person is judged. In another hadith, Muhammad affirmed that belief in the *shahada* is all that is required to guarantee the Garden. A person asks if he should inform the people, and the prophet replies that they should not in case people depend solely on the *shahada* gaining them access to the Garden.[40]

Within this spectrum is the issue of a free will. The following hadith maintains the will of Allah as the final arbitrator of those who will receive the Garden and those who receive the Fire:

The Messenger of Allah, may Allah bless him and grant him peace, said, "Allah, the Blessed, the Exalted, created Adam. Then He stroked his back with His right hand and some of his progeny issued from it. He said, 'I created these for the Garden and they will act with the behavior of the people of the Garden,' Then He stroked his back again and brought forth the rest of his progeny from him. He said, 'I created these for the Fire and they will act with the behavior of the people of the Fire.'" A man asked, "Messenger of Allah, then of what value are actions?" The Messenger of Allah, may Allah bless him and grant him peace, replied, "When Allah created a slave for the Garden, He gives him the behavior of the people of the Garden so that he dies on one of the actions of the people of the Garden and by it He brings him into the Garden. When He created a slave for the Fire, He gives him the behavior of the people of the Fire so that he dies on one of the actions of the people of the Fire and by it He brings him into the Fire."[41]

The preliminary part of the hadith states that Allah molds those destined for one realm or the other. The molding itself results in a proclivity to act a certain way. What is set is a tendency to behave as the people of each respective realm would. When the people reaffirm the actions that they were destined to undertake, they are insured of the realm that was set for them. The hadith suggests, then, that Allah has complete control of how humans are created; in essence, Allah knows the *fitra*, or the natural constitution, of an individual. What is unknown is the way an individual chooses to act through the course of his or her lifetime.

It is due to the potential of an individual reforming his or her nature that the concept of jihad plays such a large role in collections of hadith. Traditions about jihad, technically called *jihad fi sabil Allah* ("striving in the path of Allah"), have two connotations. The first refers to the militant message to fight in the path of Allah, traditions presented in chapter 1; the second is the notion of jihad being an internal struggle on the straight and righteous path to Allah. In this sense, jihad is the constant striving to be Muslim and to be a better one.

Unlike the term "conversion," which contains within it the connotation of a discrete moment of transformation, jihad connotes slower and more gradual shifts. When one constantly strives to be better in the eyes of God, one is in a process of jihad. In one hadith, Muhammad is asked what deed will ensure entry into the Garden. He replies within the framework of jihad as endeavor: "It is reported on the authority of 'Abdullah b. Ma'sud that he observed: 'I asked the Messenger of Allah (may peace be upon him) which deed was best. He (the Holy Prophet) replied: 'Prayer at its appointed hour.' I again said: 'Then what?' He then replied: 'Kindness to the parents.' I again said: 'Then what?' He replied, 'Earnest endeavor (jihad) in the cause of Allah.' And I would have not ceased asking more questions but out of regard for his feelings."[42] Given the tone of the first two injunctions, it is unlikely that here jihad has military connotations. Instead, it is based on the notion of endeavor for what Allah wills.

Yet, martyrdom through battle is also enjoined in hadiths. That martyrdom gains entry into the Garden or passage home safely with material rewards.[43] The sacrifice itself allows for dramatic transformation on the day of the Resurrection where wounds will have the color of blood and the scent of musk.[44] Martyrdom's rewards are ontological and consequential:

> Narrated Anas bin Malik: "The Prophet said, 'Nobody dies and finds good from Allah (in the hereafter) would wish to come back to this world even if he were given the whole world and whatever is in it, except the martyr who, on seeing the superiority of martyrdom, would like to come back to the world and get killed again (in Allah's cause).'"
>
> Narrated Anas: "The Prophet said, 'A single endeavor (of fighting) in Allah's cause in the afternoon or in the forenoon is better than all the world and whatever is in it. A place in the Garden as small as the bow or lash of one of you is better than all the world and whatever is in it. And if a woman from the Garden appeared to the people of the earth, she would fill the space between heaven and earth with light and pleasant scent and her head cover is better than the world and whatever is in it.'"[45]

The rewards extend to the categorical worth of the act and to the pleasures of paradise, exemplified by the gain of women in the Garden and by the superior home of the martyrs. In one dream the prophet reported that he saw the home of the martyrs:

> Narrated Samura: "The Prophet said, 'Last night two men came to me (in a dream) and made me ascend a tree and then admitted me into a better and superior house, better of which I have never seen. One of them said, 'This house is the house of martyrs.'"[46]

Martyrdom for God is determined not only by action, but also by intention. In one hadith found in Malik's collection, a non-Muslim kills a Muslim. The Muslim gains the Garden, and the non-Muslim, after Allah's forgiveness, fights in the way of God, and so he too is seen as a martyr.[47] Muham-

MATERIAL CULTURE AND AN ISLAMIC ETHIC [61]

mad is believed to have said, "Anyone whose both feet get covered with dust in Allah's cause will not be touched by the Fire."[48]

Islamic ethics does not require the actual undertaking of acts of militaristic jihad. Instead, the offering of oneself for Allah is adequate. In this sense, jihad may be seen as the highest grade of abstention, if it is followed with righteous behavior and correct action:

> Narrated Abu Hurayra, "The Prophet said, 'Whoever believes in Allah and his Apostle, offer prayer perfectly and fasts the month of Ramadan, will rightfully be granted the Garden by Allah, no matter whether he fights in Allah's cause or remains in the land where he is born.' The people said, 'O Allah's Apostle! Shall we acquaint the people with this good news?' He said 'the Garden has one hundred grades which Allah has reserved for the Mujahidin who fight in his Cause, and the distance between the Heaven and the Earth. So, when you ask Allah for something, ask for al-Firdaws which is the best and highest part of the Garden.' [The subnarrator added] 'I think the Prophet also said, Above al-Firdaws is the Throne of the Beneficent and from it originate the rivers of the Garden.'"[49]

While the martyrs are to receive the highest grade of the Garden, it is unclear if everyone else is excluded from that category. The Garden is gained through struggle that takes place in an individual's daily choices. One becomes a better Muslim by striving to meet the ethical standards set through the prophet's example recorded in hadiths. The struggle on earth involves not just behavior, but also any mechanism to bring awareness to the choices that face humanity.

While the Qur'an is clear that choices have their consequences, hadiths suggest that there is the possibility to be saved from the Fire. Some individuals implore Allah to save them from their inevitable placement. After the placement, Allah is said to take "equal to the weight of a grain of mustard seed to be taken out of the Fire." In their blackened state, they will be put in the river Haya, or "Life," and they will grow like yellow and twisted grain "near the bank of a flood channel."[50] In the case of those who have been saved, they will be given life, but not one that restores the graces and beauty that Allah first offered to them. Instead, they will be yellow and twisted. The mustard seed as a trope continues; other hadiths suggest that if a believer has a grain of goodness, even the size of a mustard seed, then he or she will be saved from the Fire.[51] Another series suggest that the mustard seed of pride will guarantee a person a spot in the Fire.[52]

Some exit the Fire through Allah's wishes and form the lowest ranks of the Garden. One of the most common traditions refers to the story of Ibn al-'Awf, referred to in chapter 2, whom Allah allowed to crawl through the gates of the Garden. In one hadith, Allah forgives a man and orders him to enter the Garden. The man tries, but finds it is full. Allah laughs at the wretch and tells him to try again: "Go and Enter the Garden, for there is for you the like of the world and ten times like it, or for you is ten time the like of this world. He (the narrator) said: He (that man) would say: 'Art Thou making fun of me? Though Thou are the King?' He the narrator said: I saw the Messenger of Allah laugh till his front teeth were visible. And it was said: That would be the lowest rank among the inhabitants of the Garden."[53] Hadiths record a sense of joy on the part of Muhammad as he laughs at God's compassion or sinners' lack of understanding. In this sense, the stories that involve the last inhabitants of the Garden not only offer a sense of the true mercy and compassion of Allah, but the stories are also framed as joyous jokes where the hero is a fallible fool, but God's generosity forgives the naiveté as well as the sin.

The articulation of what it meant to act as a Muslim was inextricably linked to a certain code of behavior that required faith in Muhammad's message and God's divine beneficence and an appreciation of, yet abstention from, material objects. With the case of adornment, Muslims were expected to deny themselves the sumptuous goods of the world in order to gain the materials of the Garden. Similarly, Muslims are promised objects such as homes, women, silks, and jewelry in the Garden if they struggle on the path and for the love of Allah. What the Qur'an and hadiths demonstrate is that the degree to which one enjoys material goods is a choice with consequences. In this world, one can be an unbeliever who enjoys a lifestyle filled with luxurious clothes and sumptuous vessels, or one can choose to abstain from these pleasures and to save them, in an altered form, for the next world. What is interesting about these distinctions is that it is unlikely that most Muslims in the seventh century—or even most Muslims in the tenth century—were rich enough to renounce a materially driven lifestyle. It is more likely, then, that the objects were used as ways to identify what it meant to be Muslim in this world and a rewarded believer in the next.

[4]

OTHERWORLDLY LANDSCAPES
AND EARTHLY REALITIES

THE GARDEN and the Fire may have been articles of faith, but within hadiths they were ultimately represented as spaces. These spaces are not abstract worlds characterized by platonic ideals or God's love. Instead, the Islamic afterworld is a designed realm with an orderly nature and an urban setting. The Fire is not just heat and flame, but also individualized cells that constitute an intricate world of punishment. The Garden is not just lush flora and abundant water, but also a multitiered world filled with tents, pavilions, and marketplaces. Neither realm is primordial. The Fire is not related to the first worldly fires, and the Garden is not the first cosmic Garden of Eden as much as it is the final aspiration for living.

The otherworldly realms are not haphazard in their details. Instead, they are deliberately structured, and their descriptions are expanded and interpreted by the human imagination. Yet, while the afterworld may be constructed through references in the Qur'an and the hadiths to form an orderly landscape, textual references are not necessarily presented in an orderly fashion. There is no text that provides an explicit tour of the afterworld; however, the Qur'an and hadiths make clear that the Garden and the Fire are structured through related markers of opposition: ethical, topographical, architectural.

As chapter 3 argues, the Garden and the Fire can be defined through their ethical orientations. One type of person is invited into the Garden, and another type is condemned to the Fire. The polarity of these two classes of humanity is reinforced by parallel structures: just as people enter the

Garden through gates, *jahannam* encloses people in its seven prisonlike gates, each one designated for a specific type of sinner: "To it are seven gates: For each of those gates is a (special) class (of sinners) assigned" (15.44). The landscape of the two realms is also understood through the metaphor of earthly behavior: "The Garden is surrounded by hardships and the Fire is surrounded by temptation."[1] In this sense, the future world is represented through an ethical framework or moral judgment.

The polarity of ethical behavior is furthered by antithetical topography and architecture. If the Garden is lusciously filled with water through underground streams, then the Fire is arid, with no shade and no respite for the flame. Whereas the Garden is spacious and its inhabitants can move along freely, in the Fire, inhabitants are contained and cannot escape. While the Garden presents the vision of luscious gardens, one rolling over another in green expanse, the Fire is a place of small closed cells in which an inhabitant sees no one. There is no hope for solidarity even through eye contact. The linking of ethical, topographical, and architectural reinforces the importance of decisions in the earthly world.

More significant, both the Garden and the Fire can be understood through earthly landscapes. The Garden is the idealized landscape that is temperate, green, filled with rivers, and, as a result, fruitful. As a landscape it is like a beautiful garden on earth; however, it exceeds earthly limitations because trees can both flower and provide fruit simultaneously—a biological process that is impossible. If the Garden is the idealized green, then the Fire is the desert intensified. It is arid, dry, barren, and intensely hotter than the purest part of flame. The Garden and the Fire, then, are based on and ultimately exceed earthly parameters.

This chapter turns to the descriptions of the Garden and the Fire as landscapes and presents the most prominent physical features of the afterworld. By focusing on geography and topography in the Qur'an and hadiths, it is possible to trace themes such as the opposition of Garden and Fire and the relationship between descriptions of the otherworld and realities of the earthly world. While each geographic feature may have varied meanings, the Qur'anic depiction of landscape is generally informed by the conditions of the Hijaz, whereas hadiths expand the landscape until they become imbued with more symbolic functions. We look closely here at the Garden rather than the Fire for a simple reason: there tends to be more description of the Garden in Qur'an and hadiths. This predominance of the Garden in early texts is in marked contrast to later texts where the Fire is of greater concern, a phenomenon that will be explored in chapter 6.

FOUNTAINS AND RIVERS

If there is one attribute that defines the conditions of the desert, it is lack of water. Both terms for desert in Arabic, *badiya* and *sahra'*, refer to terrain of limited aquatic resources.[2] The notion of the desert in Arabic, then, is one where there is no flowing water or extensive vegetation. However, that does not mean that deserts are so arid that there is no vegetation at all. Often, there is sufficient rainfall for some plants and trees. At times, the rainfall can be torrential, and sometimes it has even snowed.[3] Other than rainfall, water accumulates in two ways: it can seep into underground pools and collect into pools on expanses of level ground.[4] The level of humidity created from the transition of the hot and dry day to the cooler night creates drops of dew that the earth absorbs. This process alone allows a plant to sustain itself.[5] While these are resources sufficient for human, animal, and vegetative life, they are certainly not ample.

In the desert terrain of Mecca and Medina, located in the Hijaz, a mountain range alongside the western coast of Arabia, rainfall in the region creates pools called *ghadir*, and certain valleys contain a series of these pools that give rise to trees, such as palms.[6] However, even with the vegetation, the climate is still extreme. Central to the understanding of the power of the image of the Garden is the fact that there is not a single river in all of Arabia.

It is striking, then, that in the Qur'an and hadiths, the Garden is marked by the abundance of water, specifically in the form of rivers and fountains. In fact, in the Qur'an, the Garden is often described by the phrase "gardens beneath which rivers flow" (47.12). Perhaps the idea of the subterranean river assumes underground pools of water that are so vast that they flow underneath the earth. Such a vision is certainly antithetical to the climatic reality of the Hijaz region.

Not all rivers signify the abundance of water. Instead, rivers also indicate abundance in other realms. For example, the Qur'an references rivers of milk, wine, and honey: "Here is a parable of the Garden, which the righteous are promised: in it are rivers of water, incorruptible rivers of milk of which the taste never changes; rivers of wine (*khamr*), a joy to those who drink; and rivers of honey pure and clear" (47.15). The milk never turns, the wine always provides untainted joy, and the honey marked by purity. The liquids act as metaphors for life: milk nourishes, wine pleases, and honey sweetens. Considering the Night Journey and Ascension accounts, Muhammad chose milk for his community and as a result facilitated the right path so that in a future life they can enjoy milk, wine, and honey. The notion of a river, then, is not limited to an aquatic nature; instead, the river acts as a repository of the amplitude of all pleasing and nourishing liquids.

Building on Qur'anic description, in hadiths the rivers become enormous and include the river of water. *Al-firdaws* is said to contain one hundred levels where rivers gush.[7] It is also described as above *al-janna*, and on top of both will be the throne of the Compassionate from which flow the rivers of *al-janna*.[8] There are also four "primordial" rivers of water, honey, milk, and wine from which flow smaller rivers.[9] The notion of four rivers corresponds with the landscape alluded to in Genesis: "A river watering the garden flowed from Eden; from there it was separated into four headwaters. The name of the first is the Pishon; it winds through the entire land of Havilah, where there is gold. The name of the second river is the Gihon; it winds through the entire land of Cush. The name of the third river is the Tigris; it runs along the east side of Asshur. And the fourth river is the Euphrates" (2.10–14).

Like the reference in the Hebrew Bible, the rivers in hadiths are also identified through earthly geography; yet, the rivers are different. One hadith mentions that the four rivers that demarcate the space of the Garden include the Sayhan (ancient Saros), Jayhan (ancient Pyramus), Euphrates, and Nile.[10] The geographical span of these earthly rivers in the afterworld illustrates the expanse of Islamic territories. The Sayhan and Jayhan are both Anatolian rivers that cross Cilicia and flow into the Mediterranean.[11] The rivers were seen as symbolically dividing Muslim lands from Byzantine, Christian ones, and they were invoked during the raids into Byzantine territory in the late seventh century.[12] The Euphrates was formerly in the possession of the Sassanian Zoroastrian rulers. The Nile could have symbolized the new holdings of the Arab military garrison in Egypt. It is quite possible, then, that this hadith refers to military expansion of the late seventh or early eighth century. The significance of the rivers as being the markers between Muslim and non-Muslim territory, then, was projected upon the afterworld's geography.

If rivers provide the main underground and aboveground arteries for the Garden, it is the fountain that is the ultimate symbol of aquatic luxury. One fountain is named *salsabil* (76.18), and it will be further discussed in the section on perfumes. Another, *al-kawthar*, literally "good in abundance," is either a fountain or a river that Allah promises Muhammad. It symbolizes amplitude and appears in the Qur'an in the eponymous sura *al-Kawthar*: "To thee have we granted the fount (of Abundance)" (108.1).

The notion of water is integral to understanding the glories of the Garden. Not only do the rivers and fountains allow growth in the natural world, but they also signal abundance in terms of beneficence and success in terms of militaristic exploits. Aside from the specific meanings associated with the river, the mere image of the river acts as a trope for plenty. In this sense, the focus on the river is in stark contrast to the topographical realities of Mecca and Medina. The inhabitants of these two towns could have only known rivers to be the natural wonders of cities outside Arabia. Given the contrast between the Hijaz climate and the vision of the verdant Garden, the image of the river and its culmination of the fountain suggest that the vision of Paradise in the Qur'an was one that would have appealed to those who realized the rigors of an arid climate.

TREES

If underground and aboveground rivers make the Garden possible, then trees and vines are proof of the verdant landscape. The appearance of trees that provide shade and fruit is extremely common in descriptions of the Garden: they include generic shade trees (13.35) and date palm trees. Fruit trees are also prominent: in the Qur'an, pomegranate trees (23.19, 55.28–9) and vines will bear grapes (78.32). Other trees bear fruit in never-ending clusters (69.23, 76.14, 54.55) that hang low and in humility (76.14). The fruit will always be available and will take no work to reach. Fruit will almost present itself in a manner that makes it easiest to pluck, in the same way that in the eclipse vision the grapes were so close and near to Muhammad that he could have just reached out and grabbed a cluster. The fruit will be found in pairs, "two and two" (55.52), to emphasize the ordered symmetry and perfection; and they are abundant all season long (56.33). At times, trees both bear fruit and flower. Thus, the Garden is the place not only of bounty, but also of bounty that exceeds the natural order on earth.

These trees in the Qur'an are based on earthly models, but refined with otherworldly benefits. In the Hijaz, vegetation that survives includes plants that retain water. The most important tree is the date palm whose fruit provided a substantial staple of the daily diet.[13] There is also evidence of grapevines in the Hijaz town of Ta'if. Other types of vegetation include thorny shrubs, such as the 'idah family of trees, whose varieties included the ithl or tamarisk, which was planted as a barrier for palm trees against shifting sands.[14] One variety of the 'idah includes the lotus or sidr tree, which is thorny and aromatic. At times, it can grow to such a size that it provides shade for humans and animals.[15] Another important tree is the acacia variety called talh, which is a thorny tree found in the Hijaz. The tree is famous because gum arabic is drawn from it. It also was notable for its size: its branches are large and the trunk is so tall and wide that a person could barely wrap his or her arms around it.[16] It, too, provides ample shade.[17] Additionally, in the Hijaz, pomegranates and grapes may have been accessible, but not as easily available.

In the Qur'an, *talh* trees provide shade without any mention of their thorns (56.29). *Sidr* trees are even described as thornless (56.28). The existence of thornless *sidr* trees illustrates the parameters of the Garden's landscape. While the landscape is understood in terms of its material dimensions, particular features that are painful or inconvenient are eliminated. In the case of the *sidr*, the irony is that the tree has to exist with thorns to protect itself in a desert environment; however, since *al-janna* is not a desert, the *sidr* tree needs no thorns. Why does the Garden contain trees found in the desert but denuded of their arid characteristics? Why is there not the appearance of another type of vegetation, such as tropical trees?

The transformation of the desert vegetation suggests that the structure of the afterworld is patterned on earthly realities, but relieved of earthly burdens. In this way, a shade tree is transformed into the Garden as not only providing shade, but also as not requiring the attribute that defines it in the desert. Even trees require no defense in the Garden. The material context of the Hijaz informs the material desires of the afterworld, though the afterworld seeks to invalidate the idea that its landscape is harsh and arid. It is within this logic that trees function in ways that they could not during earthly time. Some trees perfume the air; others provide shade for a hundred years.

Trees also have symbolic functions in the Qur'an. In the Garden is found the Sidrat al-Muntaha (53.19), the Lote Tree of the Boundary, which is located on one end of the Garden near the Garden of the Abode next to Allah himself (53.20). The mysterious nature of the limit of the Garden contradicts the sense of its expansiveness described as vast as the whole heavens and the earth (3.133, 57.21) and high or lofty (69.22, 88.10). The Fire also has a symbolic tree. While the Sidrat al-Muntaha is located in the Garden near Allah, the tree of al-Zaqqum is placed in the most punitive part of the Fire. The tree of al-Zaqqum acts as the antithesis of the Sidrat al-Muntaha. As mentioned in chapter 1, the tree of al-Zaqqum was alluded to by Abu Jahl as being of buttered dates (*al-zaqqum*); after which, a revelation was sent down to rebut his words. At that point in Ibn Ishaq's text, the tree was discussed as having heads of demons on its branches (37.62–66) and was also mentioned as food for the sinners (56.52–53). Eating from it will be like eating molten brass and scalding water (44.43–50). The vision of the tree, then, is in accordance to its root word *zaqama*, which connotes the act of gobbling or eating hastily.[18]

In hadiths, the Sidrat al-Muntaha gains symbolic value as the place nearest to Allah's throne. Being near the tree, then, is akin to being in the presence of Allah. Given its spiritual value, it is interesting that contemporary Arab eschatological manuals often depict the Sidrat al-Muntaha on their covers. Hadiths also elaborate reasons to fear the tree of al-Zaqqum. Not only do its demon heads consume sinners in the Fire, but one drop of its resin or pus would also disrupt the means of life for people in the earthly world. Such a potential for contamination provides a scale to understand the pain of those who are forced to eat from it.[19]

Like the appearance of rivers and fountains, the Qur'an presents a landscape filled with trees that are informed by a desert environment. The trees that appear in the Qur'an are ones that are common in the Hijaz, and the ones that were less common, such as grapevines or pomegranate trees, were nonetheless known and sometimes enjoyed. Yet, the flora that is described does not extend to the most common vegetation such as desert grasses and shrubs. For example, *khulla* and *hamd* are the categories of grasses on which camels graze. The most common plant of the desert is a variety of *khulla* called *shih*, which provides fodder for camels, horses, donkeys, and sheep.[20] Similarly, there is no evidence of truffles (*faq'a* or *kimaya*).[21] Even the common red anemone or lavender (*khizam al-'arus*), which appears as a prized flower in pre-Islamic poetry, is missing.[22] The Garden, then, is not described through all types of vegetation; instead, only the prized shade and fruit trees figure prominently.

In hadith collections, however, the material value of the trees is not evident. Instead, trees have a greater symbolic value. While they still provide shade, they are more often discussed as metonymies for the afterworld: the Sidrat al-Muntaha epitomizes that the ultimate pleasure of the Garden is the proximity to Allah, and the tree of al-Zaqqum illustrates the types of torture that awaits unbelievers in the Fire.

PERFUMES AND SENSES

Flowing rivers, beautiful fountains, and shade-bearing trees not only form a vision of the Garden as paradise, but they also invoke the senses. One of the most intriguing aspects of the afterworld is how different realms recall different senses. In the case of landscape of the Garden, sight is the major sense in operation. The Garden, after all, is an idealized vision. By contrast, sight operates as a kind of torture in the Fire where trapped inhabitants can see the beneficence of the Garden.

Touch is also a significant way to access the afterworld. By focusing on the beneficence of water and shade, the metaphors involved in the Garden allude to the sense of touch: one can feel the coolness and the freshness of a river, run one's hand through a fountain, and feel the relief from the sun under the shade of a tree. By contrast, touch is a more *explicit* sense in the Fire where tortures are measured by their ability to inflict and maintain bodily pain. If touch were not possible, then pain could not be realized. If sight and touch are major senses, then it is curious that sound has a minor role in both the Garden and the Fire. Hearing is invoked only once in a tradition of al-Tirmidhi, where houris' voices are sonorous. There may be screams in the Fire, but the Qur'an and hadiths do not highlight them. Instead, even if the Garden and the Fire are full of life, they are remarkably silent realms.

Of all the senses, the most intriguing is the one that predominates in the Garden: smell. In the Qur'an, trees, such as the *talh*, are fragrant. Aside from the olfactory significance, landscape itself is structured by smell and composed of perfumes or spices, such as musk, camphor, and ginger. The fountain *salsabil* (76.18) produces pure wine laced with camphor (76.5) and "a cup mixed with" ginger (76.17), and musk seals the heavenly pure wine of *tasnim* (83.26). In hadiths, there is mention of soil made of saffron, as well as discussion of fountains flowing with camphor, ginger, and musk.

While camphor (*kafur*) and musk (*misk*) were not products of the Hijaz, they were known in pre-Islamic times. Pre-Islamic poets coupled camphor and musk as metonymies for white and black, respectively. Camphor is a white translucent substance distilled with camphor oil from the wood of a camphor tree. There are several varieties, indigenous to China, Japan, Borneo, and Sumatra. As a perfume and spice, camphor was prized. According to Marco Polo, it was worth its weight in gold, and the Sassanians were said to have stored camphor in the palace of Ctesiphon.[23] Camphor and musk, then, must have been expensive luxuries. The same could be maintained for ginger (*zanjabil*), although to a lesser extent. Ginger was known as a product of India and China, but also appeared in Oman and Yemen.[24] The perfumes, then, may have been available in Mecca and Medina, but if so, at exorbitant prices. One thing is certain: the perfumes were not commonly recognized goods. According to Muslim textual tradition, when the Arab armies found stores of camphor in the palace of Ctesiphon, they thought it was salt.[25] It may be the case, then, that the perfume, described in the Qur'an and hadiths, was known only by name. In this sense, access to the Garden also promised access to a luxury good never smelled during a believer's lifetime.

PRECIOUS METALS AND STONES

While the Garden smelled glorious, it also shimmered with gold, silver, and previous stones. Gold and silver were most probably understood within an Arabian context, however, the knowledge and valuation of precious stones is a more ambiguous matter. The case of precious metals and stones suggests, then, that certain objects may have been appreciated literally, while other gems had a more metaphorical significance.

Gold (*dhahab*) and silver (*fidda*) are precious metals found in Arabia; however, like perfume, they were expensive.[26] Gold was also available in mines in north and south Arabia.[27] Silver was mined in Najd and Yemen by Persians: the Shamam mine in Najd was populated by several thousand Zoroastrians, and the town had several fire temples; the Radrad mine in Yemen was also run by Persians up until the ninth century, when the mine was no longer in use.[28] The anti-Persian stance in relation to silver vessels, developed in chapter 3, is compelling given that the silver mines of Arabia were controlled by a Persian industry.[29] Thus, gold and silver were known, but too expensive to be enjoyed. The ethic that emerges in hadiths against vessels may have been an attempt to shield Muslims from the material excess produced by Persians within Arabia.

Precious stones are more difficult to understand. Pearls (*lu'lu'*)[30] and coral (*marjan*)[31] were also stones that could be dived for from Arabia, and both of the terms appear in the Qur'an and pre-Islamic poetry. While the Qur'an mentions *marjan*, it is possible that the term does not refer to coral, but a row of small pearls. The term for gem, or *yaqut*, is also present in the Qur'an. It is commonly understood as "ruby," and Yusuf Ali translates it that way in verse 50.58.

The problem with understanding the term *yaqut* as "ruby" is that *yaqut* is also used for other stones. It can refer to rubies (*yaqut ahmar*, literally "red gem"), green corundum (*yaqut akhdar*, literally "green gem"), topaz (*yaqut asfar*, literally "yellow gem"), or carbuncle (*yaqut jamri*). Thus, in eschatological texts, *yaqut* is translated loosely. To make matters more perplexing, stones understood to be rubies might in fact have been red tourmalines.[32] Nonetheless, al-Biruni (d. 1048), in his work *al-jamahir*, notes that originally there were only three gems: *yaqut*, *zumurrud* (emerald), and *lu'lu'*. Other stones, such as *'aqiq* (carnelian), *firuz* (turquoise), *jaz'* (onyx), and *ballur* (crystal), became valued only over time.[33]

While it is unclear to what *yaqut* exactly refers, it is a term that is used to describe gems of the Garden in the Qur'an. Unlike the earth, where gems are rare and unavailable, in the Garden, gems adorn believers as well as the landscape. The fact that the Garden is made of precious metals and stones distinguishes it from the earth. In the Qur'an, pearls are the predominant stones mentioned. The issue of pearls and slaves will be discussed in the next chapter, but it is worth noting here that pearls represent spiritual symbols of purity and life.

In hadiths, precious jewels are described as being part of the landscape of the Garden as frequently as the invocation of water. While gems appear in al-Bukhari and Muslim's collections, they are described in vivid terms in al-Tirmidhi's collection. In one hadith, Muhammad is asked what the world is made of, and he responds water. When questioned what the Garden composes, he replies, "A brick of gold and a brick of silver with mortar of excellent musk, and pebbles of pearls and gems, and its soil is saffron."[34] Rivers banks are made of tents of hollow pearls.[35] In a weak hadith, al-Tirmidhi records that there is a tree whose trunk is made of gold,[36] which in another tradition it is identified as the Sidrat al-Muntaha.[37] Alluding to the verse in *al-Rahman* about two heavens, one tradition claims that there are to be two Gardens, whose contents will be of gold and silver. Between the two Gardens, inhabitants will see the magnificent mantle over the face of God in the Garden of Eden.[38]

The case of precious metals and gems is complicated. It is clear that gems and precious metals would have been so expensive that they would have been out of reach for most Muslims; thus, the acquisition of these objects in the Garden must have been a powerful image. However, it is unclear why certain stones predominate over others. Why do emeralds or ivory not appear in the Qur'an, hadiths, or even eschatological manuals? If gems are so precious that few people would have even seen them, then why do pearls and *yaqut* appear frequently? It may be that these were the only gems known to the Hijaz region. More likely, the terms were known only through poetry and discourse. In this sense, the notion of pearls and *yaqut* act more as metaphors for beauty than actual artifacts. As Islam expanded into new geographies and regions of wealth, other stones were incorporated.

ANIMALS

In the Qur'an, animals do not appear in the Garden; yet in hadiths, they are mentioned. One hadith notes that there will be birds whose necks are fit to be slaughtered. When questioned if they had a good life, the prophet responded, "We ate better from it."[39] Sheep are also said to be among the animals of the Garden, and so people are enjoined to clean their pens and take care of them on earth.[40] In a series of two traditions found in al-Tirmidhi, the prophet is asked if there will be horses in *al-janna* to which he referred to a horse of gems (*yaqut*) that will fly wherever the rider desired. Another man then asked about the camels, to which the prophet replied to the man that he would receive what his soul desired and pleased his eye.[41]

The absence of animals or even vegetation for animals is striking. There are no desert animals, such as wolves, hyenas, wildcats, panthers, or even lions, famed in pre-Islamic poetry. Ibex, asses, boars, porcupines, hedgehogs, and rabbits are absent. Aside from the hadith in al-Tirmidhi, there are no birds, such as the sand grouse, ostrich, stork, or even famed falcon. There are not even domesticated animals, such as the horse, donkey, guard dog, saluki, sheep, goat, or cow.

Yet, the desire to eat any meat (52.22) and flesh of fowls is promised fulfillment (56.21). Perhaps, then, animals do not appear because they symbolize human labor. In the Garden, one can attain the pleasures of the byproducts of animals without the necessary dangers or toil involved. Interestingly, certain animal characteristics are evident in the case of houris, whose eyes are like the eyes of a gazelle, or unbelievers, whose moans in the Fire resemble the braying of donkeys. Thus, the byproducts or characteristics of certain animals are present, even if the animals are absent from the landscape of the Garden and the Fire.

FIRE

It is obvious that a desert is hot. Its heat is not only scorching, but the sun's rays can only make desert heat debilitating. In the Qur'an, the Fire is the concept of heat as metonymy. In fact, the symbol of the fire is so pervasive that fires and their attributes provide landscape for *al-nar*. It is identified as boiling, scorching, painful, fetid, insatiable, furious, blazing, and cruel. It also has a bottomless pit (101.9)

At times, the term *al-jahim* is used to describe its attributes. For example, it blasts boiling water and black smoke (56.42). The term *al-jahannam* is also employed: it is filled with men and *jinn* (7.179, 11.119, 32.13, 38.85), and its fuel is of men and stones (2.24, 66.6). It is also described as a place of ambush (78.21). Furthermore, the Fire is also personified. It draws in breath at the same time as expelling it, and it will burst with fury as each group enters to be questioned if they were not warned (67.7–8).

Hell is visible on the Day of Judgment: verses mention that *al-jahim*

(79.35–9) and both *al-jahannam* can be viewed (89.23). In fact, in one series of verses, inhabitants of the Garden see the inhabitants of the Fire (37.51–9). The inhabitants will be drinking their nonintoxicating drinks, and around them will be chaste women. One mentions to the other that he had a close companion who denied the truth of the resurrection. At that point, a voice calls to look down, and the inhabitant of the Garden sees his former companion in the middle of the hellfire (*al-jahim*) (37.55).

All the elements that exist in the Fire provide the reverse effects as the elements in the Garden. If there is water, it does not quench thirst; rather, it boils over and burns the inside of the person like a hot boiling spring (88.7). If there is food, it is the bitterest fruit called *dari'* that one eats only to regurgitate and then eat again (88.6). If there is respite, it is met by another lash.

In hadiths regarding the Fire, unbelievers first apprehend the Fire when their souls are shown their places in the next world. Hell will be brought to the unbelievers "with seventy bridles and every bridle would be controlled by seventy angels."[42] Like the hadiths regarding the landscape of the Garden, the scale of the Fire is increased. The Fire will throw off huge sparks the size of forts.[43] The quality of Fire is also intensified: it is sixty-nine parts in excess of the fire of this world,[44] and it will be not red, but blacker than tar.[45] In a hadith found in al-Tirmidhi's collection, Abu Hurayra narrates that the prophet reported that after kindling the Fire for a thousand years, it became red; after a thousand more, it became white; and finally, after another thousand, it was black and dark.[46] The depth of the Fire is also noted: if a stone is thrown, it will travel for seventy years before it reaches the bottom and makes a terrible sound.[47]

In contrast to all the materials found in the Garden, the Fire only offers the attributes of heat, burning and sparks. The Qur'an describes the Fire in terms of the senses it invokes, such as the pain of being near or touching the Fire. In hadiths, however, the Fire physically expands in both the intensity of its heat and size.

SCALE OF THE AFTERWORLD

In both the Qur'an and hadiths, the Garden and the Fire are depicted as being expansive; however, the expanse is described in different terms. In the Qur'an, the expanse is understood through the ampleness of the materials that are contained within the Garden and the Fire. If the Garden is filled with as much fruit that the hand can pick and if the Fire is filled with an intensified heat that the body cannot bear, then the places have an infinite quality to them. Yet, one of the interesting characteristics about the Garden and the Fire is that they are described as being brought near to the believer. As realms, they are close and infinite. In this sense, the Garden and the Fire can be immediate even if they are in future time and space.

In hadiths, the Garden and the Fire become more remote. They still contain bounties the eye has never seen, the ear never heard, and the heart never perceived,[48] and the tiniest space, even if the size of a bow, is better than any place on earth;[49] however, hadiths extend the geography in *al-janna* in terms of space. In a weak hadith, al-Tirmidhi reports that the Garden will comprise a hundred levels, with a hundred years between each one.[50] Inhabitants of the Garden look at the upper compartments, reserved for the most elect just as humans see the shining planets in the eastern and western sides of the horizon.[51] Another version suggests that in between the levels are individual skies and earths: *al-Firdaws* is above *al-janna*, and on top of both will be the throne of the Compassionate from which flow the rivers of *al-janna*.[52]

Another series of hadiths measure the Garden and the Fire by time. The Garden is so large that within it is a tree, sometimes specified as the Sidrat al-Muntaha, under whose shadow a rider on a swift horse would not be able to cross in a hundred years.[53] According to a weak hadith in al-Tirmidhi, the breadth of the Garden's gates will take a swift rider three years to cover.[54] As mentioned earlier, the depth of the Fire is measured by years: if a stone is thrown, it will travel for seventy years before it reaches the bottom and makes a terrible sound.[55]

The use of time is a striking way to measure distance. The Garden and the Fire are measured through steps on a journey that lasts so many years. The way of discussing the Garden and the Fire, then, indicates a mode of measurement. Instead of a parasang[56] or a cubit,[57] the scale of the Garden and the Fire is linked to a society that measured journeys by time. Such a mode of measurement was most probably likely for the Hijazi setting where the journeys of caravans were marked by the days that it took to reach the next town. These hadiths, then, either represent the infinite quality of the afterworld that cannot be measured by conventional standard units or must emanate from an earlier time period before more standard units of measurement were employed.

ANTHROPOMORPHIC LANDSCAPES

While the Garden and the Fire are places with landscapes, in hadith collections, the Garden and the Fire are also anthropomorphic beings. Hell is so hot that it burns itself by eating each part and asks respite from Allah for itself. It requests two breaths in summer and winter.[58] The two realms also argue with each other and ask Allah questions. In one series of hadiths, the Garden and the Fire dispute their respective values based on which people they house. The Fire maintains that it is more distinguished because it contains the haughty and proud, whereas the Garden wonders why it has been requested to house the meek, humble, and downtrodden. It is remarkable that the realms do not recognize their role in reward and punishment. Allah tells the Garden that it is the mechanism to show favor and the Fire is the means for punishment.[59]

Unlike Qur'anic descriptions where the Garden and the Fire oppose each other as symbols for different types of ethical and moral choices, hadiths suggest a coupling. Not only do their landscapes act as antithetical extremes of each other, but the realms also bicker with each other. In some ways, the Garden and the Fire act as twins. When the Garden is described, it is in relation to the Fire. When the Fire is mentioned, it is in relation to the Garden. The two places define each other in the same way that life and afterlife relate to each other. In the Qur'an, the Garden and the Fire involve ethical orientation and place; yet, in hadiths, they become identified as places and objectified as ways of the future.

[5]

HUMANITY, SERVANTS, AND COMPANIONS

WHEN EARTHLY time yields to otherworldly timelessness, humanity assumes its place in the afterworld and fully realizes the consequences of earthly choices. Inhabitants of the Garden and the Fire are introduced to their new lives as they enter the otherworldly realms. Those destined for the Garden will be led in crowds to the gates. As the gates open, gatekeepers will greet people by saying, "Peace be upon you! Well have ye done! Enter ye here to dwell therein" (39.73). Those destined for the Fire are not greeted with such a gracious invitation. Instead, they are violently flung into it. Whereas the inhabitants of the Garden are active agents who stroll through the gates to meet their new lives, inhabitants of the Fire are passive players who have no choice about how they are thrown into their fate.

Upon entering the new realms, inhabitants find their bodies reformed and encounter their living spaces. The purpose of the Garden is to remove earthly pollution and ugliness and replace them with heavenly perfection; by contrast, the purpose of the Fire is to contribute to earthly injury and construct an eternally painful existence. As a result, inhabitants of the Garden become physically beautiful and frolic at leisure in opulent tents or pavilions that are spacious and surrounded by glorious gardens. Meanwhile the Fire's inhabitants toil forcibly in the occupation of torturing themselves in small solitary cells that offer only confinement.

The physical state of the body reflects the judgment of the soul. Refined clothing and jewelry reinforce the beauty of believers' bodies in the Garden. By contrast, unbelievers' bodies in the Fire are not only objects of punishment, but they are also the mechanisms by which the punishment takes place. The body is not just a tortured, fetid thing, but also an instrument of punishment whose parts inflict pain against the will of the individual. The body, as opposed to being a site that reflects the beauty of the soul, becomes the deliverer of pain.

Yet, life in the afterworld amounts to more than just reward and punishment. Instead, the afterworld also provides forms of social interaction. In the Qur'an and hadiths, those awarded life in the Garden enjoy the company of their families and companions, and each companion is promised a retinue that can provide a luxurious life. In the Fire, the opposite holds true. Inhabitants have no companionship, and they can look forward only to their punishment in contained compartments. If the inhabitants of the Garden enjoy a metaphorical banquet of companionship, fine drink, and sumptuous food, then the inhabitants of the Fire encounter a bitter dish, indeed.

Just as the landscape of the Garden, which privileges the importance of trees and rivers at the expense of grasses and shrubs, sheds light on aspirations for the afterworld, the social life of the afterlife reveals which family dynamics were prized. Expectations of interactions center on earthly experiences such as life with spouses, children, companions, and at times household servants. Yet, the realities of earthly life—childhood, growing into adulthood, procreating, providing for a family, taking care of elders, and of course dying—are suspended in the afterworld, for the inhabitants (even in the Fire) do not age. In both the Garden and the Fire, there is no birth, sickness, or death. As a result, the afterworld is based on the experience of earthly living without earthly parameters or limitations.

Describing life in the afterworld through earthly frameworks is understandable (how else could Muslims and non-Muslims have discussed an unknown time and space?), but it also raises a number of questions. What kind of life can a believer or unbeliever expect to live outside the strictures of time? Is the Garden merely a more purified and the Fire merely a more putrid version of the earthly world? What happens when a believer's desires exceed the limitations of the Garden? How can a servant labor in the Garden, which is defined as a realm of no labor?

By focusing on individuals' reconfigured selves and inhabitants' social worlds, the Qur'an and hadiths offer fragmentary glimpses of how believers and unbelievers live in the afterworld. Earthly models of social relations did not always accord with the inherent principles that structure the Garden and the Fire, and the Qur'an and hadiths address these inconsistencies by describing parts of the afterworld, including certain beings, as objects. The significance of the objectification of the material nature of the after-world can encompass even humans as part of a social landscape. More importantly, seeing the afterworld as being made up of objects becomes a mechanism that replicates earthly models of a slave class in otherworldly images of leisure.

PAIN AND PUNISHMENT IN THE FIRE

What marks life in the Fire is solitude and emptiness. Inhabitants of the Fire enjoy no companionship from friends, family, or household members. They also have no homes. Instead, their settings are only described as sites of punishment, such as mountains, fires, or valleys. While the flames crackle and roar (25.14), hot boiling water surrounds inhabitants as they wander around (55.44). People sigh and sob because there will be nothing left for them to do (11.106).

Not only will the inhabitants or unbelievers be scorched from fire, but their faces will also be covered with the Fire and their garments will be made of liquid pitch (14.50). In another verse, their garment is described as being cut from the Fire (22.19). Their only adornments are objects and the results of punishments: chains of 70 cubits (69.32) and the wounds they create (69.36). Mostly, they are yoked either physically or mentally: "The yokes (shall be) round their necks, and the chains; they shall be dragged along—In the boiling fetid fluid then in the Fire shall they be burned" (40.71, 40.72). The yokes are elsewhere described as "yokes of servitude" (13.5), which may represent their payment for the burden of unbelief.

While unbelievers lose a sense of living without social interaction or familiar spaces, they retain their physical selves in an altered state. The transformation of the earthly body begins during eschatological time, and all of humanity experiences fear in anticipation of punishment. At death, the unbeliever's soul smells in the grave; in one hadith, Muhammad puts a cloth to his nose to block the stench.[1] At the time of the Last Judgment, humanity gathers barefoot, naked, and uncircumcised. In essence, human-ity will revert to the way that Allah made them as opposed to the way that they changed themselves.[2] Some will try to prostrate themselves, but they will not be able to because their backs will revert to one bone of a single vertebra.[3] When they stand before Allah, people will be drenched in per-spiration that flows so copiously that it reaches halfway to their ears.[4]

According to one hadith, the extreme range of pleasures and punish-ments are so great that the person forgets the pains and pleasures of earthly life. A future inhabitant of the Fire would be dipped in the Fire and would not find any blessing; a future inhabitant of the Garden would be dipped in the Garden and would not find any hardship.[5] The physical punishments of the Fire are not only ones that pain them and force them to live a life of eternal fear and excruciating pain, but also the punishment of a lesson understood far too late. That lesson is the majesty of God, which was ignored in the pursuit of the world's riches: "The mutual rivalry for piling up (the good things of this world) diverts you (from the more serious things)" (102.1).

After the end of eschatological time, those destined for the Fire undergo another transformation. Their bodies are enhanced with both a greater ability to withstand and greater sensitivity to feel all forms of pain. As a result, punishments in the Fire cut deeper than their earthly versions. Pain is felt in a greater capacity at the same time as the body is able to manage the pain without physical collapse. In this way, the Fire can promise a future of eternal pain.

In the Qur'an and hadiths, there is sparse reference to beings that administer punishment. While the functioning of the Garden is at the hands of the well-guarded youths and houris, nineteen punitive angels administer punishment (74.30–31), and guards flank the gates of the Fire. These angels and guards are under the authority of Malik, the keeper of the Fire (43.77). The only other mention of beings in the Fire appears in the hadith collection of Muslim where women, whose piled hair on their heads resemble camel humps, roam the compartments to tempt men sexually.[6]

Instead of depending on others to manage their punishments, unbelievers are compelled to cause themselves pain. Yet, although they are agents in their own divine retribution, they are passive, since they cannot control their own bodies or their own wills. In the most gruesome manner, punishments take on an infinite quality of unceasing torment. When they are punished, their scorched skin renews itself. They drink fetid water, and they still cannot die (14.6–7). Instead, they cannot stop sipping it, and no amount will damage the person: "In gulps will he sip it, but never will he be near swallowing it down his throat: Death will come to him from every quarter, yet will he not die: and in front of him will be a chastisement unrelenting" (14.17).

Once in the Fire, body parts become separated from the individual as self-contained punishment. Muhammad saw 'Amr b. Luhayy dragging his intestines, as mentioned in chapter 1. An unbeliever's molar or canine tooth will be like the rocky, plateau-topped Mount Uhud north of Medina. Inhabitants' skin will also thicken to the length of a three-night journey.[7]

In another hadith by al-Tirmidhi, "an unbeliever drags his tongue a league and then two leagues while people tread on it."[8] The conditions of the Fire also transform bodies. The Fire's heat alters the body: the color of an inhabitant will change to a darker hue. The Fire will roast an inhabitant until his lower lip retracts to the middle of his head and his lower lip to his navel.[9] Inhabitants are quenched of thirst, but their desire is never satiated: "The believer drinks in one intestine and the unbeliever drinks in seven."[10]

The greatest transformer of bodies, however, is the infliction of boiling liquids. Dregs of olive oil will become like molten copper that is so hot that when it comes near the face, the scalp and face fall into it.[11] Boiling water will be poured over inhabitants' heads, and it will penetrate them until it comes out; in the process, it will burn the person to such an extent that his innards will emerge at his feet. The person, then, becomes restored to full form, presumably to face the torture again.[12]

Another punishment involves the drinking of boiling liquids: "He will be given to drink some liquid pus which he will gulp" (14.16), and, "They will be given to drink a boiling liquid and it will cut their entrails to pieces" (47.15 and 18.29). The inhabitant will be given liquid pus; when it is brought near, it will burn his face and scalp. When he drinks it, it will cut his entrails until it emerges from his posterior.[13] The purulent matter is so pungent that if a bucket of it were poured on the world, the people of the world would stink.[14]

Aside from the general torment that occurs to inhabitants' bodies, punishments are sometimes based on earthly sins. As mentioned in chapter 2, during his Night Journey and Ascension, Muhammad saw usurers whose bellies were like camels maddened by unquestionable thirst since they consumed income that was unnaturally generated. Male fornicators were faced with good fat meat and lean stinking meat, but chose to eat the latter, presumably since in earthly life they sought female flesh that was not theirs for the taking. Female adulterers were hung by their breasts to emphasize their sexual indiscretion. Those who consumed the wealth of orphans were forced to eat the fire that would then emerge from their posteriors since they took what was not theirs by right.[15]

In the Qur'an, there is also mention of specific torments for specific sinners. A sura is dedicated to one of Muhammad's main detractors 'Abd al-'Uzza whose father nicknamed him Abu Lahab ("father of the flame") because of his beauty.[16] The nickname allows a play on words in the sura, for his punishment is to burn in the blazing flame (111.3). Meanwhile, his wife will carry wood as fuel for the flame. Around her neck will be the twisted rope of palm leaf fiber (111.4–5). The scandalmonger or backbiter also acquires wealth, thinking that he is saved and protected. Instead, "he will be sure to be thrown into that which breaks to pieces" (104.4). The Fire he builds encompasses unbelievers and creates a vault around them so they suffocate. The blaze will mount to the hearts, cutting off each from the other, and be upheld by "columns outstretched" (104.9).

In hadiths, categories that involve political rule also develop. A ruler who does no good for his people will never smell the Garden.[17] A person who rules without doing good circulates around the Fire like a donkey grinding a mill.[18] One of the forms of punishment in the Fire is the lack of authorities to whom inhabitants can appeal. In one hadith recorded by al-Tirmidhi, the inhabitants cry for food and are fed the bitter *dari'*; they cry for water, and then boiling water poured from iron hooks approaches them and scorches their faces. When they drink the water, it cuts their stomachs to pieces. They turn to the guards, who tell them that the appeal from unbelievers is futile. Then the inhabitants call out to Malik. He responds a thousand years later and tells them, "You are remaining" (43.77). The punishment is one of solitude where no one can intercede on their behalf.

Muhammad alludes to unbelievers' torment at the battle of Badr. After Abu Jahl b. Hisham, Umayya b. Khalaf, 'Utba b. Rabi'a, and Shayba b. Rabi'a died and their bodies went unburied for three days, Muhammad is said to have sat near them and asked if they found the promises of the Lord correct. 'Umar listened to the prophet and asked if they could hear him. Muhammad replied: "By Him in Whose Hand is my life, what I am saying to them, even you cannot hear more distinctly than they, but they lack the power to reply."[19] Muhammad then reassured him that his enemies would live with bodily mutations resulting from punishment.

Given that the purpose of the Fire is to make the unbeliever feel pain, the body becomes the prime site of punishment. Yet, the punishment is both physical and mental. The everlasting physical torture is experienced in solitude. Whereas the inhabitants of the Garden have transformed bodies and homes that allow them to share companionship, the companions of the Fire are trapped alone in compartments that sometimes have four walls with forty years in distance between each.[20]

The transformation of unbelievers' bodies is one of the main ways that the Garden and the Fire distinguish themselves. Just as in the Garden bodies are relieved of their earthly smells, pains, and decay, in the Fire bodies become the prime mechanism to inflict punishments that yield greater stench, pain, and decay. Living in the Fire is as much an external transformation as an internal one. It is not just the world that transforms into a more blissful or more terrifying place, but it is also the physical and mental self that contributes to the bliss and terror.

BODIES IN THE GARDEN

Life in the Garden is an everlasting banquet. In the Qur'an, the Garden creates the opportunity to experience fully the joy that could not exist for those who toiled on earth for Allah. Believers are finally restored, endowed with perceptions and knowledge that they did not enjoy on earth. Transformed versions of themselves, they will be resurrected to an ageless age. They will experience the span of their lives without temporal gradation.

In their beautiful residences (*masakin*) in "gardens of eternity," inhabitants will enjoy peace (61.11). Removed from their hearts will be "any lurking sense of injury: They will be brothers joyfully facing each other on thrones of dignity" (15.47). Inhabitants of the Garden, then, not only have altered bodies, but also altered mentalities. They are rid of any earthly based jealousies or ill will. They are guaranteed bliss, no matter the residue of their attitudes from the toil of earthly life.

Beaming, laughing, and rejoicing will be the order of the day (80.38–9). Believers will never be weary from work (35.35), and life will be peaceful with the trials and toils of earthly life left behind. The righteous will be surrounded by joy and will feel joy in all that they do (36.55). After all, the Garden is also the dominion of Allah: "His throne doth extend over the heavens and the earth, and he feeleth no fatigue in guarding and preserving them" (2.255).

Hadiths focus on the transformed physical state of the inhabitants of the Garden. In the Garden, believers' hearts will be like the hearts of birds, while the stature of each group to enter the Garden varies.[21] Those who entered the Garden would not be destitute, have worn-out clothes, or declining youth.[22] A weak tradition in al-Tirmidhi notes: "Inhabitants of *al-janna* would enter hairless, beardless, eyes anointed with collyrium, age thirty or thirty three."[23] Inhabitants' health would be perfect so they would never fall ill or die; they will always remain young, and they would be reminded, "This is the Garden. You have made to inherit it for what you used to do."[24]

The transformation of bodies is also determined when an inhabitant enters the Garden. The first group to enter would be sixty cubits, or the size of Adam, but the inhabitants' sizes would diminish group by group until they would be contemporary human sizes.[25] The first group would also have a number of characteristics that symbolize their new lives in their transformed bodies. Their faces would be as bright as a full moon during the night, and the next group would have faces as bright as shining stars.[26]

Bodies would not be marked by bodily pollution. "They would neither pass water, nor void excrement, nor will they suffer from catarrh, nor will they spit, and their combs would be made of gold, and their sweat will be musk."[27] The significance of the lack of pollution is that believers will be restored to a state where they will not have to be encumbered by earthly necessities. When they are relieved of these bodily processes, it is as if their body is fully restored to its pure state, as opposed to being corrupted by worldly experiences.

According to one *gharib* hadith in al-Tirmidhi, men will be given additional strength for sex. When the prophet was asked about sexual capability, he responded that the believer would have the sexual strength of a hundred men.[28] The enhanced energy would be used, since no one would be without a wife in the Garden.[29] One hadith refers to each inhabitant having two wives whose shank marrow glimmers beneath the flesh.[30] While hadiths clearly specify sexual enjoyment, it will not detract from worship of Allah: "Their hearts would be like one heart, glorifying Allah morning and evening."[31]

Just as the landscape is blissful, the inhabitants of Garden become more beautiful. They would come to a street every Friday and when the north wind blows, it would scatter fragrance on their faces and clothes and enhance their beauty and loveliness. When they returned to their families later in the day, they would be greeted with statements that they have increased in beauty and they would find the same of their families.[32]

TEXTILES IN THE GARDEN

Beauty will not only surround inhabitants of the Garden, but it will also adorn them. Believers will be clothed by, recline on, and walk upon fine textiles. In the Qur'an, believers recline on thrones or couches adorned with silks and brocades; cushions will be by their sides and rich carpets, mostly silk, at their feet (88.8–16, 55.76). Their clothes will be of silk (22.23, 35.33), sometimes green garments (76.21, 43.31), and fine and heavy brocades (18.31, 76.21, 44.53), laced with silver and gold and pearls (76.12). They will also wear bracelets of gold and pearls (56.19) and perfume or *riyhan* (56.89). Hadiths continue these descriptions, and sometimes extend them to the landscape so that trees too are bejeweled.

In terms of fabrics for clothing, the Qur'an mentions silk (*harir*), thin silk brocade (*sundus*),[33] and thick silk brocade (*istabraq*).[34] As mentioned in chapter 3, Persian silk and brocade were renowned during the time of Muhammad. Aside from luxurious fabrics that adorn believers, the opulence of the Garden is also evident through the multitudes of carpets that believers can walk upon. Carpets in the Garden are described by three terms: *furush*, *'abqari*, and *zarabi*. *Furush* generally connotes "carpets;" however, in the Qur'an they are characterized as extraordinary: "carpets whose inner linings will be of brocade" (55.54).

While the *furush* exemplify the sumptuary environment, the connotation of *'abqari* or *zarabi* is of a fantastic, marvelous object. 'Abqar was understood to be the land of *jinn* located somewhere in the desert. Certain texts also identify it as a town in Yemen or al-Jazira, the Iraqi region in between the Tigris and Euphrates rivers where there was the production of variegated or figurative textiles. 'Abqar, then, has two meanings; the first is as a magical and unlocated land, the second as a specific region that produces exquisite textiles. These fabled carpets were used to describe Muhammad's prayer carpet. In the Qur'an, they appear as "carpets of beauty" (55.76). *Zarabi* were carpets of all sundry colors and perhaps made of silk brocade. The *zarabi* were often likened to plants, since their image was of thick carpets spread widely like foliage. In the Qur'an, they are described as "rich carpets spread out" (88.16). All three terms depict types of carpets and rugs that are extraordinarily expensive or contain qualities that are only attributed to rich, developed artisan and trading areas.

Believers will also rest upon cushions or *namariq*, a term that is used to describe cushions that are placed on saddles to soften the impact of travel.[35] The term, while used to depict the more urban setting of the Garden, is also understood as cushions to place on animals as well as cushions in the home.[36] The use of the term suggests a society that still appreciated the process of journeying on pack animals. Both the carpets and the cushions, then, would have been appreciated in Mecca, a trading center that exported coarse textile.[37] Like gem-studded jewelry, the exquisite silks and brocades would not have been available to most believers. Instead, they would have to wait until entry into the Garden to wear their fine, fantastic fabrics and jewels.

FAMILIES AND HOUSEHOLDS

To be placed in the Fire is to forgo meaningful connections with other humans. Social life is nonexistent for the unbeliever. Unbelievers live a fragmented existence where they have no companions to provide comfort and no opportunities to reunite with their families. By contrast, sharing otherworldly rewards with the family is one of the joys of life in the Garden. Believers enjoy time with parents, spouses, and offspring (13.23). Just as bodies are made whole and perfected in the Garden, families also reunite in ways that defy earthly temporal realities: believers will not only meet the full genealogical line of their progeny, but they will also be able to greet their ancestors for the first time. There are limitations in this otherworldly reunion: those ancestors (and presumably progeny) who did not follow the faith will not be included (52.21). In otherworldly time, faith in God and Muhammad's message either makes or breaks the constitution of a family.

The continuation of the family in the Garden illustrates the possibilities of living in a timeless realm. In the Garden, one is able to meet all branches and generations of the family line. Since everyone enters the Garden after the end of time, humanity can be gathered together. Families will become whole in the Garden in a way that is impossible for families on earth. However, neither the Qur'an nor hadiths discuss how families will be organized or how they will relate to one another: there is no discussion of patriarchs, matriarchs, uncles, aunts, cousins, or siblings.

Yet there is discussion of spouses and children. One series of hadiths illustrates the paradox of catering to an individual's wishes to have children in the Garden, a realm where there can be regeneration of Allah's earthly creations, but limited possibility of generation. Al-Tirmidhi records that if an inhabitant wishes a child, it will be conceived, delivered, and full grown to the age it wishes. This hadith is considered *gharib*, and al-Tirmidhi discusses the consensus of religious scholars who argue that the believer can have a child, but he will not wish it.[38] The hadith exemplifies the inconsistency of continuing the earthly family and granting believers their desires for new family. The case of generation of children illustrates that even the Garden, a realm of otherworldly promise, has limitations. The Garden is supposed to be made up of whatever the individual desires so if an individual wants a child, he or she should be granted one. However, life in the afterworld is based on the human relations in this earthly world so there can be no new additions in the Garden. Children are born in earthly time; and in the realm of no time or growth, new creations are impossible.

The logical problem that the desire for children raises exemplifies one of the main tensions of understanding life in the Garden. The Garden is supposed to be what every individual desires, but the Garden is also understood within the limitations of natural landscape and human relations. In the Qur'an and hadiths, material conditions of the world still define what is possible in the afterworld so that there is a limit to what an individual can be provided. Is the Garden, then, a more purified and restful version of the earthly world or a realm for individual desire?

In a certain respect, the Garden actualizes desire and fantasy. For example, one hadith records a believer asking Muhammad if there will be horses in the Garden. He is said to have replied that there will be horses of gems.[39] The exchange suggests that believers can enjoy whatever their minds can conceive. Other issues, such as having children, are more complicated. Al-Tirmidhi's hadith takes a diplomatic path by diffusing the tension between individual desire and structural possibility: the believer's desire for children is acknowledged, but it is also accompanied by suggestions that the desire for the impossible would be muted by the sheer joy of the Garden.

Family life in the Garden occurs within domestic space. The Qur'an refers to scenes in beautiful residences (masakin) in "gardens of eternity." In the Qur'an and hadiths, homes are described as places of rest and not as castles or courtyard mansions. Family life not only takes place in opulent homes, but also involves a large retinue. One hadith suggests that aside from his wife, even the lowest-ranked man in the Garden will enjoy eighty thousand servants, seventy-two wives, and a pavilion of pearls and gems. He will also wear a crown of pearls that will light up the space between east and west.[40] It is in the home, then, that families will enjoy what was most probably an expensive or impossible luxury of earthly homes: space, privacy, and bejeweled setting among a large household.

There are two types of homes in the Islamic afterworld: tents and pavilions. The two homes illustrate different topographical expectations of future life. The vision of the tent suggests an urban afterworld that still has contact with near-nomadic conditions. Allusions to tents appear in the Qur'an and the Sira and are further developed in hadiths. The appearance of pavilions, by contrast, has an urban vision of the afterworld that is separated from the conditions of the desert. Pavilions appear in the Qur'an, Sira, and hadiths; however, they become more prominent in later eschatological texts written by authors who did not necessarily experience the realities of desert life.

While both types of residences are opulent domiciles in the Qur'an, in hadiths they are described more fully. Tents are referred to in the Qur'an in terms of both luxury and their ability to unify the family. Often, these two motifs are combined into one image. Inhabitants of the Garden are described as living in a single hollow pearl whose breadth would be sixty miles[41] or thirty miles high.[42] Each corner could house a family; due to its vast size, families would be out of sight of each other, and enjoy utmost privacy.[43] Also during the Night Journey and Ascension, Muhammad was said to have seen small tents of pearls and the earth of musk.[44]

What is striking about these two examples is that they both involve visions of a modified tent. The tent is not one made of hide or coarse cloth; instead, it is described as a pearl, a precious item that often symbolizes purity in the Qur'an. What marks this kind of domicile is that it affords another kind of luxury: privacy. Whole families can reunite under the shelter of one luminescent roof. Not only is there the promise that families will meet their ancestors, but each branch has its own space. For this reason, hadiths often mention that the tents are so wide that they equal a hundred-day journey.

The model of the pavilion also emerges early in the Islamic textual tradition. The Qur'an mentions one specific place for Muhammad's first wife Khadija. According to hadith collections, Muhammad and Khadija learned of her palace from Angel Gabriel. One day, Khadija was bringing Muhammad some soup while he was in Gabriel's presence. Gabriel instructed Muhammad that he should tell Khadija that she has a palace in the Garden where there will be no noise and fatigue.[45] Presumably, he was indicating that the palace would be a reward for the labor of her present life. While in the Qur'an this place is only designated as Qasab, in hadiths it becomes identified as a palace.

The expectation of the pavilion is also represented in the *Sira* of Ibn Ishaq. In an exchange, described in chapter 1, Meccan leaders adversarial to Muhammad try to negotiate with Muhammad so he will stop reciting the verses that he hears from Allah. At one point of frustration, they ask Muhammad to ask God for a sign: "Ask God to send an angel with him to confirm what he said and to contradict them; to make him gardens and castles, and treasures of gold and silver to satisfy his obvious wants."[46] Here the leaders ask for a residence within the model of a pavilion.

While both types of residences are invoked in early texts, the tent and the pavilion represent different visions of luxury. The tent represents a rewarding life where believers can enjoy time and utmost space with family members. In life in the otherworldly tent, the privilege is space. The pavilion is also spacious, but carries with it a connotation of heightened luxury. What makes the pavilion a paradisiacal home is it reinforces an urban vision and also transcends earthly models of luxury.

Eventually the pavilion as the domestic model of the Garden overtakes the tent beginning in tenth century texts. The later pavilions are only populated by servants and are no longer residences whose principle purpose was to house families throughout time, as will be discussed in the next chapter. The transformation from tent to household, then, erodes the concept of the family in the afterlife, eliminates women and children, and replaces them with a world that caters to individual desire. What results is a vision of a Muslim male's otherworldly home as one that is designed solely for his pleasure.

MARKETS

In the Qur'an, there is no commercial exchange in the Garden. The only exchange that exists is the spiritual one established on earth with God: believers offer their lives in veneration, and in return, they are rewarded a more glorious life in the Garden. However, in a series of hadiths found in al-Tirmidhi, there is mention of a marketplace in the Garden, which male inhabitants reach after meeting Allah. Wives do not visit the market; rather, they stay within the home. The only females who interact in the public sphere are houris.

The visit to the market occurs on Friday when men would visit Allah, and they will see Allah's throne and presence in the garden of Paradise (al-firdaws). "Pulpits of light, pulpits of gold, and pulpits of silver will be placed for them, and the lowest of them, for there is no worthless among them, will sit on mounds of musk and camphor, not considering that those who are on chairs are in a better position than they."[47] Allah will remind them of the things they have done in this world. When believers ask if Allah will forgive them, Allah responds that it is only out of forgiveness that they have received the elevated station of being in the highest heaven of al-firdaws.

At this point, Allah instructs believers to take what they desire. They arrive at a market surrounded by angels and things of which their eyes had never seen, ears had never heard, and hearts had never known. Although the place is identified as a market, there will be no buying and selling; instead, people will greet each other. A man of an exalted station would meet a man of a lower station and perceive his clothes to be charming, and they would become more beautiful as they conversed. When the men return home, their wives notice that they have become even more beauti-ful in the presence of Allah.[48] In another *gharib* hadith, Muhammad is to have said that in "*al-janna* there will be a market with no buying and sell-ing except forms of men and women and if a man wants something he enters the form."[49]

The presence of markets illustrates the problem of modeling the after-world on the world. Markets appear in al-Tirmidhi's hadith; however, they are denuded of their import. There can be no buying and selling in the Garden because there can be no exchange. If each inhabitant can receive what he or she wants, then there is no need to barter or negotiate. There is also no need for monetary units. With no discernible way to measure wealth, there can be no distinction between the rich and poor. The lack of functioning markets ensures a greater equality within the social environment of the Garden.

The only hierarchy presented in the Qur'an and hadiths is a result of righteous behavior on earth that is rewarded by proximity to Allah. The earthly hierarchy within the family, tribe, or economic society is not evident. Yet, even within al-Tirmidhi's hadith, the remnant of hierarchy still exists. The man of exalted status greets the man of lesser status, and as he imagines his clothes as charming, they become more beautiful. Presumably, the clothes were rough at the moment of meeting, and they transform through their exchange. The hierarchy of the Garden, then, is not just reflected in the different levels of the Garden where the highest level is for the most elect; instead, differences can also be seen through the adornments and interior beauty of the individual. What is interesting about the hadith is that the differences are not static: the man of lesser status, after all, becomes more beautiful through his exchange with the man of higher status.

Is there equality in the Garden? While all believers in the Garden live in a blessed condition, some are more elevated than others. What is remarkable is that the process of reform can happen within the Garden. If the man of lesser station has clothes that become more beautiful, then there can be growth and transformation. The transformation, though, is only related to the proximity of Allah. Yet, the issue of equality is made more complicated by the articulation of the hadith. While the man of higher station respects the man of lower station, the distinction of his superiority is still asserted to illustrate a society without hierarchy.

The presence of the market illustrates how the afterworld is understood through the models and institutions of the earthly world. However, the appearance of the institution does not necessarily have the same significance as it would have in the earthly world. The exchange in the market is intriguing because it is the main space where inhabitants meet each other. There is no other space, such as a mosque, in the Garden. In some ways, the market approximates the social aspect of the mosque since it takes place on Friday, the day of congregational prayer on earth.

The approximation of market for mosque brings into high relief what earthly activities are missing in the afterworld. No one prays in the Garden. For that matter, other obligations, such as fasting or giving charity, are not evident. Muhammad is also absent: he does not appear in the Garden in Qur'an, hadiths, or even later eschatological texts. Instead of enacting practices that defined believers as Muslims in earthly time, the inhabitants of the Garden have only one purpose—reaffirming their relationship with Allah and themselves.

BEING SERVED

In the Garden, believers are served; in the Fire, they serve themselves. The Garden is the realm antithetical to toil and work. Believers are never employed. They do not provide necessary services to maintain their lives, and there are no emergencies that require their attention. By contrast, in the Fire, inhabitants toil in order to create their own punishments. While there is mention of angels and demons in the Fire, its punitive state and constant punishment is maintained by the inhabitants themselves. If extreme labor defines the Fire, then it is the absence of strain that marks the Garden.

While the perfection of the Garden does not require labor, there are helpers who ensure that believers live the blissful life. In the Garden, beings form a retinue who serve inhabitants. They include angels, youths, and pure companions (*azwaj mutahhara*, which refers to persons of a coupled pair [2.25]). The function of these beings is to serve. Yet, they serve in an invisible manner. While the Qur'an, hadiths, and later eschatological texts mention their existence, they form a nameless, faceless work force. They are living beings; yet, they are not human. Instead, they are beings who, unlike believers and unbelievers, did not live on earth and face judgment.

The Qur'an explicitly mentions male servants. Both young men (*wildan*) and slave boys (*ghilman*) are depicted as "well guarded as pearls." Believers will be surrounded by "youths of perpetual (freshness): If thou seest them, thou wouldst think them scattered pearls" (76.19 and 56.17). Another verse also depicts *ghilman* serving "a cup free of frivolity, free of all taint of ill" (52.24). These male servants are linked particularly with easing the life of the Garden through serving food and drink. Like angels, they function as objects in the landscape, as opposed to sentient, sensitized beings. If the function of the angel is to do God's biding, then the function of the *wildan* and *ghilman* is to serve the banquet. In the Qur'an, the vision of the opulent life centers on the food and drink. The males are not general laborers in the Garden whose duties just *happen* to include serving nonintoxicating drinks. Instead, it is the life where one does not even lift a finger that requires that a drink, the focal point of pleasure, be poured by one of the males. One object serves another.

In Qur'anic verses, it is clear that the *wildan* and *ghilman* act as servants. To what extent are they slaves? *Ghilman* in Arabic denotes "male slaves," and it is reasonable to assume that *wildan* or "boys" is a euphemism for them.[50] Yet, the Qur'an does not use the terms to denote slaves in other contexts. Instead, male and female slaves are designated as *'abd* ("slave"), *raqaba* ("nape of the neck"), or *ma malakat aymanukum* ("that which your right hand possesses"). Furthermore, while in the Qur'an the distinction between free and slave is part of the natural order, verses also present the emancipation of slaves as a meritorious act (2.177, 90.13) and command certain ordinances to safeguard the dignity of slaves.[51] The *wildan* and *ghilman* cannot be slaves in a conventional sense because they cannot be freed from their function.

Given the practice of slavery in Islamic society, it is not far-fetched to assume that the *wildan* and *ghilman* were understood as kinds of other-worldly slaves. Slavery was common in both pre-Islamic and Islamic Arabia. In particular, slaves of Ethiopian origin were ample commodity. In fact, Bilal, the first caller to prayer (*muezzin*) in Islamic history, was of Ethiopian origin. There may have been some white slaves, but they were not numerous.[52] Arab slaves, who were captured as a result of raiding and ransoming, were also available.[53] If there were slaves in the world, why not slaves in the afterworld?

The presence of the male servants raises interesting questions about the implication of their functions in the Garden. If the practice of slavery arose out of both economic and social considerations, do the male servants appear because they are needed or because the afterworld would not be socially complete without them? Clearly, the servants do perform a task: they serve food and particularly nonintoxicating drink. Through the services they provide, then, the male servants have an "economic" function, even if the Garden has no commercial economy. More important, the slaves complete the approximation of the earthly world. Yet, unlike earthly slaves, they cannot be transformed into free people. Since the *wildan* and *ghilman* are part of the retinue of the Garden, there is no chance that they will one day transform into believers.

The descriptions of the servants as being "well guarded as pearls" or "scattered as pearls" offer some clue into the social and spiritual value of the servants. As mentioned in the previous chapter, pearls (*lu'lu'*) have a spiritual significance; yet, the term *lu'lu'* also appears in later texts as a name for a black slave. Referring to the male servants as having characteristics like a *lu'lu'*, then, may have had several registers of meaning. The term may have been a linguistic marker to show the spiritual worth of the servant. It could have also indicated a black slave or conversely a very fair white slave. More likely, the invocation to pearls confers an iconic quality on the servants so that *wildan* and *ghilman* are not just servants, but also represent archetypal beauty and youth. In this function, they share the function of the cupbearer (*saqi*), who conferred youth and immortality in classical Arabic poetry.[54]

Whether white or black, *wildan* and *ghilman* are considered pure. The metaphors about pearls used to describe them suggest that they have an otherworldly quality that transcends earthly form and limitation. Their function in the Garden is to provide beauty and ease, and they do so with purity, the highest state of spiritual and aesthetic existence. For this reason, they are akin to rivers, fountains, jewels, and textiles. While they appear human, they are still objects.

FOOD AND DRINK

While the servants may seem invisible, what they serve is pronounced. Male servants offer sumptuous food and nonintoxicating drinks on dishes of gold and silver. The variety of cuisine reaches perfection and is always available for believers. As for food, one can choose from a variety of dishes. Explicitly mentioned is the flesh of fowls (56.12) and any fruit and meat desired (52.22). The banquet is not just an exquisite experience; it is an *everlasting* exquisite experience. Sustenance or satisfaction (*rizq*) is given morning and evening (19.62), and believers will be told "Eat ye and drink ye to your heart's content: For that ye worked" (43.77).

What distinguishes the banquet in *al-janna* from an earthly banquet is that appetitive pleasures are soulful endeavors built into the landscape of the Garden. One drinks a drink that does not intoxicate: "Nor will they suffer intoxication therefrom with goblets, (shining) beakers, and cups (filled) out of clear-flowing fountains" (37.47). The drink does not produce aftereffects; instead it is designated as "holy" (76.21) and is filled from a clear flowing fountain. Other verses mention pure drink (*rahiq al-makhtum*) sealed with musk (83.25) that can be sipped from a fountain located near Allah (83.27). The pure drink is created for the pure soul in the pure realm. The cup will be "free of frivolity, free of all taint of ill" (52.23).

While the landscape is filled with rivers of wine (*khamr*), none of the descriptions of the drink in the Garden refers to wine directly. Instead, the Qur'an refers to pure drink that does not intoxicate. What does it mean to drink nonintoxicating drinks? While the type of libation is not clear, its nature reinforces the notion of the Garden as a place where pleasure can be experienced without any spiritual taint. One enjoys the drink, then, without earthly limitations of becoming drunk, losing control, and proving to be a nuisance. Additionally, the pleasure is something that is granted by God, as opposed to being an act that detracts from his reverence.

Muslim tradition records that people of Mecca and Medina used to get drunk and gamble; thus, the need to prohibit wine and gambling games (*maysir*). In one instance, Muhammad's uncle Hamza b. 'Abd al-Muttalib became drunk and mutilated 'Ali's camels.[55] The types of wine that were available in the Hijaz may have included *khamr* and *nabidh*. *Khamr* was generally understood to be the drink from fermented black grapes, whereas *nabidh* was the drink of raisins or fermented dates, such as *tamr* and *busr*. Unlike the soil of Mesopotamia and Palestine, the soil of the Hijaz was not suitable to grow grapevines for wine; however, there is some evidence of wine production in the town of Ta'if, located north of Mecca.[56] Most wine, then, was probably imported from Iraq or from Syria, fabled as the land of wine in pre-Islamic poetry. Like the link of silver with Persians, Jews and Christians were linked with the sale of wine in Arabia,[57] and Syrians were linked with the sale of wine in Medina before the prohibition of alcohol.[58] With the prohibition of *khamr* (5.90), Muslim jurists debated the question "What is wine?" There were also attempts to answer the question and apply it to other drinks such as coffee.[59]

Thus, whether the intoxicating drink was made of wine, raisins, or dates, there was consumption of alcohol in the Hijaz. While wine is ethically corrosive on earth to such an extent that its excessive consumption is one of the signs of the apocalypse, in the Garden, wine turns into beverage of reward.[60] Because there is nothing to tempt believers, wine is stripped of its cosmological threat. For the drink to be nonintoxicating in the Garden, then, may have indicated that it would taste as delicious, but not lead to the unruly earthly behavior associated with intoxicants and gambling. The drink was associated with destructive behavior. In the Garden, however, inhabitants could enjoy all food and drink without fear of maleficent consequences.

FEMALE COMPANIONS

There are no female servants in the Garden. While *wildan* and *ghilman* represent male servants, females are referred to through different terms. These females provide services, but they are not servants in the same fashion as the male youths. They are integral to the vision of the paradisiacal banquet, but they do not serve food and drink. Instead, their function is to provide companionship.

While the role of companionship is clear, there is no single term for the companions. Instead, the Qur'an refers to the notion of female companions in a number of ways. Some references invoke the notion of *hur*: "wives with beautiful eyes" (*zawwajnahum bi hur 'ayn*, 44.54, 52.20); "hur restrained" (*hur maqsurat*, 55.72); "*hur 'ayn* like pearls well guarded" (*al-lu'lu' al-maknun*, 56.22–23). Other references focus on the notion of companionship: "companions of equal age" (*kawa'ib atraban*, 78.33). Yet, others emphasize the notion of purity: female plural pronoun as virginal (*abkaran*) (56.35–37); male plural pronoun with the phrase "around them restraining their glances" (37.48, 38.52); female plural pronoun with the phrase "like gems (*yaqut*) and small pearls (*marjan*) whom no man or jinn before them has touched" (55.56). These various phrases make it difficult to ascertain if there are different categories for women. For example, one verse mentions the general term for wives (*azwaj*) in connection with the Garden: "Enter ye the Garden ye and your wives in beauty and rejoicing" (43.70). Yet, this verse is different in tone from the descriptive phrases of women listed above. Interestingly, not all the verses even have a name for these females; instead, the descriptors are in apposition to a feminine pronoun.

Although there is a wide range of interpretation about the houri, there is no definitive account of what constitutes the meaning of the term. Is *hur 'ayn* meant to be a feminine being? If so, are they wives or concubines? Do earthly wives transform into houris, as some scholars suggest? Or are these female companions in a category separate from a male believer's wife? Some scholars argue that in fact the two possibilities are really an evolution of the houri from feminine beings to wives in the earlier to later verses in the Qur'an.[61] Yet, Smith and Haddad suggest that purified wives (*azwaj mutahharah*; 2.25, 4.57, 3.15) are definitely not houris, since the houris are pure from the beginning.[62]

While understanding the original nature of the houri is challenging, there is an evolution of the houri from pure to sensual female companion that can be traced in the Qur'an, hadiths, and eschatological literature. Houris are mentioned four times in putative Meccan suras (52.20, 56.22, 55.72, 44.54). In two of the suras, the righteous will be joined "with companions with beautiful, big and lustrous eyes" (44.54, 52.20). There is also mention of "(companions) restrained glances" (55.72) and "wide eyes" (56.22). It is in the sura *al-Rahman* that their conditions are discussed: they live in pavilions or tents, neither man nor jinn has touched them before, and they recline on green cushions and rich carpets of beauty.

In the Qur'an, houris are marked by large eyes and purity by virtue of being untouched. Hadiths develop their description. Their white limbs are so fair and fine that their bones can be seen through them. Their white gauzy garments flow in the breeze.[63] When they walk in the marketplace, they have a scent that wafts for miles. Composed of saffron, the houri is adorned with jewels. Like all people of the Garden, she will not spit or go to the bathroom. Unlike women on earth, she will not menstruate. In al-Tirmidhi's collection, the houris also speak in their melodic voices: "We live forever and never pass away, we are affluent and never austere, we are content and never discontent. Blessed are those who belong to us and to whom we belong."[64] This hadith is unusual in that it is the only sound other than laughter that is heard in the Garden.

Whereas the houri served as a nurse to the wounded in chapter one, hadiths begin to describe her in a more titillating way. With her translucent flesh and her untouched, restrained manner, the houri as an object draws on sensual perception. But is she desexualized or hypersexualized as an untouched being? Given modern commentators' effort to neutralize her sexuality and conflate her with believers' wives, it is probable that the popular understanding of the houri was (and continues to be) a sexual one.[65] Interestingly, the purity of not having to experience any bodily fluids does not invalidate sexual activity and satisfaction.[66] In later eschatological texts examined in the next chapter, the houri is equated with a virgin designated to each believing man.

The houri is one of the more enduring objects in the Garden; contemporary eschatological manuals still discuss the qualities of houris and forgo detailed discussions of food, drink, and male servants. Yet, the meaning of the houri is highly contested. While there may have been an insistence to see her purity in the Qur'an, hadiths develop her alluring, virginal attributes. References to the houri in hadiths suggest that she must have been understood more as a concubine or a female singer or musician (qiyan) than a wife.[67] In the Qur'an, however, the categories are at times conflated: believers are promised a wife from the houris. Yet the houri as wife is not necessarily someone who has lived on earth and faced judgment. In this sense, while she may not provide labor in the way that a wildan or ghilman does, she too was understood in terms of an object to be relished in the Garden.

The social dynamics of the afterlife lend insight into what makes both the Garden and the Fire such visions of pleasure and pain. What structures the Fire architecturally and socially is the lack of social interaction. By contrast, the Garden completes social life by easing life, providing domestic space, and ensuring physical and spiritual beauty. Within the transformation that occurs to bodies in the Garden, believers are able to enjoy experiences that would be impossible in earthly time. Meeting one's ancestors and progeny is one of the rewards of the Garden. Other rewards include enjoying the companionship of pure females while a retinue of servants ensures that the banquet is everlasting.

While the social life in the Garden is meant to be glorious, it provides a glimpse into the construction of idealized visions of human interaction. In this sense, the importance of family in the Qur'an and hadiths is preeminent. So, too, is the notion of a servant class that provides the believer services and companionship. Although not articulated in the texts, these beings form another class within the afterworld. Their existence is understood through the prism of objectification in the same way that earthly slaves would be objectified. For this reason, social life in the afterworld is defined as much as by textiles and food as it is by its beings, which also act as objects.

[6]

INDIVIDUALIZED GARDENS
AND EXPANDING FIRES

T HE TERRORS of the apocalypse and the possibility of life in the Fire led to anxieties about death and promoted a religious culture of exhortation. From admonitory hadiths to highly performative storytelling, exhortation was one of the ways that Muslims learned about what awaited them in eschatological time. The Garden and the Fire became objects of rhetoric for the religious learned (*'ulama*), who aimed to develop believers' religious sensibilities and behaviors.

Eschatological warnings, in both oral and written forms, sought to instill the importance of moral education and behavior. Preachers and storytellers often employed dramatic warnings about the punishments that awaited misguided believers. Because preachers and storytellers could interact with the audience, their narrations could be tailored to instill fear. Often, the preaching sessions included eschatological motifs that were exaggerated in order to make an emphatic point. As long as the traditions conformed to ethical guidance, some embellishment was allowed. As a result, traditions about the Garden and the Fire may not have been treated with the same scrutiny as other traditions that affected law codes. Theologians also developed eschatological manuals in order to satisfy believers' curiosities about the afterlife.

The first manual about the afterlife was probably Ka'b al-Ahbar's *Kitab al-akhira* (Book of the Hereafter).[1] There is no extant copy of this seventh-century text, but given the traditions from Ka'b al-Ahbar found in other collections, it is likely that the work was a compilation of the traditions that he transmitted. These traditions addressed the topics of death, the Resurrection, and the Garden and the Fire. Aside from hadith collections, there are several extant primers from the ninth century that described future life. The texts, written by both orthodox and heterodox theologians, provided clear and often simplified narratives of eschatological events. Typically, the texts contained references to both the Qur'an and hadiths. Yet, those texts did not merely compile verses and traditions. Instead, they ordered the canonical textual fragments within a framework in order to develop a fuller picture of the afterworld. As a result, authors of eschatological manuals often presented their own dramatic rendering of life after death in order to create a narrative that reinforced the reader's moral and spiritual welfare. The composition of these eschatological manuals continued over the centuries (even until the present day) and eventually shaped the way that Muslims understood and accessed eschatological traditions.

While all eschatological texts lead the reader to the point where eternity begins, not all of them discuss the Garden and the Fire explicitly. Some texts are dedicated solely to considerations of the soul (*ruh*) from creation to the grave to the final judgment.[2] Other texts are more focused on the Resurrection (*qiyama*) and lead the reader from the grave until entry into the Garden or the Fire.[3] Many of the texts that involve the soul and Resurrection allude to the afterworld through discussions of the terrors of eschatological time, but they do not always discuss the soul or account for life *after* the Resurrection. Instead, the narrative stops "at the precise point where history becomes eternity."[4] There are also texts that focus mainly on the characteristics of the Garden and the Fire. Some texts, such as Ibn Habib's *Kitab wasf al-firdaws* (Book of the Depiction of Paradise), al-Maqdisi's *Sifat al-janna* (Characteristics of al-Janna) and *Dhikr al-nar* (Remembrance of Death), and Isbahani's *Sifat al-janna*, list the characteristics under topics and address questions about the afterlife. Other texts describe the characteristics within a larger spiritual narrative that takes the reader through a *mi'raj*-like ascent or through the stages of eschatological time. These texts include al-Muhasibi's (d. 857) *Kitab al-tawahhum* (Book of Imagination), al-Samarqandi's (d. 1002) *Kitab al-haqa'iq wa-l-daqa'iq* (Book of Realities and Intricacies), al-Qadi's (ca. 1100) *Daqa'iq al-akhbar fi dhikr al-janna wa-l-nar* (Intricacies of the Matter of the Remembrance of al-Janna and al-Nar), and al-Suyuti's (d. 1505) *Kitab al-durar al-hisan fi al-ba'th wa-na'im al-jinan* (Book of the Beautiful Pearls During the Resurrection and the Blessing of the Garden). Finally, beginning in the twelfth century, texts such as al-Ghazali's *Kitab dhikr al-mawt wa ma ba'dahu* (Remembrance of Death and the Afterlife) and Qurtubi's (d. 1273) *al-Tadhkira fi ahwal al-mawta wa-umur al-akhira* (Remembrance on the

Terrors of Death and Matters of the Hereafter) created a synthesis of the considerations of the soul, Resurrection, and described life in the Garden and the Fire. Eschatological texts, then, were not monolithic in their out-looks. Instead, they focused on particular aspects of eschatological time. What unites each manual is the objective to impart the importance of a rightly guided life. Sometimes that educational aim is demonstrated through a presentation of otherworldly rewards and punishments. Other times the aim is made manifest through a series of questions about the state of the soul and its possible resting places.

This chapter offers an examination of manuals from the ninth to the sixteenth centuries. While it considers the interrelated themes in all types of eschatological manuals, its focuses primarily on works that describe the Resurrection or characteristics of the afterworld. In doing so, it demon-strates how the narrative form of the manuals privileged certain aspects of the Garden and Fire over others and eventually gave shape to the ways that Muslims understood the Islamic afterworld. In assessing the dynamic quality of eschatological traditions, the chapter focuses particularly on the development of descriptions of houris, architecture, and demons. The structure of the eschatological manuals privileges certain traditions over others and suggests that over time the Garden and the Fire were under-stood through the prism of individual experience. The focus on the sensual aspects of the afterworld provided a realm of spiritual pleasure that did not include familial companionship. With an emphasis on individual tor-ment, the Fire also became a more dynamic site for discourse. In the manuals, the way that the Garden and the Fire were discussed expanded in both form and topic.

PREACHING AND STORYTELLING

At the heart of exhortation is moral edification, which may have involved modes of entertainment. Exhortation is meant to be sobering, perhaps terrifying, but as a form of warning, it is also highly performative. The entertainment would not have necessarily detracted from religious pur-poses, yet it added an element of theater. The multiple meanings embedded within the delivering of religious warnings are best illustrated in the case of preachers (*wuʿʿaz*) and storytellers (*qussas*) who entertained Muslims with moral and edifying stories. As in any kind of performance, preaching and storytelling necessitated a relationship with the audience. Preachers would want to convey their messages in dramatic and effective ways in order to reach their audience. The audience may have wanted to hear the religious lesson, particularly in the form of stories that instilled fear for the last days and reverence for the awesome quality of God.

Because the performers' interpretations were sometimes innovative, they undermined the theological opinions of scholars. As a result, the relationship between the preachers and storytellers and theologians was not always smooth. Yet, preachers served an important function of disseminating hadiths and edifying stories in an accessible and compelling fashion. Not only did hearing the story allow for a more dramatic impact than reading, but conveying religious traditions from person to person was also considered a more legitimate way to transmit knowledge.[5] No matter the inherent tension between religious performers and theologians, preachers were essential in the process of Islamic learning. Their influence was significant during a time of fluid religious authority and the rise and development of urban centers.[6]

The preachers and storytellers' innovations elicited works that critiqued their behavior. The most renowned of these works is Ibn al-Jawzi's (1112–1201) *Kitab al-qussas wa-l-mudhakkirin* (Book of Storytellers and Preachers). In his work, Ibn al-Jawzi presents several cases of storytellers and preachers narrating and exhorting people to remember the inevitability of judgment and life beyond. The work may have been written to serve as a textbook for the science of preaching and contains frequent reference to the afterlife, which produced the most fruitful material to manipulate or goad an audience.[7]

The aim of the storyteller, then, was to use the afterlife in order to encourage people to maintain righteous behavior. For example, one tradition, in Ibn al-Jawzi's work, suggests that the afterlife was a central concern for storytellers: "Ibn Hanbal reported on the authority of his father Hanbal b. Ishaq: 'I asked my paternal cousin about the *qussas* and he replied: "The [true] *qussas* are those who speak about the Garden and the Fire, who arouse people to fear, and who are upright in intention and honest in matters of hadith. However, as for those, who introduce fabricated narratives [*akhbar*] and false traditions, verily with such persons I shall have nothing to do."'"[8] The Garden and the Fire may have been a motif for the storyteller, but they also functioned as the ultimate goal. If storytellers were able to ward people from bad behaviors through their performances, then they may have been able to save them from the Fire. As the text suggests, the best storytellers are those whose words were able to influence a believer's behavior and attitude. Yet, the text also has an inherent critique. The successful storyteller was able to arouse fear through narratives that were deemed credible. Those storytellers who fabricated traditions may have achieved the same ends, but they did so outside the bounds of verified narratives.

An example of a true *qass* is Ka'b al-Ahbar, a Yemenite Jew who converted around 638 and wrote several works on the afterlife. In a story about Ka'b al-Ahbar, Ibn al-Jawzi suggests that his preaching took place daily. What is interesting about his performance is that the impetus may have come as much from his audience, the caliph 'Umar, as it did from Ka'b al-Ahbar himself.

'Umar b. al-Khattab also frequently used to ask Ka'b to give exhortations. Ka'b himself related the following:

> One day 'Umar b. al-Khattab said while I was with him: "O Ka'b! Instill fear into our hearts!" I replied: "O Commander of the Faithful! Do you not have in your possession the Book of God and the wisdom (*hikma*) of the Prophet?" He replied: "Yes, but I want *you* to instill fear into our hearts!" So I said: "O Commander of the Faithful! Perform the deeds of a man! If I were to present at the judgment the deeds of seventy prophets you would find your deeds inadequate, as you will see." 'Umar hung his head in silence for a while after which he recuperated and said: "O Ka'b! Exhort us again!" I said: "O Commander of the Faithful! If the door of hell in the east were open the width of a bull's nose, a man's brain in the west would melt because of the excessive heat." 'Umar again bowed his head in silence for a period after which he recovered and said: "Exhort us still more O Ka'b!" I said: "O Commander of the Faithful! On the Day of Judgment hell will send forth exceedingly hot gusts of air, and no favored king or chosen prophet will be too great to escape prostrating himself upon his knees and uttering: 'Lord of my soul, my soul! Today, I plead only for myself!'" 'Umar bowed his head in silence for a while after which [Ka'b] said: "O Commander of the Faithful! Do you not realize that the following words are to be found in the Book of God: 'On that day every soul will come pleading for itself, and every soul will be repaid what it did, and they will not be wronged.'"[9]

In this exchange, 'Umar is the one who initiates the session with Ka'b in order to hear about the Fire. For 'Umar the purpose was to feel fear in order to reinforce his moral rectitude. In fact, part of the exchange was not only to discuss the ferocity of the Fire, but also to value 'Umar's deeds in relation to others. The Fire's flames feel even more immediate because 'Umar's actions pale in comparison to other prophets. The number seventy signifies plentitude or infinity so the deeds of seventy prophets mean that an infinite amount of a prophet's good works would also not save them from the Fire.[10] With such calculation, 'Umar's placement in the Fire is a possibility.

Interestingly, Ka'b not only tells 'Umar that these traditions are found in the Qur'an and the wisdom of the prophet, but he also ends his exchange with words from the Qur'an, reminding 'Umar of the truth of Allah's words beyond their exchange. Indeed, each of the traditions that Ka'b al-Ahbar chose to relate came to be considered sound. He did not invent traditions; rather, he chose select traditions that would evoke the terrible fear that 'Umar desired to experience. Here we see not the desire to know, but the desire to experience the Fire vicariously so that 'Umar is reminded of the importance of staying on the straight path. Invocation and discussion about the Fire were types of religious practice. In this sense, Ka'b acted as a teacher who instilled and crystallized the values and lessons that were presented in revelation and hadith. For 'Umar the power of the message was expressed through oral transmission. In similar moments, believers would have known the stories and their outcomes, but they sought to hear them from those gifted enough to make the impending reality present within the time of the storytelling.

Not all types of exhortation were conventional. Ibn al-Jawzi writes about those people who sought to imitate preachers and as a result introduced innovations. One case of innovation was particularly literal:

Abu al-Husain al-Khayyat reported the following: "I passed by Abu 'Abd Allah Ghulam Khalil while he was conducting a meeting in Baghdad during which he got down on all fours. I said to one of the persons present in the meeting: 'Woe unto you! What is the matter with Abu 'Abd Allah?' The man replied: 'He is illustrating how 'Abd al-Rahman b. 'Awf will cross the [Bridge of] Sirat on the Day of Resurrection.'" Abu al-Husain continued: "On another occasion I passed by one of his meetings, and he was stretching out his hands while standing in a stooped posture. So I inquired with one of those present: 'What is the matter with him?' 'He is illustrating how God will cast His protection around his servant on the Day of Resurrection,' was the answer."[11]

In this example, the storyteller reenacts his tale with dramatic gestures. First, he crawled on all fours in order to convey how 'Abd al-Rahman b. 'Awf crosses the Bridge of Sirat after Allah has interceded on his behalf. Then he tries to indicate with his hands how God will shelter believers on the Day of Resurrection. In these instances, the gestures aim to mirror the events during apocalyptic time; the incongruence between the scale of human gesture and cosmic upheaval is apparent. Not only was the use of gesture in this fashion seen as an innovation, but it also made a slight mockery of the storyteller and others at the meeting who would have witnessed him crawling about on the floor in such farcical enactment.

Aside from performance, some storytellers and preachers fabricated stories or passed along stories not knowing that they were false.[12] At times, however, the falsification was deliberate. Ibn al-Jawzi presents one anecdote of a preacher who related a story that the prophet's grandsons Hasan and Husayn went to 'Umar, and he presented them with a thousand *dinars*. They reported this to their father 'Ali, who then said, "I heard the Prophet of God say: 'Umar is the light of Islam in this world and the lamp of the people of the Garden in the Garden.'" The boys returned to 'Umar and reported this "tradition," whereupon 'Umar ordered that it be written and placed with him over his tomb. Added to the tradition were praises of Hasan and Husayn. Ibn al-Jawzi adds: "Now when the qussas are of this kind how can they be censured?"[13] For Ibn al-Jawzi, people who claimed such stories were not those who knew the science of tradition. Instead, they distorted truth by willingly fabricating traditions: "These are the ones who buy and sell on the market of time. It thus happens that they preach to ignorant persons who, among the masses, belong to the ranks of the dumb animals. They do not refute what they relate nor what they quote. They can be heard saying: 'Such and such a learned man said so and so.'"[14] In a world of irresponsible preachers and audiences willing to accept any story, there was the possibility of fabrication.

Ibn al-Jawzi exposes the manipulation of select preachers through another tale where the preacher clearly set out to make fun of his audience. The preacher not only highlighted people's lack of reason and judgment, but he also enjoyed demonstrating how willing they were to follow his outlandish suggestions.

> 'Uthman al-Warraq said: "I saw 'Attabi eating a piece of bread in the street by the Damascus Gate. So I said to him: 'Woe unto you! Are you not ashamed of yourself?' He said to me: 'Do you suppose if we were in a place where there were cattle that you would be ashamed to eat while they were watching you?' I replied: 'No.' He said: 'Wait until I show you that [the people] are cattle!' So he rose up and preached and narrated stories until the crowd around him grew large. Among the things he said to them was the following: 'Several persons have narrated traditions to the effect that the person whose tongues can reach the tip of his nose

will not go to hell.' Then all of them stuck out their tongues pointing them toward the tips of their noses to see whether they could reach them. When the people had gone their separate ways 'Attabi said to me: 'Did I not tell you they were cows?'"[15]

In this case, the preacher draws on peoples' desire to know whether they will be in the Fire or the Garden. The preacher's point was that people are as stupid as cattle to comply with his wishes. What was meant to be a narration resulted in a demonstration of how easy it was to fool others. From Ibn al-Jawzi's perspective, the actions of the preachers exhibited irresponsible behavior. What is interesting about the case of crawling on all fours or having an audience try to reach their noses with the tip of their tongues is that the motivation in both cases was avoiding the Fire.

The anecdotes in Ibn al-Jawzi's text illustrate the popularity of invoking the Garden and the Fire. Preachers and storytellers could draw on them to inspire or affect certain behaviors. Beyond rhetorical devices, the Garden and the Fire also functioned within the very acts of preaching and storytelling. Preachers and storytellers were supposed to bring people closer to the Garden by helping them to maintain good behavior and to be fearful of the majesty of God and the apocalypse.

Preaching and storytelling depended on rhetorical force as well as faith in the impending possibility of being placed in the Fire. In this sense, preaching and storytelling about the Fire could have met people's curiosity, or it could have fed their need to be told stories, to have them enacted, and to feel the heat of the flames. The case of 'Umar is a dramatic example, since he was renowned for his piety. Yet, it is possible that narration provided a way for Muslims to experience the fear of the Fire while still on earth. Storytelling and preaching, then, helped continue belief in the Garden and contributed to a religious culture that heightened the inherent drama of eschatological time by transforming it into popular narratives. The case of storytelling also provides a model for understanding the dynamic involved with the reception of eschatological manuals. The increasing drama of the manuals may signal the development of rhetorical tools of theologians as well as demonstrate a literate audience's desire to find all the traditions of the Garden and the Fire in an accessible and comprehensible form. Why hear or read stories about your impending doom? At the heart of the performances and texts about eschatology is the process of religious edification. If one entertains the Fire as possibility within earthly life, perhaps one can save one's soul before it is too late.

ESCHATOLOGICAL NARRATIVE
AND TEXTUAL DRAMA

The structure of eschatological manuals further dramatized the events at the end of time by creating narrative frameworks that reinforced the power of the Garden and the Fire as realms of existence. Not all the narratives were similar in approach. Some were more descriptive; others were geared for more mystical contemplation; yet others aimed for moral edification. Each manual shared the objective of making the afterlife understandable. In doing so, the manuals reflected concerns over certain topics (such as houris, for example) over others (such as clothing in the Garden). By the twelfth century the different approaches of the manuals began to yield to one dominant model that framed the manuals as moral exercises.

The narrative developed in the manuals often follows central eschatological events. Eschatological time has three inherent narratives. The first is an individual narrative that begins upon dying and continues into the grave as the angels Munkir and Nakir record the deeds of the soul. The second is the collective narrative of the apocalypse, which begins when the lesser signs of the end of time are made manifest.[16] Lesser signs are dramatic events that signal that the world will soon be ending. After the lesser signs and with the imminent destruction of the world are the Greater Signs of the Hour. They include the appearance of al-Dajjal, Jesus' descent to battle the al-Dajjal, and the coming of Gog and Magog. After the appearance of lesser and greater signs, humanity faces the Resurrection, the Gathering, the Judgment, and the crossing of the Bridge of Sirat. The third narrative is the Night Journey and Ascension, which may have occurred during earthly time but was located in a temporal and spatial zone that was otherworldly.

The Garden and the Fire are closely linked to eschatological time because they are the end result of all three types of narratives; however, they do not follow the same temporal guidelines. The afterworld, after all, is a timeless realm. As a result, manuals that focus more on the Garden and the Fire as realms organize traditions in a few ways. Ibn Habib's book *Kitab wasf firdaws* is a ninth-century work that illustrates the kinds of choices that are made by putting the Garden and the Fire within a narrative, and hence temporal, structure. The text is divided into sections that create categories for hadiths and exegetical material. Unlike Muslim's hadith collection, there is a greater logical progression to the exposition of traditions. The work does not just present categories of traditions in discrete units. Instead, it offers some temporal markers. The first part of the work starts with the creation of the Garden and ends with the first and last to enter the Garden. The second part of the volume draws on Ibn Habib's work as an exegete and is dedicated to events that occur from death to the torment of the grave.

In the first section, the text focuses on the creation of the Garden, the names of its doors, and its topography. It offers sections describing the Garden and its food and drink. It then turns to the people of *al-janna*, the first and last to enter, and the houris. The description ends with a section on inhabitants' households, including their mansions, their ability to have sex, and their children and wives. Interspersed through the individual sections are exegeses that Ibn Habib offered on topics such as the term *al-janna* in the Qur'an.

Ibn Habib's text is unusual because it does not follow the temporal gradation from death to grave to afterworld. Instead, the afterworld is more prominent than eschatological events. The structure of Ibn Habib's text both exemplifies the importance of the afterworld and reinforces a very particular way of looking at it. Ibn Habib's divisions indicate an interest in the human condition in the afterworld. From describing the palaces to rivers to the people of *al-janna* to the markets and houris, the text tries to create a vision of what life would be like for the believer. Through traditions and exegesis, the Garden is understood as a future *domestic* space.

While all descriptions of the Garden focus on the quality of believers' lives, not all of them aim to provide a tour of the afterworld. Instead, each manual can have a different purpose. The case of al-Muhasibi's *Kitab al-tawahhum* provides an interesting example of how eschatological events can be used to develop a more mystical argument for the union with God. Al-Muhasibi (d. 857) was a mystic who was renowned for his encouragement of the individual to examine his or her conscience. It is due to this mission that he earned the moniker *al-muhasibi*, or "he who calculates his actions."[17] Replete with description of jewels, clothes, and the glories of angels, al-Muhasibi's text leads the soul through a journey that culminates in the union with the divine. The text is remarkable for both its vivid descriptions and its use of the second person. In this sense, the text is more active since it draws the reader into its journey. The realm that al-Muhasibi introduces to the reader is one of full dramatization. While al-Muhasibi draws on the Qur'an and hadiths, he does not just account for the characteristics of the Garden and the Fire. Instead, he writes of a journey to the realm where he acts as a guide for a presumably male reader.

The text begins with the soul facing the angel of death and seeing all of creation during the Day of Resurrection. The fear of the Resurrection and

Judgment is made more palpable because of the use of the second person. The terror continues with the recognition of *jahannam* and the eventual encounter with the Bridge of Sirat. After passing through the trials, the soul finally begins to approach the Garden. There the soul sees fathers, mothers, brothers, and sisters who have placed themselves in the hands of God.[18] When the soul finally enters the Garden, he visits his palace of emeralds, rubies, and pure pearls.[19] The beauty is not just in the palace, but also the fragrance of Paradise. As the soul enters the palace, servants call out to his spouses that he is arrived. The soul appreciates the beauty of the houris and domestic servants. After an exchange with one of the houris, the text discusses the marvels of the Garden and the praises of God.

Al-Muhasibi's text provides an early example of the drama contained within eschatological narratives. While the drama is made evident through the use of the second person, the account is also compelling because of the focus on details. The terror of the day of Resurrection and the encounter with *jahannam* is made manifest through the various creatures that stand nude and trembling before the judgment of God. The Garden is made more impressive through the invocation of sensual imagery such as sight and smell. In fact, the exchange with the houri, which will be addressed later in this chapter, not only depends on the senses but also shows how the soul can interact with the retinue of the Garden.

Al-Muhasibi's account is one of the most sensual of the eschatological narrative, yet it reinforces the notion of moral edification. The journey is one that leads the soul to God, and for this reason it is also a *mi'raj*-like text, since the soul journeys through eschatological time and space to enter the heavens and see his particular place there. Yet, the use of the Garden and the Fire as sensual motivational devices was viewed as crude. Because of its introspection and employment of the dialectic, al-Muhasibi's work was attacked by Ibn Hanbal as part of the larger theological and philosophical battle between theologians. Ibn Hanbal found his early work *Kitab al-tawahhum* particularly heterodox for the way it used the descriptions of the Garden and Fire as symbols of God's favor or disfavor.[20]

In contrast to al-Muhasibi's imaginative journey to the soul's personal palace, al-Samarqandi's (d. 1002) *Kitab al-haqa'iq wa-l-daqa'iq* presents a cosmological framework that accounts for the creation of the world. The text begins with the creation of Adam and the nature of angels. He presents eschatological events within discreet topics such as the Day of Resurrection and then Paradise. Interestingly, al-Samarqandi's account, like al-Qurtubi and al-Muhasibi's texts, does not describe or develop the Fire.

Al-Ghazali provides another kind of eschatological journey in two principal texts: *Durra al-fakhira* and *Kitab dhikr al-mawt wa ma ba'dahu*. While there are differences in the works, they are both moral in their aims. The *Durra al-fakhira* narrates the events from God's division for those destined for the Garden and those destined for the Fire to the time when souls face the eschatological events of the trumpet of resurrection, the waiting in the grave, the intercession of the Garden and the Fire, the tablet and messengers, the Reckoning, the Bridge of Sirat, and the accusation of rich and troubled. The text cuts off before reaching the Garden and the Fire, but the two realms play an important role as ending places. For example, in one passage during the Gathering, the Fire breaks away and approaches humanity with the intention of consuming it.[21]

Al-Ghazali's second text treats the Garden and the Fire more explicitly. The text is divided into two parts. The first deals with the consequences of death until the trumpet blast, records the death of the prophet and the Rashidun caliphs, offers sayings of death, the true nature of death, and dreams about the dead. The whole purpose of the first part is to remember the terrible nature of death, its loss, and how it creates widows. As a result, the contemplation of death is an exercise that hastens the heart towards the straight path. Just thinking about death is a way to atone. "When the remembrance of death touches his heart and comes to make some impression upon it his contentment and pleasure in the world will wane and his heart will break."[22] To think of the dead is also to "recall how they appeared in their former positions and circumstances, and meditate upon the way in which the earth has now obliterated the beauty of their forms, and how their parts have been scattered in their tombs, and how they made widows of their wives and orphans of their children; how they lost their property, and how their mosques and gatherings have become voided of them, and of how their very traces have been wiped away."[23] The second part of the text presents the eschatological narrative from the trumpet announcing the Day of the Resurrection to depictions of the Garden and the Fire. The text ends with the beatific vision.

The framework of al-Ghazali's text, then, reinforces the importance of the contemplation of death within earthly life in order to realize the full extent of the pleasures of the Garden and more importantly the pains of the Fire. The first part about death is reinforced by the second part that presents what will become a standard description of the Garden and the Fire. *Kitab dhikr al-mawt wa ma ba'dahu* presents the Garden and the Fire within the framework of how to exercise morality and humility.

Like the previous texts, al-Qadi's *Daqa'iq al-akhbar fi dhikr al-janna wa-l-nar* also presents a moralizing text, but its drama and detail demonstrate how the narrative form encourages elaboration in terms of both the pains of the Fire as well as they beauties of the Garden. Like al-Samarqandi's text, the work is cosmological in nature since it offers a chronological account of the creation and destruction of the world. However, it is mainly devoted to describing the events during the Resurrection.

The narrative begins with God creating Light, which sweated out of modesty because it was before Allah. Its sweat from various body parts formed the world. After the creation of Adam and the Angels, the work turns to the Angels of Death and narrates the specific events of the Resurrection, which includes the role of Satan, the shouts and weeping of the dead, the role of Munkar and Nakir, the recording of the scribes, the call of the trumpet, the rising of humanity, the bringing forward of the Garden, and the Judgment when attempting to cross the Bridge of Sirat. What is striking about al-Qadi's text is the space devoted to the traditions about the Fire. Whereas al-Qadi's text functions as a primer for moral edification, like other texts, it privileges the Fire in ways that other texts do not. The Fire, then, becomes a more developed realm for contemplation with its demons and specified punishments. The development of the Fire also shifts the eschatological manuals from one that presents suffering during apocalyptic time to one that fully develops the consequences of being doomed eternally. In this way, al-Qadi's text reverses the propensity to privilege the Garden.

If al-Ghazali and al-Qadi's texts demonstrate the developed form of eschatological manuals, then texts such as al-Qurtubi's (d. 1273) *al-Tadhkira fi ahwal al-mawta wa-umur al-akhira* show the form of the eschatological manual at its fullest articulation. The text combines different eschatological narratives of death, resurrections, the afterlife, and apocalyptic signs in one volume. The result is one larger, comprehensible account of what happens after death and what happens at the end of time. Like al-Qadi's text, al-Qurtubi develops a considerable amount of attention to the traditions of the Fire. Like Ibn Habib's and al-Ghazali's works, al-Qurtubi also records traditions of those people who will benefit from intercession and will be saved from life in the Fire. Yet, even the traditions of the Garden are further developed. Al-Qurtubi does not just record Qur'anic verses and hadiths, but he also presents exegetical material and Arabic poetry.

The structure of the work enhances the understanding of eschatological drama within earthly life. The work begins with the accounts of death, turns to the events of Resurrection, and then presents the descriptions of the Garden and the Fire. It is only after this eschatological chronology that al-Qurtubi presents the apocalyptic narrative. Structurally, al-Qurtubi has taken readers from the future moment of their deaths to their judgments and placements in the afterworld. After an understanding of what is to come, he presents the more immediate reality of the apocalypse.

Eschatological narratives transformed over the centuries. From the traditions recorded in hadith collections, they eventually became more focused and organized within topics. Sometimes the traditions presented would convey the full *isnad*, other times they would be abridged or eliminated. The manuals were never just merely compilations of hadiths, though. Instead, their authors framed them to present accounts that inspired greater spirituality and moral behavior. With this moral purpose as the objective, manuals presented different forms until the twelfth century, when a narrative model began to predominate. By the thirteenth century, that model was fully crystallized to present the drama of the apocalypse alongside the events of eschatological time.

HOURIS, WIVES, AND CHILDREN

Because eschatological manuals mostly draw on hadiths for their individual subsections, one of the ways to determine how much attention they pay to a certain topic is the number of traditions they present. For example, whereas in each individual hadith collection the discussion of children and earthly wives in the afterlife is scant, authors of the manuals culled all the possible hadiths in order to present as complete a picture as possible. For this reason, the manuals are both compilations of previous material, as well as records of what concerned theologians and perhaps their readers.

Within the dynamic of textual compilation, the houri is one of the most enduring motifs of the Garden. Not only do the manuals exhibit intense interest in the houri, but they also record the houri as having greater sensuality. In some ways the sensuality mirrors the trend for the manuals to increase the embellishments of the Garden. In order to attempt to describe its ineffable nature, the Garden becomes more opulent and new jewels are named as part of its landscape. For example, a common tradition for the manuals claims that houris have faces created in white, green, yellow, and red. Their bodies are composed of saffron, musk, amber, and camphor, and their hair is of raw silk. The smell is delineated by part of the body: toe to knee is saffron, knee to breast is musk, breast to neck is amber, and neck to head is camphor. "If they had spat once in the world, the world becomes musk."[24] Yet, aside from the description, manuals also suggest a character for the houri. While still an object to be possessed, the houri sees an inherent competition with earthly wives.

In Ibn Habib's collection, the section on houris is startlingly developed. It includes more common traditions, one that the houris are so fair that their marrow can be seen through their clothing just as "red drink can be seen in a white glass."[25] Yet, there are other traditions that present strikingly new material. For example, one tradition introduces a houri named La'ba around whom the other houris gather.[26] Houris also interact with believers. In these exchanges, houris are active beings who received believers in their new abodes and greet them as their reward.[27] Yet, the houri is not just reward; sometimes she embodies the beneficence of the Garden. One tradition claims, "Written on the chest of the wife of the believer of the people of the Garden is You are my love, I am your love, my eyes are only for you and my soul leads to you."[28] Here the houri is not just a female being of the Garden who is promised to the believer, but also a teleological end of the Garden. Just as the believer finally makes his way to his final abode, so will the houri finally unite with her beloved.

The reference to the houri as a wife is further supported by a tradition that every man will receive seventy-two of them. Yet, Ibn Habib also records traditions that show concern for earthly wives, especially in regard to women who have married twice. Someone asks who would be her husband in the Garden. Two hadiths suggest that she would marry the previous.[29] In a related hadith, a woman asks if she will be able to marry her dead fiancé in the Garden. The answer is affirmative if she remains unmarried.[30] The question itself shows concern for women and in particular the continuity of familial structures.[31] What is clear is that women will only have one husband each.[32] Ibn Habib's collection also addresses what happens if a husband and wife want a child. There would not be pregnancy, birth, and growth. Instead, the child would appear in a moment like a pure pearl.[33] These types of hadith must represent the types of questions that people raised about the continuation of the family in the otherworld.

While there is often a distinction between earthly wives and houris, sometimes the two categories are conflated. In al-Muhasibi's text, houris are referred to as both *hur al-'ayn* and wives (*azwaj*) of the believer. The houri, then, occupies both spaces as the beloved wife and the otherworldly object of the believer. Al-Muhasibi does not elaborate on the terms. Instead, in his eschatological drama, he places houris in a central role. When the soul finally enters the Garden, he sees the face of God. As he is touring the Garden and taking in its gardens of saffron and its dunes of musk, a call is made to announce the believer's entrance.[34] It is after the retinue is informed of the believer's presence that he meets the houri.[35] She is not the only object of beauty. The steward of the household is also beautiful because of the light that surrounds him. The believer asks if he is an angel; he replies, "I am only your attendant in your service, and there are seventy thousand attendants with me."[36] Aside from the beauty of the attendants, al-Muhasibi introduces the reader to the beauty of the heavenly palace with its trees. As the believer watches in astonishment, the servants make a short declaration, calling to the spouses, "That is the one, the son of that one. At the door of his palace, he is entering."[37]

The description continues as the reader is enjoined to imagine the beauties of the Garden. Part of the beauty includes the houri. She walks toward the believer clad in brocade and silk, and her perfume is of musk. As she passes, the saffron plants awaken.[38] The sensual description of the houri extends to the reunion with the believer: "Imagine that she ascends with her splendid gentle body until she takes her place there sitting balanced. Then you lift yourself on the couch (*sarir*) and like her you take a place with her. She faces you. You face her. You glance at the beauty of this woman sitting in her robes and her adornment, the case of her face which would light morning, her gentle body. On her wrists, she has bracelets, on her hands rings, and on her ankles rings. A precious belt is tied at her waist." As the believer and the houri admire each other, angels circle about the pavilion, trees incline on the banks of your alcove, their branches full of fruit. The rivers flow on the circumference of the palace and their streams run of wine, honey, milk, and *salsabil*.[39] The houri offers the believer wine (*al-khamar*), *salsabil*, and *tasnim* in pearl goblets and silver cups.[40]

The purpose of al-Muhasibi's journey is to take the believer through the levels of afterworld in order to culminate with the greater experience of communing with God; however, the way in which al-Muhasibi presents his journey is by emphasizing the materiality of the afterworld so that the believer is invited to imagine his fate through the senses. In this way, al-Muhasibi creates a language that allows him to express the most ineffable of experiences: the human encounter with God. Yet, within the sensual drama, the houri acts as a central object of sensuality. She is connected through landscape, since her beauty can even affect plants. She is also the member of the household retinue who has the greatest interaction with the believer. While she has a clear role in the Garden, she also embodies the idea of the Garden as a place of repose and marvel.

By the twelfth century, texts repeated the same traditions as found above. At times, however, new material is introduced, such as the naming of a place called *al-bidukh* where women are secluded in bejeweled tents.[41]

Sometimes there are scenes where the value of children is asserted. For example, in al-Ghazali's *Durra al-fakhira*, at the time of the Resurrection children give cups of water from the rivers of the Garden to their parents. One man who is parched of thirst asks for some water and is met with the question, "Do you have a son among us?" When he answers in the negative, the children counsel him on the advantages of marriage.[42] Presumably he does not receive the coveted cup.

The repetition of material about the houri suggests that the popularization of that figure occurred as early as the ninth century and continued well into the twelfth century. By then, the houri had become a kind of metonymy for the Garden, as well as an accepted object. A new role of the houri as the superlative being of the Garden emerged through the use of traditions, and most of all the structure of the text. Al-Qadi's text provides an excellent example of the importance of the houri. In al-Qadi's text, the houris are described by common traditions such as the composition of precious smells, or that their spouses' names will be written on their chests.[43] They are adorned with gold bracelets. On each finger are ten rings, and on each ankle are ten anklets of jewels and pearls. One particular houri is referred to as "al-'Aina' who is made of musk, camphor, ambergris, and saffron."[44]

The houris have a new status in the text. As the preeminent women in the Garden, they also have servant girls. One tradition explains the houris by painting a scene where every woman has seventy robes, every man seventy couches of ruby. On the couches are seventy rugs, and on each rug is a woman, and each woman has a servant girl (*wasifa*).[45] In this tradition, the term "houri" and "woman" are conflated, yet they are cast within the meaning of the houri. Every woman in the Garden, then, is a houri. The text does not address if these are spouses transformed. More likely, the use of the number seventy suggests that these women are beings of the Garden. What is most surprising about the tradition is that the houri has servant girls who attend to them. The female companion, by the twelfth century, has her own attendants. The expanding nature of beauty and luxury even extends to the servant girls. In another tradition, angel Gabriel sees one of these girls (*al-jaria*), and she smiles at him. Her teeth are so luminous that he mistakes the vision for the light of God.[46] She informs Gabriel that she is created for those who prefer the pleasures of God to the whims of their own souls.[47]

Within these traditions, the houri not only emerged as the highest-ranking female in the Garden, but she also became part of the Garden, acquiring servants of her own. The elevation of the houri is more intriguing when considering who is missing from the Garden. In al-Qadi's text, there are no family members, such as wives and children. The emphasis, then, is not on the benefits of female companionship in addition to the extended family, but the reward of female companionship without any appearance of family members. The tension between balancing individual desire and family structure in the afterworld, which was evident in hadiths in chapter 5, does not exist in the later eschatological manuals. Families have been removed from the landscape of the Garden, and houris have become the main source of companionship.

ARCHITECTURE OF THE GARDEN

While the Garden has an inherent landscape and urban design, the eschatological manuals present the Garden through a series of motifs. These items, such as thrones, gates, and pools, form a schematic architecture that introduces the reader to the Garden through objects that have spiritual value. The Garden, then, is a space of spiritual significance, which is expressed through the bejeweled nature of the Garden. For example, invocations to gold and silver bricks signal both opulence and the purity of the afterworld.

Like the architecture of the Fire, the Garden is often expressed through gates and levels. While there are several variations of these two motifs, there are often eight gates and eight levels. For example, in both al-Samarqandi's and al-Qadi's texts, the first gate is for prophets, messengers, martyrs, and those who were generous. The second gate is for those who prayed. The third gate is for those who gave charitable offerings (*zakat*) willingly. The fourth gate is for those who commanded the good and forbade the reprehensible. The fifth gate is for those who desisted from their desires. The sixth gate is for those who did pilgrimage (*hajj* and *'umra*). The seventh gate is for those who struggled in the way of God (*jihad*). The eighth gate is for those who turned their eyes from forbidden things and respected parents, relatives, and others. The gates signify an evaluation of behaviors on this earth and accord each one a level. This gradation of behavior is not seen in earlier hadiths.[48]

Beyond the hierarchy of behavior, each level is associated with a garden, name, and jewel. In al-Samarqandi and al-Qadi's texts, the first garden of white pearl is called the Abode of Majesty, and it is of white pearl. The second garden of red ruby is the Abode of Peace. The third garden of green chrysolite is the Abode of Shelter. The fourth garden of red and yellow coral is the Garden of Immortality. The fifth garden of white silver is the Garden of Bliss. The sixth garden of red gold is the Garden of Firdaws. The seventh garden of white pearl is the Garden of 'Adn. The eighth garden of red gold is the Abode of Rest, which is raised over the Gardens.[49]

The identification of each level with precious stones, especially pearls, marks the Garden as the ultimate spiritual place and realm of pleasures. The focus on the jewels is also matched by the invocation of gold, silver, and other luxurious items. The eighth garden, for example, has two gates, and the two leaves are of gold and silver. Between each of the two leaves is what is between heaven and earth. It is built on gold and silver bricks. Its mud is musk and its earth is amber and its straw is saffron. Its castles are of pearl and its rooms are of ruby. Its doors are of jewels, and in it are rivers.[50]

Gates and levels of the Garden provide the external structure of the space, but the Garden is also understood through the different waters. *Kawthar*, the pool or river given to Muhammad, is prominent in the eschatological manuals.[51] Al-Samarqandi and al-Qadi's texts also involve identifying the origins of the rivers of the Garden. The prophet asks Gabriel from where the rivers of water, milk, wine, and honey (47.15) emanate and where they flow. Gabriel tells him that they go to the basin of *kawthar*. Muhammad is taken to a tree where there is a dome of white pearl with a door of green corundum and a lock of red gold. Four rivers flow from under the dome. After walking away, Gabriel commands him to open the door with the phrase *Bismillah al-Rahman al-Rahim* (In the name of God the Compassionate and the Merciful). Muhammad utters the words, and then inside the dome an angel shows him the four corners of the dome on which *Bismillah al-Rahman al-Rahim* is inscribed. Water comes from the letter *mim* of *Bismillah*, the river of milk from the letter *ha* of *Allah*, the wine from the *mim* of *Rahman*, and the honey from the *mim* of *Rahim*.

The inhabitants will drink from these letters: water on Saturday, honey on Sunday, milk on Monday, wine on Tuesday, and then they will be intoxicated. In their drunken state they will fly for a thousand years and then land at a mountain of musk where *salsabil* will flow. They will drink from it on Wednesday. Then they will fly for a thousand years and reach a lofty castle where there will be couches and goblets set for them.[52] They will recline on the couches and drink ginger on Thursday. Finally, they will fly a thousand years until they reach a Seat of Veracity. That will be Friday. They will sit at the Table of Immortality and drink *rahtaq* (nectar).[53]

Aside from the rivers and fountains of silver and gold is the importance of trees. Another tradition notes that when the trees strike each other they make a beautiful sound.[54] While the Lote Tree of the Boundary is the paramount tree in Qur'anic verses and hadiths, in Ibn Habib, al-Qadi, and al-Samarqandi's texts, the tree called Tuba is highlighted. It is as large as a one-thousand-year journey, provides wonderful fruit, and is described in opulent terms: its roots are of pearl, its trunk of ruby, its branches of chrysolite, and its leaves of silk brocade. Aside from its opulence, the branches of the tree are connected to the leg of the Throne, while its other branches are in the nearest heaven.[55] The greatest of the monuments in the Garden is the Throne of God itself. In al-Ghazali's text, prophets and *'ulama* will be on smaller thrones below. The thrones of each messenger will be in proportion to his standing.[56] The Qur'an even appears in al-Ghazali's text on the day of resurrection in the form of a man with a beautiful face.[57]

The architecture of the Garden, then, includes entry points such as gates and levels to create a hierarchy among people. However, within the Garden itself, the topography is understood through the throne of God, the tree Tuba, and the rivers that emanate into the many gardens. These motifs act as a vocabulary set that introduces readers to the Garden. By following the progression from Throne to rivers, readers would have been able to create a map of the Garden, as we will see in the next chapter.

DEMONS AND UNBELIEVERS

In Qur'anic verses and hadiths, the Fire was a gruesome place of punishment that always acted in counterpoint to the Garden. Whatever characteristic the Garden offered, the Fire usually offered the opposite conditions. In this way, the Garden and the Fire may have signaled distinct concepts of reward and punishment, but they were not entirely realms independent of each other. Instead, they were tied together with more discursive space dedicated to the pleasures of and the ways to enter the Garden. Eschatological manuals develop the Fire in more deliberate ways. Some manuals are dedicated solely to the Fire, such as Ibn Abi al-Dunya's *Sifat al-nar* and al-Maqdisi's *Dhikr al-nar*. Others, such as al-Ghazali and al-Qadi's texts, show the growing interest in exhortation regarding the Fire. In their manuals, the Fire is a rich site for narrative forms of exhortation. Not only do the manuals dramatize life in the Fire, but they also present new punishments, different types of sinners, and the appearance of a multitude of demons.

Al-Ghazali demonstrates the greater drama of the Fire by personifying the Fire itself. On the Day of Judgment, *jahannam* approaches a group of people "clattering and thundering and moaning."[58] The sight is so terrifying that even prophets fall on their knees, and Abraham, Jesus, and Moses cling to the throne. Only Muhammad, in a testament to his preeminence, grabs the Fire by the halter and commands it to go back until it is time for the group to enter it.[59] Aside from its attack on humanity, the Fire is also described through hadiths that try to understand its amplitude. When God commands that the Fire be brought forth, the Fire "walks on four legs and is bound by seventy thousand reins. On each of the reins are seventy thousand rings; if all the iron in the world were collected it would not equal that of one ring. On every ring are seventy thousand guardians of hell; if even one among them were ordered to level the mountains or to crush the earth he would be able to do it."[60] The Fire is also described as sounding like the braying of a donkey.[61]

New types of punishments for different categories of sinners enhance the threatening, loud, chaotic nature of the Fire. One who does not offer crops in alms has on his back a pair of sacks with things he withheld.[62] A bald monster called *zabibatan*, whose tail falls into the sinner's nose and coils around his neck, plagues those who refused to give alms.[63] Other sinners have enlarged pudenda that emanate pus so putrid that they nauseate their neighbors.[64]

The more detailed punishments of the Fire are best exemplified through the narrative drama presented in al-Qadi's text. In some ways, al-Qadi's descriptions are based on the traditions in chapter 4; however, in his text, greater attention is paid to landscape, architecture, and beings that administer pain. For example, al-Qadi cites traditions where snakes have the tails of camels and scorpions are as large as mules. While these traditions are mentioned in the collection of Ahmad ibn Hanbal, in al-Qadi's account, the beings are the center of a dramatic scene. People flee the snakes and scorpions, running from one fire to another. Even rushing into the Fire does not save them from the chase. The snakes and scorpions eventually capture them by clasping at the unbelievers' mouths and skin between their hair and nails.[65] Another tradition notes that snakes have necks like camels, and that their sting extends for forty years. People who are eternally trapped in the Fire will sigh and moan and their voices will resemble a donkey: "It begins with a sigh and ends with a bray."[66]

Like al-Ghazali's collections, the Fire also has a more clearly articulated architecture of seven named gates with a designated group associated with each gate (54.14). While the Qur'an mentions the Fire as having individual gates, in al-Qadi's account, each gate and its corresponding populace is explicitly named. The lowest gate, named *hawiya* (Abyss), is for hypocrites and those who reject the truth. The second gate, *jahim* (Hellfire), is for those polytheists or those who associate deities with God. The third gate, *saqar* (Blaze), is for the Sabians. The fourth gate, called *laza* (Flame), is for Zoroastrians (referred to as Magians) and anyone who follows Iblis or Satan. The fifth gate, *hutama* (Furnace), is for Jews. The sixth gate, *saʿir* (Fire), is for Christians. The inhabitants of the seventh gate are Muslims who committed serious wrongs.[67]

This tradition shows two characteristics of later traditions of the Garden and the Fire. The first is that often chains of transmissions are not quoted. The second is the elaboration of the motifs of the gates of Hell (*jahannam*). Like the earlier traditions of the gates of the Garden, each gate is reserved for a special class of sinner, and each of the categories forms a group that refused to follow the tenets of Islam. Furthermore, each gate has a portion of men and women, and women are not mentioned as the majority of the inhabitants of the Fire, as in the case of the series of hadiths explored in chapter 3.

The tradition presents the category of sinners as well as the names of the gates. For the first time, there are designated realms for people of other religious traditions, such as the Christians, Sabians, Jews, and Magians. Each of these groups were considered historically to be *Ahl al-Dhimma*, or "Peoples of the Book," a term that applied to those groups who were recognized as having revealed religions and as a result considered as protected peoples. Unlike Qur'anic verses and hadiths, there is no mention of local Arabian tribes or religious practices. Another innovation is that the different names for the Fire in the Qur'an are co-opted as different names of gates. Unlike earlier traditions that evaluated behavior within the Muslim community, later traditions put a greater emphasis on the superiority of Islam over other religious communities.

In al-Qadi's depiction of the Fire, beings that administer pain are explicitly described. The greatest torturer is the personified Fire itself, called *jahannam*. Like the tradition in al-Ghazali's text, *jahannam* has four legs. Each leg is the size of one thousand years and has thirty heads. Each head has thirty thousand mouths, each mouth thirty thousand teeth, each tooth the size of a mountain. Each mouth has two lips with iron chains. On each chain are seventy thousand rings, and on each ring are innumerable angels.[68]

Jahannam is not the only being of the Fire. Angels and *shayatin* (satans) also populate the landscape. Malik, who becomes a fearful overlord, looks into the Fire and sees the phrase *Bismillah al-Rahman al-Rahim*. Its nineteen letters equal the number of angels who take people by their hands and feet—ten thousand in each hand and foot—and push them into the Fire. These nineteen who administer punishment are referred to in the

Qur'an as the *zabaniya* (96.18). The Angel of Fire oversees the *zabaniya*. He is said to have as many hands and feet as people in the Fire, and he can employ his appendages to enchain them. The leader of the *zabaniya* is Malik, and the other eighteen are like him. They are large enough to have between them the distance of one year, and if one plunges in the Fire for seven years, the flame does not touch him. The *zabaniya*, then, are the mechanism by which punishment is delivered. Interestingly, the *zabaniya* probably refers to the Islamic verse about the nineteen angels who will punish unbelievers in the Fire (as discussed in chapter 1).

A new entity seeks and enforces punishment. A tradition from Abu Hurayra describes something called *Harish* that will come from the Fire. Its size is so enormous that its head will be in the seventh heaven while its tail under the lowest earth. Scorpions are born from it. *Harish* calls out for different types of sinners: those who withheld tithe (*zakat*), those who abandoned prayer, those who were usurers, and those who spoke of worldly matters in mosques.[69]

Aside from the elaboration of descriptions and beings, the text develops an uninterrupted drama: people will be brought into the Fire and others will inflict punishment. According to one passage, an unbeliever (*kafir*) will have a blackened face, green eyes, and a sealed mouth. One chain will be placed in his mouth and come out of his back, will bind his left hand to his neck and the right hand, and will go through his breast and come out of his shoulders. Bound in chains, each man is chained to a *shaytan*. He will be dragged on his face while angels beat him with iron staffs.[70]

Muslims will receive better treatment. Their faces will not be blackened, eyes not turn green, and mouths will be opened. No *shaytan* will accompany them, and no chains and shackles will be fastened on them. Angels will lead old men by their white hair, young men by their beards, and women by their forelocks.[71] As for punishment, the descriptions are based on the hadiths in chapter 5, with some elaboration. The punishments tend to be grouped together: those who are unbelievers, fornicators, and usurers, and those who abandoned prayer. There is also explicit mention of the punishment of wine drinkers. Like the punishment for other sins, they will eat the food of al-Zaqqum, drink the boiling water called *hamim*, and be attacked by snakes and scorpions in a valley called Wayl, "one of the valleys of Jahannam."[72]

Although al-Qadi's Fire develops the sense of the despair, like the manuals of Ibn Habib, al-Ghazali, and al-Qurtubi, there is the possibility of intercession. After a thousand years, Muslims cry out to Allah, who commands Gabriel to investigate. In one long, drawn-out drama, Muhammad intercedes for his people. He is astonished by the wretchedness of their state and the narrowness of their quarters, and releases them from their tortured conditions. In the river of Life near the gate of the Garden, they will bathe and emerge young, beardless, hairless, with kohl on their eyes, as mentioned in hadiths in chapter 5.[73]

Al-Qadi's text, then, illustrates how the Fire had become a developed site for punishment. Unlike the role of the Fire in other texts, in al-Qadi's work the Fire becomes a place that is replete with beings, demons that punish, and different kinds of sinners. No longer is the Fire the realm for general punishment. Instead, the Fire has an inherent structure where each type of sinner belongs to a specific place. These places also include members of different religious communities. Even in the Fire, Muslim sinners are in a better position than other kinds of unbelievers.

The texts that characterize the Garden and the Fire vary in their functions and forms. Qur'anic verses present glimpses, sometimes enigmatic, of the afterworld through warning and spiritually imbued imagery, such as the references to pearls. Hadith collections aimed to classify and record sayings of the prophet or about religious experience. As a result, they were more a compendium of authorized traditions than a collection of traditions that we can be sure circulated in Islamic society. By contrast, the traditions in eschatological manuals illustrate the images that theologians found useful for explaining the afterworld and at times reflected the social concerns of both theologians and people who may have questioned them about the nature of the afterworld.

Aside from the traditions employed, manuals also exemplify the different forms of exhortation. Whether the text was dedicated to explaining the beauties of the Garden or the terrors of the Fire, the purpose of the manuals was religious edification. Even as early as the ninth century, writers of eschatological manuals sought ways to make the traditions of the afterlife accessible and to address the questions and problems that arose in later centuries. Issues such as the problem of women having more than one husband in earthly life might have indicated that people were trying to understand the consequences of their earthly behavior.

The form of exhortation, as reflected by the eschatological manuals, shifted the way that the afterworld was presented. While still the realms of respective pleasure and pain, the manuals presented the Garden and the Fire through the vantage point of individual experience. In hadith collections, there was a tension in the Garden between individual desire and replicating earthly, familial life. By contrast, eschatological manuals erase markers of earthly life and social dynamics and replace them with visions of pleasure palaces for the soul. The transformation from hadiths to eschatological manual is equally dramatic when it comes to the Fire. In hadiths, the Fire was a realm where unbelievers were forced to punish themselves in a world of solitude. Eschatological manuals heighten the drama by depending on external punishment through demons, scorpions, and snakes so that the punishment of the unbeliever provides a more dramatic scene.

It is at this point that the materiality of the Garden and the Fire shows the power of its attraction. Eschatological manuals employ the power of the materials to paint a picture for readers. These materials, themselves, became more expansive in their descriptions. While in earlier texts descriptions of materials were the means to understand the ethical polarization of the Garden and the Fire, in later texts, the materials amplified the inherent drama of both realms. Materials were not the only way to explain why the Garden was better than the Fire, but they became the way to understand why the gruesome life will be one of the Fire, and the blessed life will be in the Garden.

[7]

LEGACY OF GARDENS

THE GARDEN and the Fire are not realms that believers can enter until the end of time. Believers can dream about or create narrations about the afterworld; however, according to Islamic narratives, only Muhammad was privileged with an actual visit. For everyone else, the Garden and the Fire were unseen worlds whose signs only God could manifest in the earthly world. For believers, a cool stream, a vision of a houri, and dreams of living in a palace were some of the ways that Paradise could have been invoked within earthly life. To enter the actual Garden while on earth would have been impossible for a believer.

In chapters 4 and 5, I argued that the material structure of the afterworld is related to earthly objects and social dynamics in complicated ways. Given that the earthly world is filled with materials similar to those promised in the Garden, how were believers supposed to distinguish true religion from its pretender? How could believers recognize that the Old Man of the Mountain's Paradise was not the one believers waited for at the end of time? Ultimately, how could one see the unseen world within the seen world and at the same time recognize truth from artifice? These epistemological questions focus not on how one recognizes true theology versus heresy as much as how one can perceive truth in a world of possible artifice. The Old Man of the Mountain's Paradise and the actual Garden are composed of similar motifs. If believers were tricked into accepting that some part of the earthly world was really the Garden, it was because the place fashioned to impress them was modeled after an image they recognized.

While previous chapters traced the developing image of the Garden and the Fire in texts ranging from the eighth to the twelfth centuries, this chapter focuses on the later artistic forms that may have allowed believers to approximate glimpses of the Garden and the Fire on earth. By the twelfth century, an image of the Garden and Fire had begun to crystallize and assume a more definite vision with a repertoire of set themes and motifs. From this point onward, the Garden and the Fire were not dynamic, developing realms; rather, they were becoming more static. Instead of being places informed by earthly realities and expectations, they presented a form that gave shape to how believers understood their future lives and provided a model by which artists could provide reflections of heaven on earth for their patrons. While a doctrine of belief, the Garden also became an aesthetic. After addressing epistemological fears of deception and possibilities of perception, this chapter presents the aesthetic of the Garden by tracing some of the ways that Muslims represented aspects of the afterworld on earth. The legacy of the belief in the Garden may be found in the various ways Muslim rulers, painters, poets, and architects incorporated cosmologies of heaven and earth within earthly productions.

DECEPTION AND PERCEPTION

Believers require signs to see divine connections in the world and to recognize their placements in the cosmological order. Yet, in a world where objects or words can be interpreted as manifestations of the unseen world, a sign from someone other than God could cloud the direction of faith. An infamous example is the issue of Satanic verses, revelations delivered to Muhammad but later revoked on the basis that they were not sent by Allah. Eschatological traditions are also replete with the warnings of deceptive signs. For example, one of the portents of the end of time is that al-Dajjal is said to bring to believers a hell (*jahannam*) that resembles the Garden.[1] The issue of deception is central to appreciating the threat that heretics or even the Quraysh posed to the faith of believers. How can believers read signs of the unseen world without being deceived? Moreover, what is the role of material objects and artistic production within the process of deception? A story about Mani in Persian poet Nizami's (1141–1197) epic *Iskandar-nama* (Book of Alexander), provides an excellent illustration of the multiple ways that deception can threaten theological truths.

In an effort to spread the Manichean faith, Mani, whom Islamic heresiographers regarded as both a Zoroastrian heretic and a supremely gifted craftsman, decided to make his way to China. The Chinese were not eager for him to enter their land. In order to thwart his path, they created an impressive illusion. On a vast pool of crystal, they painted tiny waves. The artificial pool appeared like a large, impassable body of water. Its form was so real that Mani approached it with thirst and tried to draw water from it. When his flask broke on the crystal, he realized that the intended purpose of the artifice was to dissuade him from continuing the journey. In response to the artistic deception, he took out his brush, and on the crystal pool of gentle waves, he painted a dead dog whose body oozed with writhing worms. The Chinese, renowned in the Islamic world for their artistic abilities, were so impressed by the vividness of Mani's creation of death that they allowed him to enter China and decided to listen to his religious instruction.

Inspired by this story, painter Sur Gujarati depicted the scene of Mani painting on the pool of crystal for the Mughal emperor Akbar's (r. 1556–1605) copy of the *Khamsa* of Nizami (figure 7.1). For Sur Gujarati the miniature was an opportunity to illustrate the artist at work. The focus of the composition is Mani's act of painting the dead dog. Upon the crystal slab, the dog is emaciated from sickness and death. The body of the dog is splayed flat, and worms have made their way through his stomach to form a writhing heap on the crystal pool. Other worms are crawling out of body orifices. Alongside the dog on the crystal pool are the flask and tools of the painter. The depiction of the dead dog becomes as much a representation of the story as an opportunity to study the methods of the painter. Yet, within the context of Nizami's praise of Mani as painter, there is another meaning embedded in the scene.

Through illustrated manuscripts of Manichean texts, Mani was identified as a superb artist. His success as both religious leader and artisan depended on his ability to depict truth in a compelling fashion. As in the case of the story in the *Iskandar-nama*, Mani is praised for having the ability to make the artificial appear authentic. The Chinese inclination toward his instruction, after finding his creation, reveals Muslim perceptions of Chinese religion and arts. The Chinese could be fooled because they valued what was religiously false, yet artistically extraordinary. Yet, while Mani may have been celebrated as a representative of the power of artifice by artistic tradition, theological authorities feared his power to delude people into believing that he created paradisiacal conditions on earth. Mani's legacy in Islamic culture, then, provides a model for understanding the relationship between religion and art in historical and theological traditions of the Garden.

Mani embodies the connection between heresy and artifice in Islamic

7.1 Mani paints a dead dog. Painted by Sur Gujarati in the *Khamsa* of Nizami, ca. 1595.

heresiography. Heresy diverts from perceptions of "true" faith because it deludes people into believing that the heretic is a prophet or God. By posing as something that he or she is not, the heretic creates a theological order that does not accord with mainstream perceptions of truth. In the same pattern, artifice diverts the eye from the world of God's creation to the world created by the artist. By pretending to create, the artist mirrors a divine act. While Plato would have us believe that poets should be ousted from the Republic, we know that not all artists were inherently heretical and not all heretics were artful. Yet, if Mani's depiction of the dead dog appears so real that only renowned Chinese artists could recognize its artifice, then what chance do believers have in a world of objects?

Just as the Old Man of the Mountain fooled his adherents, Mani convinced people that his art was real. In both cases, the leaders were considered dangerously heretical because their creations rivaled God's: the Old Man of the Mountain and Mani both promised a version of Paradise on earth. Furthermore, they deceived people into believing that their creation was the real one. Yet, what connects the Old Man of the Mountain and Mani is not just their intentions to deceive. Instead, their deception takes a material form. Mani can make a painting appear real through his talents; the Old Man of the Mountain can recreate the Garden through the use of landscape, invocations to houris, and the hallucinogenic effects of drugs. Both were threatening because they offered a theological and material alternative to God's being and creation.

How are believers, then, to trust their perception of the world? How do believers enhance their perception in order to see the linkages between the seen and unseen worlds? In the work *Niche of Lights*, al-Ghazali suggests that with proper guidance, the faithful are able to comprehend the literal, metaphorical, and spiritual composition of an object. Within this form of perception, believers are not only able to discern the difference between truth and artifice, but they are also able to enjoy opportunities to perceive the world within its divine logic. Believers are able to live in the world and also see meaning *beyond* it. The ability to stand in one world and appreciate other worldly manifestations is what Ebrahim Moosa identifies as al-Ghazali's ability to inhabit the liminal space of intellection and create multiple narratives of thought.[2]

The *Niche of Lights* is one of the many commentaries of the light verse in the sura entitled *al-Nur*, "the Light:"

Allah is the Light of the heavens and the earth
The parable of His Light is as if there were a niche

And within it a Lamp
The Lamp enclosed in Glass
The glass as it were
A Brilliant star lit from the blessed
Tree an Olive, neither of the East
Nor of the West
Whose Oil is well-nigh
Luminous though fire scare touched it
Light Upon Light Allah doth guide whom he will
To his light
Allah doth set forth parables
For men
and Allah Doth know all things.

Commonly inscribed on glass mosque lanterns, the verse has inspired artistic forms. At times the verse was invoked by the shape of a lantern in designs of carpets or even a tombstone.[3]

Al-Ghazali's first chapter explicates the first section of the light verse by explaining how different strata of light are perceived by different strata of people: the common, the elect, and the elect of the elect. True light is the light of God and can be perceived by a believer with a purified heart and eye that can see the world.[4] In assessing the difference between metaphoric and literal levels of existence, al-Ghazali suggests that the eye is, in fact, two eyes: an inward and an outward. "The outward eye derives from the world of sensation and visibility, while the inward eye derives from another world—namely, the world of dominion."[5] The faithful can gain access to both the visible world through the senses and the world of spirit through God and the revealed books. The two worlds are related. The visible world is a shell for the world of spirit: "Then everything that enters into the senses and imagination will become his earth, and this includes the heavens; and whatever stands beyond the senses will be his heaven."[6] When a person has reached this first ascent, he or she is on the way to understand the relationship between the seen and unseen and between object and shadow, and realize that "manifestation may be the cause of hiddenness. When a thing passes its own limit, it reverts to its opposite."[7]

Accessing a similitude simultaneously through literal and metaphorical levels exhibits the ability to receive divinely ordained wisdom. Al-Ghazali's use of the similitude can provide a model to understand the material correspondence of the afterworld with the world. For example, when looking at a bejeweled garden scene, a viewer may see both a depiction of a garden as well as the Garden. Islamic artistic tradition embodies these visual clues that allow the viewer to see both a physical space as well as metaphysical manifestation.[8] Take an etching of a lantern on the tombstone, as an example. According to al-Ghazali's use of the two eyes, the outer eye can appreciate the form of the lantern etched on the stone, while the inner eye can apprise God's presence made manifest within the object.

Beyond the different ways to perceive the world is a different understanding of what the world constitutes. Instead of seeing the world as one plane of existence that is followed by an afterworld, Sufi thinker Ibn al-'Arabi (1165–1240) discussed cosmology in terms of three interlinked realms. These realms included the spiritual, the imaginal, and the corporeal worlds. The intermediate state of the imaginal world connects the physical or corporeal world to its spiritual source. Inherent in Ibn al-'Arabi's philosophy is a spatial eschatology. He called the intermediate space *barzakh*, the same term employed for the space in between earth and the heavens.[9] A believer who could connect the spark of the individual within God's being would be able to access all three worlds at the same time. In his opus *al-Futuhat al-makkiyya* (Meccan Illumination), Ibn al-'Arabi develops the eschatological themes further by discussing the Garden and the Fire.

Al-Ghazali and Ibn al-'Arabi's works suggest some thinkers were formulating ways that people could live within the world and see its sanctified meaning through religiously guided perception. Perception of the physical world, then, was a realm of opportunity. Cunning heretics who could twist a believer's notions about divine creation in order to support their agendas could manipulate that perception. Yet, deception of divine truths was not the only result of interpreting and bringing meaning to the world. Instead, al-Ghazali and Ibn al-'Arabi's theories suggest that when believers were able and willing to look beyond the object and into its divinely created manifestation, their perceptions could also yield greater insight into the world.

CONGREGATIONAL MOSQUES

The Dome of the Rock and the Umayyad mosque in Damascus both offer multivalent ways to explore eschatological themes. Umayyad rulers built both mosques around the seventh century, but they were not necessarily constructed as paradises on earth. Instead, their eschatological import developed in later centuries when they became common sites for pilgrimage (*ziyara*). Medieval Muslims considered Mecca, Medina, and Jerusalem to be holy cities. While Damascus in al-Sham (Greater Syria) was not as preeminent as those three cities, it was nonetheless considered a holy land.[10] By the eleventh century, texts consisting of sayings of the prophet and companions fully articulated the sanctity of the city.[11] Muslims eventually viewed Mecca, Medina, Jerusalem, and Damascus (like Karbala for the Shi'a) as sacred spaces that offered blessings (*baraka*). Josef Meri argues that these spaces form a sacred topography made up of natural sites, such as mountains, and buildings, such as monuments, tombs, houses, shrines, mosques, synagogues, and churches.[12]

What is intriguing about the notion of sacred topography is that the land is not considered sanctified because of the buildings or natural sites that people recognize as holy. Rather, the topography itself was recognized as having sanctity, and it is for that reason that monuments and shrines were developed in the area. Sacred spaces create sacred places.[13] For example, Damascus was understood as a sanctified space since it provided a setting for the apocalyptic drama and was believed to be one of the earliest settlements of human existence with Mount Qasiyun as the site of Cain's murder of Abel. As a result, Damascus played a role in the "broader context of Islamic sacred history" of which the Umayyad mosque eventually assumed a central role.[14] Muslim perceptions of sacred topography did not just seek to draw on preexisting sacred histories; instead, they articulated a worldview that claimed sites as their own and contributed to their sanctity.

The Dome of the Rock played a significant role in the Muslim articulation of self in a religiously diverse environment. The Umayyad caliph 'Abd al-Malik commissioned the Dome of the Rock in 692 on one of the highest points of Mount Moriah in Jerusalem. The actual site of the Dome was considered in Jewish and Christian traditions to be sacred ground. Jews believe that Abraham had sacrificed his son Isaac on the rock in the center of the platform of the actual site and that Solomon built his temple of the plateau. Christians regarded the site as the Temple Mount, the place of Jesus' ministry and temptation. In the Islamic tradition of the Night Journey and Ascension narratives, the rock is considered the point from which Muhammad ascended to the heavens.[15]

While the Dome was probably not built to commemorate the Night Journey and Ascension, it became associated with it. The Qur'anic verse that referred to the farthest mosque (al-Masjid al-Aqsa) was understood as the congregational mosque in the southwestern part of the site of the Dome of the Rock complex (Haram al-Sharif). By the eleventh century, the al-Aqsa mosque had a covered arch that included a quote from the Qur'an containing the words "Masjid al-Aqsa."[16] Yet, the direct association between the Dome of the Rock and the prophet's Journey may not have been made until the twelfth or thirteenth century.

An inscription in the inner face of the east door also provided support for the later eschatological interpretation. Part of the inscription asks God for intercession on the Day of Judgment:

> We ask you, our God, by your mercy, by your beautiful names, by your noble face, by your immense power, by your perfect word by which heaven and earth stand together and by which, and with your mercy, we are preserved from *shaytan* and we are all saved from your punishment on the day of resurrection, by your abundant grace, by your great nobility, by your clemency, your power, your forgiveness, and your kindness, that you bless Muhammad, Your servant and your prophet, and you accept his intercession for his community. May God bless him and give him peace and the mercy of God. And this is what was ordered by the servant of God 'Abdallah, the imam of al-Ma'mun, commander of the Faithful, may God prolong his life, under the rule of the brother of the commander of the faithful Abu Ishaq, son of the Commander of the Faithful al-Rashid, may God prolong him. By the hand of Salih ibn Yahya, client of the Commander of the Faithful. In Rabi' al-Thani 216 (May June 831).[17]

Over time, all the buildings on the eastern side of the complex were associated with eschatological themes. According to one hadith, the Golden Gate is regarded as the Gate of Mercy and Repentance and since Umayyad times was recognized as the gate where the Last Judgment would occur.[18] At another structure, the Dome of the Chain, the sifting between the just and the damned would take place. The chain was supposed to stop the wicked and allow the just.[19] The Bridge of Sirat was also understood to cross the Haram to the Mount of Olives.[20] Even the shrine of Muhammad was believed to contain a piece of the rock of the footprint of Buraq during the Ascension.[21]

The significance of the mosaic decoration, which covers 1,280 square meters, is contested. Some scholars argue specifically that the images present paradisiacal patterns of trees and jewelry.[22] Others connect the mosaics with legends about Solomon's temple.[23] Yet others argue that the building of the Dome of the Rock was an act establishing political legitimacy based on the model of David and Solomon, and the religious interpretation took over only when the caliphate center had lost its political potency.[24]

Aside from the formal analysis, there is an argument about eschatological events taking place near the complex structure.[25] One tradition claims that the Golden Gate and Bab al-Rahman, or "Gate of Mercy," will be locked by 'Umar and unlocked on Judgment day.[26] Al-Wasiti, in his

Fada'il al-bayt al-muqaddas, makes similar statements from a Muslim platform. In this work, he identifies the Dome of the Rock as a temple. The throne of the Day of Judgment will stand on the rock before the congregation. Another tradition claims that the Dome of the Rock will stand on a palm tree resting on one of the rivers of Paradise under which Pharaoh's wife and Miriam (Moses' sister) will string pearls for the inhabitants of Paradise until the Day of Judgment.[27]

Thus, the Dome of the Rock presents a varied history. It was not built as a reflection of the Garden. However, over time it became associated with the Garden by local Muslims eager to extol the virtues of the city and by pilgrims who were seeking the otherworld by way of their travels. After the Crusades, the traditions about the eschatological character of the Dome began to develop and were spread extensively.[28]

Unlike the Dome of the Rock, the Umayyad mosque has a stronger formal connection with images of Paradise. The mosque was built on an existing sacred site. In the second millennium, the Semitic god Hadad was assimilated with the Roman god Jupiter. Under the patronage of Septimius Severus (r. 193–211), the temple was restored. After Christianity became the imperial religion and perhaps under Emperor Theodosius (r. 379–395), the inner pagan shrine was eliminated and the temple was transformed into a Christian church dedicated to Saint John the Baptist. The church remained a site of worship by Christians well after the Arab conquest of Damascus in 636. The Umayyad caliph al-Walid (r. 705–715) negotiated with the Christians for the sacred space that offered a large congregational capacity. Work on the mosque began in 708 and was completed in 714–715, after al-Walid's death.[29]

While the site of the Umayyad mosque has a rich multivalent religious history, its eschatological significance rests within its mosaics, which were said to cover the entire surface of the mosque, including its walls and floors, and the high parts of the prayer hall. According to al-Maqdisi, the walls were covered with marble to the length of two people, and then the length was followed by pure mosaic.[30] Yet, the mosaics faced severe damage over the years. A fire damaged the mosaics in 1069.[31] Tamerlane burned the mosque in 1401.[32] An earthquake hit the region in 1157, and a fire once again destroyed mosaics in 1893.[33] In 1963 many of the mosaics in the courtyard were restored. Some scholars have complained that since the restoration employed different techniques, the mosaics are not true to their original form. Similar complaints were made about the restoration in the 1990s.[34]

However, enough remains of the paneling in the facade of the transept, western arcade, and north portico to obtain some sense of the original

7.2 Barada panel of the Umayyad mosque.

form of the mosaics. The Barada panel on the western wall (figure 7.2) and the unreconstructed, albeit darker, version of it in the western section (figure 7.3) gives an excellent sense of the original. Each of the panels offers scenes of palaces or sumptuous homes that are interlaced by trees. Underneath many of the panels are flowing rivers.

Another important aspect of the mosaics is the hanging pearls and the hanging lanterns or pearls in the archways. Finbarr Barry Flood asserts that pearls or ovoids in the shape of pearls that were hung on golden chains in the surviving mosaics may have a common heritage with Byzantine mother-of-pearl pendants. Both are related to the iconography of Heavenly Jerusalem or Islamic Paradise.[35] Flood links the pearl with the bejeweled architecture of the Garden and suggests that its appearance added to the heavenly connotations.[36]

The use of jewels emphasizes the otherworldly nature. Nasser Rabat, reading al-Maqdisi and Yaqut, reports that al-Walid I decorated the mosque's niche indicating the direction of prayer (*mihrab*) and the area around it with sapphires and agates. A large jewel was used "as a diacriti-

7.3 Barada panel of the Umayyad mosque.

cal mark in the last word of a Qur'anic verse inscribed in gold on the *qibla* wall of the mosque." One of the gems in the *mihrab* was so famous that it had a proper name, al-Qulayla,[37] and was allegedly taken by an Abbasid prince.[38] Golden vines set between the mosaics and the marble may also have conferred a paradisiacal imagery.[39]

Based on his reading of Ibn 'Asakir, Flood also claims that there may have been lost inscriptions that were located between the marble and the mosaic in four superimposed narrow bands along the southern wall. Of the five inscriptions (2.255–256, 1.1–7, 79.1–46, 80.1–42, 81.1–29), three make reference to the Day of Judgment, two of which are evocative verses from the suras *al-Nazi'at* and *Tawkir* that dramatically recount the Last Judgment and Resurrection and the moments "when the blazing fire is kindled to fierce heat; and when the Garden is brought near" (81.12–13). The inclusion of these putative dramatic inscriptions suggests another layer of eschatological meaning to the structure of the mosque. Although it is unlikely that the inscriptions were to be read, they do support, in formal terms, the notion of a decorative scheme with eschatological themes.

Even in the later medieval period, the meanings of these panels were divided between those who suggested that they showed the grandeur of the world under the Umayyads, and generally Islamic rule, whereas others suggested that they invoked paradisiacal imagery. Al-Maqdisi was one who identified with the image of grandeur being linked with caliph's rule on earth. Other commentators sided with the representation of Damascus itself, while still others identified palaces promised in Paradise with the rivers flowing underneath.[40]

While a worldly meaning of the mosaics is compelling, an otherworldly one is just as plausible since over time the sites were understood to have an otherworldly dimension to them. Within the framework of al-Ghazali and Ibn al-'Arabi's theories, the meaning of the mosaics can exist on different registers as both worldly and otherworldly sites. What is significant for the purposes of the chapter is that the best of this world carries the resonance of the best in the next world. In fact, given the opulence of materials painted in the Qur'an through jewels, vegetation, and carpets, the two mosques may have been sites where Muslims not allied with court life would have had an opportunity to see jewels and fine mosaics.

As major pilgrimage sites, the beauty of the mosque and its decoration may have reinforced a religious aesthetic of the Garden based in the Qur'an, elaborated in hadiths, and further interpreted as the centuries passed. Pilgrims traveled to religious sites to enter sanctified space. Given the religious import of their journeys, it is quite possible that they saw the image of the Garden with its bejeweled residences, flowing rivers, and lush greenery within the colorful, elaborate mosaics of the Umayyad mosque. In the case of the Dome of the Rock, it is clear that by the tenth century, eschatological themes were fully developed in pilgrimage guides, even if those beliefs may have formed and evolved earlier. The correspondence that al-Ghazali encourages may have been what the pilgrims were seeking. Muslims journeyed to receive *baraka* and perceive divine beauty at religious sites. They must have known of the Garden promised to them in the Qur'an, and may have seen its approximation on the walls and within the religious space of the mosques.

COSMOLOGIES

By exploring eschatological events and fantastic places within worldly geographies, certain texts invoked the ideas of the Garden and Fire in order to bring meaning to earthly life. The reception of these cosmological texts would have been limited to readers associated with the court, and so the books themselves would have not been widely experienced the way a pilgrimage site may have been. Yet, the range of topics in the manuscripts gives us a sense of the ways that eschatology was reflected and represented. Beyond mere representation, cosmologies showed the numerous ways that writers and illustrators expressed their understanding of the fantastic within their earthly worlds.

One of the most popular cosmological treatises was al-Qazwini's (1208–1283) *Kitab 'aja'ib al-makhluqat wa ghara'ib al-mawjudat* (Wonders of Creatures and Marvels of Creations). The text is part of the genre of wonders that describe the fantastic creations of the world. The wonders begin with the first elements of creation and end with the explanation of the various climes and their odd characteristics. Eschatological traditions appear early in the work. The opening sections are devoted to the eschatological narrative, which includes angels who will bring about the Day of Resurrection, angel Israfil blowing the horn, angels of the dead recording deeds, and angels Mikhail and Gabriel. At times, manuscripts also illustrate the angels of different levels of heaven or four animal-headed angels (figure 7.4).

The four-headed angels depicted here illustrate the often complex ways that eschatological images play out religious themes. In the illustration, each one of the angels has a different animal head: eagle, lion, ox, angel. Marie-Rose Séguy suggests that the man and bull are meant to intercede in favor of men and beasts of burden, while the eagle and lion intercede for birds and wild animals.[41] Yet, some animals may also have significance as a symbol for Christian apostles: Mark is often symbolized by a winged lion, and Luke by a winged ox. The angels, then, may have referred to both the idea of the heavenly realm where God's throne is surrounded by his attendants as well as Christian symbolism.

Yet, the eschatological current within al-Qazwini's text is not limited to otherworldly realms. The invocation of the Garden also occurs in the descriptions of islands in the Pacific where houris with wings are said to reside.[42] The beings are not represented as actual houris of the afterworld; however, in describing the fantastic qualities of the Pacific islands, the text identifies the female creatures as "houris." In this sense, the term *houri* entered a general vocabulary that describes otherworldly places, whether real or imagined. To have a houri in a tree in the far-off land is to signify that the land is as marvelous to the reader as Paradise is to earth.

The mapping of heaven and earth was not an activity that was solely undertaken by writers of marvels and geographical texts. Another text

7.4 Four angels surround God's throne. Al-Qazwini, *Kitab 'aja'ib al-makhluqat wa ghara'ib al-mawjudat*, ca. 1475.

also literally maps out eschatological time and space within a schematic drawing. The Ottoman Turkish work *Ma'riftename* (1756–57) by Ibrahim Hakki is an eighteenth-century encyclopedia of the world. The work has a number of remarkable maps of which two depict the levels of earth, the Last Judgment, the different motifs of eschatological time, and the levels of heaven themselves. The first map (figure 7.5) presents an eschatological

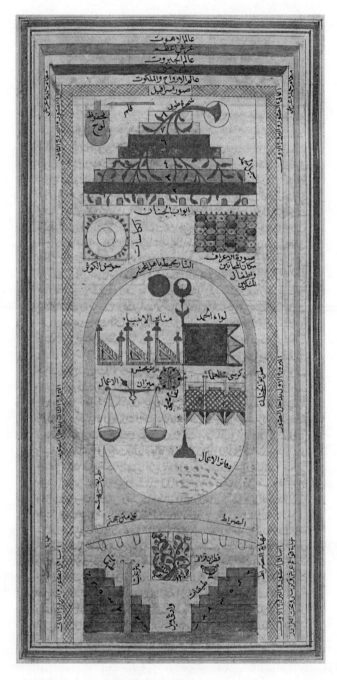

7.5 Depiction of heaven and earth. *Ma'rifetname* of Ibrahim Hakki, ca. 1756–57.

cosmology. The lower part of the composition displays seven levels under the Bridge of Sirat, which divides the lower levels from the center of the composition that depicts the Last Judgment. The Last Judgment is represented by the scales on top of which are the *minbars* of prophets. Muhammad has a reserved space before the other prophets and above humanity. The top register depicts the seven levels of heaven with the branches of the tree Tuba connecting all levels. On the top left is the tablet and pen upon which all of humanity's deeds are written. The second map (figure 7.6) mirrors the first in its eschatological themes, but the center is the Ka'ba. Both the top and lower registers of the map are the same. The two maps demonstrate how heaven and earth are linked. The maps present a continuum from celestial to mundane that is connected through the Ka'ba. The Ka'ba then acts as a central point for Islamic faith, but it also links the realms of heaven and earth.

The most common eschatological depiction, beyond angels and houris and maps, is of the actual *mi'raj*. There are numerous versions of the Night Journey and Ascension narrative in legends of prophets, general histories, resurrection literature, and poetry.[43] While each may vary in details, they all have the central concept of Muhammad's journey to the heavens with Angel Gabriel and Buraq. The scenes of the Ascension and Night Journey typically show Muhammad traveling on Buraq through the night sky. Often Muhammad is surrounded by a nimbus of fire to signify his special position, and sometimes his face is erased or occluded to comply with more orthodox standards against the depiction of figural images. Other miniature paintings do show Muhammad's face. One of the most renowned works that depicts the Night Journey and Ascension is an illustrated copy of poet Mir Haydar's translation of the Turkish *mi'raj* in eastern Turkish, which the calligrapher Malik Makhsi of Herat wrote in the Uighur script. Its illustration is extensive with sixty-one illuminations. In illustrating Muhammad's journey, the painter depicts Muhammad on Buraq flying through the night skies (figure 7.7). Muhammad is surrounded by a number of angels, each with a different vessel.

This telling of the *mi'raj* is remarkable because it provides sixty-one illustrations that give visual form to an extended Night Journey and Ascension narrative. It tells the entire story of the journey and provides illustrations of all the levels of the Garden and the punishments of the Fire. In this version, the angel Gabriel awakens Muhammad and takes him to Jerusalem. Then he visits each of the levels of heaven and meets their respective prophets, various angels, and other fantastic creatures. As he approaches the seventh Paradise, he sees the bejeweled Lote Tree of the

7.6 Depiction of heaven and earth, with the Ka'ba at the center. *Ma'rifetname* of Ibrahim Hakki, ca. 1756–57.

7.7 *Mi'raj*: Mohammed rides on Buraq across the night sky.

BIBLIOTHÈQUE NATIONALE DE FRANCE.

Boundary and bows down to worship God. He then ventures beyond into Paradise to see the houris frolicking in the Garden (figure 7.8).

The houris are enjoying the bounties of the Garden with flowering trees and flowing water. Some are picking blossoms from the trees while others are conversing at ease. There is such peace in the composition that even birds come to them and sit on some of their heads unperturbed.

7.8 Houris frolicking.

7.9 Women guilty of loose behavior.

The manuscript also provides some of the only depictions of punishments in the Fire. The punishments that are illustrated include categories that were not mentioned in Ibn Ishaq's *Sira*, such as those who were evil speakers, sowed discord, bore false witness, and were falsely devout. In all, fourteen punishments are illustrated. Two regard women in particular. One is a depiction of the adulterers who hang from their breasts,[44] while the other depicts shameless women who engaged in dishonorable acts. These women are hanged by their tongues over the blazing fire (fig. 7.9).

7.10 Punishments for drinkers of wine and fermented drinks.

The punishment of the drinkers of wine and fermented drinks illustrates the reciprocal nature of punishment: what was enjoyed immorally on earth is the source of pain in the future. In this illustration, the sinners are being forced to drink their libations eternally by their tormentors (figure 7.10). Punishments are generally administered by demons as opposed to being inflicted by the sinners themselves. In the depiction of the dreaded tree of al-Zaqqum, demons cut off the sinners' tongues. Above them is the tree, whose branches contain various demon heads. Before the tree is a blue demon (figure 7.11). Here the theme of self-punishment, reflected in the Qur'an and hadiths, is not evident, since the pain is at the hands of various kinds of demons.

Not all cosmologies involve eschatological time and happenings. In fact, one of the greatest cosmologies is found in the pages of the Persian poet

7.11 Tree of al-Zaqqum.

Nizami's *Haft Paykar*, completed in 1197. The title of the poem embodies its several layers. *Haft* is the Persian term for "seven," and *Paykar* is the Persian term for "temple" or "pavilion." The poem, about the Sassanian ruler Bahram Gur, presents several narrative frames. The work begins with a prologue that includes praise of God and Muhammad, description of the *mi'raj*, the poem's composition, praise for the patron, the discourse of the poem, and advice for the poet's son. The poem then launches into its main narrative of Bahram Gur. Within that narrative of his youth, Bahram Gur goes on a hunt and then discovers a room in the palace with portraits of seven princesses from seven climes. Afterward, he seizes the crown and rules Iran. As the shah of Iran, the poem describes his love affair with strong-willed Fitna and his defeat of the ruler of China. After his defeat, he seeks the seven princesses as his brides, and his architect builds a palace with seven pavilions for them. He eventually enters the narrative world to visit each of the princesses in their different pavilions. When Bahram Gur emerges, he finds his kingdom in chaos. He restores justice by eliminating his corrupt vizier, renounces his seven princesses, and dedicates himself to justice. The tale ends in a hunt where a lovely female donkey leads Bahram Gur into a cave. His soldiers cannot find him and his kingdom passes to his heir.

The central tale of Bahram Gur's encounter with the seven princesses is in some ways a *mi'raj*-like journey. Like the later developed traditions of heaven, each pavilion has a gatekeeper (princess), stone (color), designated star (attribute), and day of the week. The tale that each princess tells relates to the themes of love and frustration: the hero is with his beloved in some tales and is estranged from her in others. On Saturday, Bahram Gur visits the princess of India, whose color is black and who is ruled by Saturn. On Sunday, he visits the princess from Turkestan, whose color is yellow and is ruled by the sun. On Monday, his time is spent with the princess of Khwarazm, whose color is green and who is ruled by the moon. On Tuesday, he visits the princess of Slavonia, whose color is red and who is ruled by Mars. On Wednesday, his time is dedicated to the princess of Maghreb, whose color is turquoise and who is ruled by Mercury. On Thursday, he visits the princess of Byzantium, whose color is sandal and is ruled by Jupiter. And finally on Friday he visits the Iranian princess, whose color is white and who is ruled by Venus. The final tale of the Iranian princess ends in the fulfillment of love. In her story, the hero recognizes the illicit nature of love and marries his beloved, thus allowing and ultimately legitimating their union.

The tales are similar to paradisiacal traditions, since they involve the themes of reunion and ultimately yield a moral conclusion. Julie Scott Meisami argues that poetic gardens in medieval Persia, found within the verses of Nizami, Rumi, and Hafez, share the feature as being allegorical paradises of love.[45] In their moral dimension, the tales also serve as allegorical "mirror for princes."[46] For example, in the third tale, a certain Bishr goes on pilgrimage to purify himself of the feelings of temptation after he caught sight of a woman when she walked by and her veil fluttered; he wins her in the end of the story when he returns the belongings of his unethical traveling companion and discovers that she was the deceased man's wife.

The setting of the *Haft Paykar* is dependent upon and extends paradisiacal garden imagery. The use of the pavilion as the centerpiece for the narrative draws on the notion of the pavilion garden homes that are mentioned in the Qur'an, described by hadiths, and further employed in eschatological texts. Within the garden imagery of the *Haft Paykar* are also stories that reinforce the developed vision of Paradise as a courtyard Garden. The lady in the tale of the first princess lives in a palace, "a place like Paradise." She tells the tale of the king who dressed in black because he was depressed that he never won the lady in a land of China that is identified as a Paradise.[47] Traveling by way of fantastical bird, the king lands in a garden:

I looked around, myself again,
and scanned that place before, behind,
I saw a garden untouched by
the dust of men; its earth the sky.
A myriad of flowers blossomed there,
its water seeping, grass aware.
Each flower was of a different shade;
the scent of each for miles did spread.
The lassos of the hyacinths
bound up the tresses of the pinks.
Jasmine bit roses' lips; deep grass
silenced the flowering Judas-trees.
The dust was camphor, ambergris
the earth, sands gold, the stones all gems.
Streams flowed like rose-water, and hid
pearls and carnelians in their midst;
A spring from which our turquoise fort
begged both its hue and luster bright.

The fish in those bright streams did play
like silver coins in mercury.
Girt by a mount of emerald hue,
where cypress, pine, and poplar grew,
Its stones were all of rubies red,
its poplars with their colour dyed;
Sandal and aloes everywhere;
with them the breeze perfumed the air.
It seemed of houris' forms devised
who taxes paid from Paradise.
'Heart's-ease' its name by Iram given,
and by the turquoise sphere called Heaven.[48]

Within the description of the garden is a highly formalized way of talking about the sensual delights of sight, smell, and sound. The landscape is verdant, is filled with fragrance from various flowers, and alternates between silence and the sounds of water. This version of Paradise is so beautiful that even the houris have to pay taxes. Its descriptions are based on the models of the Garden through the appearance of jewels, such as pearl and carnelian. In the following verses, it is also compared to Iram, a city of marbled columns that takes on mythic proportions in Arab and Persian poetry. While there are several explanations for Iram, it was later understood to be built by the Arabian king Shaddad of the tribe 'Ad in Aden in order to imitate Paradise.[49] Qur'anic verses note that God destroyed it because of Shaddad's excessive pride (89.7–15).

Nizami's *Haft Paykar* redefines the understanding of poetic and cosmological texts. The verses within the poem are rich with history, myth, philosophy, theology, and cosmology. The tales tell the story of passions; yet, ultimately, love is always righteous. The entire epic itself is framed within the theme of ascension to the heavens in the ultimate pursuit of God. After illustrated manuscripts of al-Qazwini's *Kitab 'aja'ib al-makhluqat wa ghara'ib al-mawjudat*, Nizami's *Haft Paykar* is the most frequently used composition for illuminated manuscripts. Manuscripts usually depict the seven temples in their glorious color with their accompanying princess (figure 7.12). The most extraordinary never give the reader a clue whether they are inside the pavilion watching the lovers play or if they are outside the walls looking into the tale. In this sense, the very best miniatures are paradisiacal in their depictions of flora and fauna, and also in that they invite the viewer to taste the potential of the Garden while turning the pages.

7.12 Princess in the black pavilion. *Khamsa* of Nizami, ca. mid-17th century.

GARDENS

While the metaphor of the Garden is central to the image of Paradise, the reverse is not true: not every poetic and earthly garden is a Paradise on earth. Gardens are far more complex in forms and meanings. What unites the multitude of differences is that gardens are a way that humans attempt to shape the natural world, and for this reason gardens offer an "intimate history of human relationships to nature."[50] The ability or desire of humans to build a natural world around them is central to understanding the garden as a site. The garden is not untamed expanses of land. Instead, it is a contained place crafted for human subsistence and repose. It is through the distinction between open, wild and closed, controlled space that the word "paradise" finds meaning. "Paradise" derives from the Old Persian *pairi-daeza*, meaning an enclosed space such as a walled garden. The idea that Paradise is enclosed is predicated on a vision of a created world that stands apart and provides respite from the hardships of the natural world.

As a created world, gardens are often seen as the result of divine favor or evidence of the splendor of a ruler. If a ruler can create a garden that mirrors *al-janna*, then his or her realm has as much majesty as possible for God's agent on earth: the best rulers build the best gardens. Within this framework of political and religious legitimacy is the Persian tradition of poetic gardens renowned for their splendor to create Paradise on earth.[51] For example, Ghaznavid gardens were memorialized in verse. In an extended description that William Hanaway argues provided a poetic model, Farrukhi describes Sultan Mahmud's garden in Balkh as a realm where the shadow of Tuba falls and Kawthar bubbles up.[52] Poet Mu'izzi celebrated Malik Shah's garden and compared its roses and cypresses beside the stream to a houri's face or a beloved's figure.[53] Beyond the demonstration of splendor, Ghaznavid gardens were also a way that the ruler establishes the primacy or glory of his power on earth. The garden complex became a way of demonstrating power and might of a ruler who had the capacity to mirror heaven on earth. In a *qasida* by Farrukhi Sistani (d. 1032–33), the poet celebrates the birth of Amir Abu Ya'qub Yusuf ibn Sabuktigan's (d. 1031) son and his new palace. The opulent palace is described through its inscriptions of gold, vistas that look to the garden, mountain slope, sea, and land, walls of camphor and rosewater, use of marble and Turkish jade, ceiling of white balsam and red sandalwood, and floor of black musk and amber. As Julie Meisami notes, the palace is not meant to reflect Paradise as much as it is supposed the rival it. What has been created is an "earthly Paradise which is the envy of the heavenly Garden itself."[54]

One remarkable description comes from an ode written to celebrate the completion of a new garden by the son of a Ghaznavid *wazir* (minister). The garden is described as an earthly representation of the paradise garden with its flora and its palace whose terraces are as broad as the heavens. Yet the garden also contains peculiar Ghaznavid decorations: "Three hundred thousand idols stand in it, each one such as would amaze the great Buddha of Balkh."[55] Given the archaeological record of Ghaznavid sites, it is likely that the account of the idols is exaggerated.[56] Significant, however, is the sense of a model of Islamic paradise containing within it the spoils of other destroyed religions. Just as Mahmud of Ghazni used captured idols as decoration in his palaces to act as symbols of power, the idols in the garden not only celebrate Islamic glory as Paradise, but they also do so because they triumph over other religious traditions.

Within the realm of metaphor, poetic Gardens can mirror or even rival *al-janna* itself. Yet, the relationship between the Garden and actual gardens depends on the interplay of intention and reception. One of the problems with ascertaining if an earthly garden is meant to mirror the heavenly Garden is the power of the image of Garden in the Qur'an. Gardens are described in abstract terms as green with flowing waters. As a result, gardens that contain elements of flowing water within green expanse seem to support the ideal vision within Qur'anic terms. Often the Qur'anic invocation is expressed through the Persian form of *chahar bagh*, where cross-axial channels of water create a rectangular garden made up of four plots. The Qur'anic ideal and the pre-Islamic form thus become conflated. What results is that many gardens built by Muslim rulers are understood as being paradisiacal *chahar baghs* even when they do not contain four plots or cross-axial water pathways.[57] There are two lessons we can learn from the propensity to look for essentials within Islamic garden imagery. First, not every garden was intended to invoke Paradise. More important, the image of the Garden is so dominant that when invoked it collapses earthly detail and difference.

Why is there a tendency to read earthly gardens as Paradises on earth? D. Fairchild Ruggles provides an interesting answer. The Mughals built many of the surviving Islamic gardens, and many of those gardens express paradisiacal programs. The privileging of Mughal gardens, especially before the study of gardens such as Madinat al-Zahra' in Cordoba, skews the study of the garden.[58] As a result, the iconography of the Islamic garden is understood through the Qur'an and a limited set of monuments.[59] Reading paradise into every garden also mistakenly encourages reading religion into monuments when the intention or reception requires further study. What results is a particularly colonial approach of appropriating religious categories since scholars invoke the Qur'anic vision of the garden in order to claim and identify Muslim landscape. Yet, Ruggles makes an interesting point: the Qur'an creates a distinction between *al-janna* as a garden (6.141) and *al-janna* as *the* Garden: "If the Qur'an itself distinguishes between the garden that is paradise and gardens that are simply gardens, so must historians."[60]

Assessing the intention to build a garden complex becomes more interesting when considering architectural elements that could be intended for different functions. For example, Yasser Tabbaa suggests that gardens that take on the qualities of the western Islamic courtyard garden intersected by a channel of water are a result of hydraulics and perfection of the courtyard garden initiated in the twelfth and thirteenth centuries.[61] What made the gardens possible was the advent of the *salsabil*, a fountain made of a spout that spills water over a curved marble slab. The water then flows down a narrow channel into a pool of water in the center of the courtyard.[62] As Tabbaa notes, the architectural form creates the interplay of movement and stillness, of solidity and ephemerality, and controlled and free water that may have had both secular and sacred potential for reflection. Just as the visual and aural interplay could be stressed for meditative purposes, it could also be the object for palatial environments. Neither the religious nor the sumptuary trumped the other.[63] If we follow this line of argument, there is no clear function for or even type of "Islamic garden," and the gardens may have been enjoyed on various levels.

While we cannot assume that all gardens built or enjoyed by Muslims were seen as paradises on earth, we also cannot discount the gardens whose intentions created correspondences with the developed aesthetic of the Garden. For example, Cynthia Robinson argues that the Aljafería built by the Banu Hud, lords of Saragossa during the last half of the eleventh century, were understood as paradisiacal surroundings due to the poetics of the metaphorical *badi'* style. By readings al-Jurjani's exposition of poetic imagery, Robinson identifies one type of metaphor, *isti'ara*, as central to the equating the Aljafería with the Garden. This type of metaphor recognizes that the subject and object can have similar effects on the viewer. By drawing on the collective imagination of the viewers through phrases such as "you think you see," the poet uses the senses of the viewers to create an analogy with the senses experienced in Paradise. With Paradise and Aljafería aligned, the literary evocation makes the palace a paradise.[64]

Another example that illustrates how intention can make an earthly garden site a reflection of Paradise on earth is the example of Ottoman Kağithane gardens during the Tulip period (1718–1730). Deniz Çalış argues that the Kağithane Commons, a site that epitomized luxury and consumption during the Tulip period and was eventually destroyed, drew upon eschatological motifs. By reading the poetry of Nedîm and exploring his relationship to Ibn al-'Arabi's philosophy, she suggests that gardens were seen as an intermediate space of *barzakh* that was manifested in garden rituals practiced by the whole society.[65] Çaliş suggests that the garden had a bridge called Sirat which visitors had to cross to enter the site. In between the Sultan's gardens and the public commons was a garden that commoners could view over a low fence or access through two doors. Identified as the "Paradise Garden on Earth," it would have contained pools with underground channels of water. This garden site, whose only records are in the poetry of Nedîm, invoked both the Sirat as an entry into the afterworld and also the Qur'anic promise of "gardens underneath which rivers flow."[66]

Both examples show how earthly spaces were understood as otherworldly gardens through the use of epistemology and metaphor. Yet, many Mughal funerary gardens were built with the explicit intention to house the deceased in a paradisiacal setting until the end of time. Not only do the sites surround the deceased with a vision of the afterworld with its trees, shade, and running water, but often an explicit connection with the afterworld is also inscribed within the tomb structure. For example, the inscription of Emperor Akbar's tomb draws on paradisiacal imagery:

Hail, blessed space happier than the garden of Paradise!
Hail, lofty building higher than the Divine Throne!
A paradise, the garden of which has thousands of rizvan as its servants
A Garden, the terian of which contains thousands of Celestial Paradises.
The pen of the mason of the Divine Decree has written upon its threshold:
There are the gardens of Eden, enter them to live forever.[67]

The most dramatic funerary garden is the Taj Mahal. Built by Shah Jahan to house his beloved wife Mumtaz Mahal, the Taj Mahal is a mausoleum set in a riverine garden space. The intention of the site was to build a burial place for Mumtaz Mahal that would provide an earthly image of her heavenly mansion in Paradise.

The inscriptional program of the Taj Mahal reinforces the connection with paradise. Shah Jahan's cenotaph invokes it, since it refers to him as *firdaws ashyani* (Dweller in Paradise). The southern facade of the Taj Mahal consists of the entire sura *al-Fajr* (89), which ends with "Enter Thou my Paradise."[68] Other verses are also found within the structure. The last two verses of the sura *al-Bayina* (98), which invoke the Gardens of everlasting bliss with flowing streams, can be found in the east arched niche around the door. The arch of the southwest niche of the central tomb chamber refers to the sura *al-Insan* (76), which presents a vision of the Garden as sitting on couches under shady branches. The upper cenotaph of Mumtaz Mahal quotes the sura *al-Fussilat* (41.30) twice: "As for those who say, 'Our Lord is God' and take the straight oath towards Him, the angels will come down to them and say, "Have no fear or grief, but rejoice in the good news of Paradise, which you have been promised."[69]

Aside from the inscriptions, other elements of the garden structure reinforce the vision of paradise. Shah Jahan and his designers created flower and plant imagery in inlaid stone to create an image of a permanent garden for the inhabitants.[70] Ebba Koch suggests that even the interior dome of the mausoleum was built to evoke eternity, since it held a single tone for nearly half a minute. What is remarkable about the Taj Mahal is not only the complete and sophisticated program that included architecture, inscriptions, and floral imagery to project a permanent garden, but also the intention that the complex would be visited by a larger public purpose. Koch argues that the "The Taj Mahal was built with posterity in mind: we, the viewers, are part of its concept."[71] The Taj Mahal was intended as an earthly reflection of paradise not just for Mumtaz Mahal, but also for all the visitors who would visit it over the years. In fact, the larger Taj complex with its forecourt of the Jilaukhana complex and the surrounding bazaar and caravanserai zone were meant to accommodate travelers.[72]

The Taj Mahal is a special case because it illustrates both intention to represent a Paradise on earth and reception of its message. While it is unique in its scale and ambition, it also exemplifies the special place that gardens held for the Mughal dynasty. Even the founder of the dynasty Babur, in his memoir *Baburnama*, makes a special point to note the gardens during his travels and conquests, even though he does not evince any intention to replicate Paradise. Beyond the founder of the dynasty, the Mughals built gardens and were remembered for their gardens. Sa'ib of Tabriz praises Mughal princesses Jahan-Ara's garden in Kabul: "Praise God for the garden which adorns the world and this city. The Tuba would wither from jealousy at its trees. Like the cypress, its trees are safe from losing their leaves for autumn cannot rust them here. Khizr tried his luck in the Darkness searching for the Water of Life; you are invited here to take eternal life from its streams."[73]

Within the larger tradition of Mughal gardens, one map attributed to Delhi during the 1800s illustrates the Mughal fascination with the garden

7.13 *Higher regions of paradise and heaven,* ca. 1800s.

FREER GALLERY OF ART, SMITHSONIAN INSTITUTION, WASHINGTON, D.C. GIFT
OF PROFESSOR ALBAN G. WIDGERY OF WINCHESTER, VIRGINIA. F1968.3.

as an imperial complex. The map (figure 7.13) presents a topographical
schema of the connection between the earthly and paradisiacal gardens.
In the map, the door of faith (*bab al-iman*) at the bottom of the composition opens to a cultivated garden in which four rivers flow. Above the
garden, marked by both earthly production and heavenly allusion, is the
throne of God flanked by angels. Above the throne is the presence of God,
represented by the word *huwa,* the third-person masculine singular that
often is used to refer to Allah.

The Gardens of Iran and Mughal India draw on earlier Persian tradition of landscape design as well as on Islamic meanings of the Garden.[74] Whether through poetic or earthly form, rulers asserted the blessedness of their sovereignty on earth by building gardens. Sometimes the gardens were intended to represent a paradise on earth. At other times they were solely designed to provide a realm of pleasure and repose for the ruler. For those projects that were intended to reflect Paradise on earth, we can return to the question raised earlier in the chapter about perception and deception. Why is the Old Man of the Mountain a heretic for attempting to re-create Paradise, but Shah Jahan the embodiment of the true love for building a monument meant to house his wife in an earthly paradise? The answer rests both with the builders' intentions and the consequence of their agendas. Hasan-i Sabbah meant to deceive believers from the divinely created world, and he is remembered as a heretic. Shah Jahan sought to enhance perception of the world to come, and he is remembered for his piety and devotion.

Theological texts may form the classical doctrine of a faith, but they do not monopolize the ways in which believers can access the meaning of a doctrine as lived historical experience. The previous chapters approached the developing Sunni tradition of the Garden and the Fire as theological and historical phenomena; however, the belief in the Garden and the Fire also had a cultural life that could reflect theological concerns, but was not limited by them. The cultural life did not necessarily emanate from theological texts, but stood alongside them, sometimes reinforcing and at other points competing with religious doctrine. Faith in the Islamic afterlife, then, can be accessed through nontheological sources, such as stories, paintings, and gardens.

When analyzing each site, object, or painting within its specific historical and artistic contexts, it becomes clear that not every artistic production was meant to recall the Garden. Instead, the invocation to the Garden was more complicated. The case of the Dome of the Rock and the Umayyad mosque illustrates that even if there is an argument that the sites were meant to represent aspects of the Garden, they were only fully understood over time as eschatological sites that emanated *baraka*. Cosmological texts drew on the notion of eschatological time and architecture of the Garden in order to further explore human understanding of worldly geography or the end of time. Ironically, gardens present the trickiest case because while some gardens had explicitly eschatological meanings, most are better understood through the prism of rulers' ambitions to establish and enjoy a monument meant both to enhance nature and to battle natural entropy: gardens, after all, require constant maintenance.

All these cases, however, illustrate the legacy of the Garden as an enduring idea of perfection. By the thirteenth century and beyond, the Garden became an ideal of perfection and wonder. The legacy of the Garden, then, is the power of this ideal within the process of artistic production. The material culture that invokes the Garden is an evolving category whose meanings shift with the changing tastes of beauty on this earth: there is not just one way to represent *al-janna*. Yet, the legacy of the developing image of the Garden from the seventh to the twelfth century is the notion of a realm of true beauty. The Garden within later artistic invocations is as much an idea of perfection as it is a future place of residence.

EPILOGUE

I N MARCH 1997, *Time* magazine reported on the belief in the afterlife with the cover story, "Does Heaven Exist?" After treating the intellectual developments and controversies of the afterlife from Genesis to the twentieth century, the article presented a poll of Americans' religious beliefs. It found that the majority of those polled believe in a heaven where people live forever with God and in a hell where others are punished after they die. Other questions drew out the enduring faith in Saint Peter and angels. In another development, in the summer of 1999, *La Civiltà Cattolica*, a Jesuit magazine closely affiliated with the Vatican, endorsed the belief that hell does not exist but is rather a state of psychological torment. The Vatican soon gave its nod to the opinion, and Pope John Paul identified hell as the "pain, frustration, and emptiness of life without God."[1] *U.S. News and World Report* followed the story and, after interviewing scholars, suggested why hell had ended after centuries of profitable existence.[2] The twentieth century thus concluded with the continued belief in heaven and the waning faith in hell.[3]

While the topic of heaven and hell may occasion cover stories for American newsmagazines, there has been a sustained developing interest in religious literature in both American and Arab publishing markets. In the United States, religious fiction has become a publishing category, with Tim LaHaye and Jerry Jenkins's *Left Behind* multivolume series as its star. The series bases its plot on the events of the Rapture, the coming Apocalypse, and the return of Christ. Written with the tone of a thriller, the series dramatizes the events of the Apocalypse through the lens of an airplane pilot who has his own doubts about faith. As he witnesses those good souls (including his wife) who have been taken from the earth in a single moment, he soon realizes that he is part of humanity who has been left behind to face the Apocalypse. The events are set within contemporary political events, with the Antichrist eventually assuming the position of secretary general of the United Nations. The novels alternate between accounting for the events at the end of time and modeling Christian faith for the reader.

Eschatological drama is not limited to the American publishing market. Popular belief, rarely recorded and often censored from historical record, has an articulate form in contemporary Arab eschatological manuals. Commonly sold in bookstores, marketplaces, and outside large congregational mosques in Amman, Cairo, and Damascus, these booklets and pamphlets act as edifying primers that illustrate Islamic theology through religious traditions and inspirational stories. The first of these manuals may have been published starting in the 1970s; however, their numbers have increased dramatically since the mid-1980s. Alongside Friday sermons, the manuals offer a rich source for understanding the contemporary status of Muslims' beliefs and practices. The manuals contain religious stories and hadiths that have often been omitted from theological guides over the centuries because the textual material did not meet theologians' criteria of verifiability. For example, a common saying enjoining reverence for mothers is, "Paradise lies at the feet of mothers." While this is one of the most popular traditions, readers would be hard pressed to find it in one of the six hadith collections. Through the technological advance of printing, these traditions have surfaced in the religious manuals.

Studying the manuals allows a glimpse into the formation of popular theology for the Muslim individual, family, and community. The works provide easy and inspirational reads for Muslims, and some of the works are published for specific readership, such as distinct Sunni and Shi'a biographical accounts of companions of the prophet. Works for families, such as *The Key to Paradise: Stories for Mothers* and *The Key to Paradise: Stories for Fathers*, narrate inspirational stories to inspire good religious parenting. Other works address what happens after death and prepare the reader for the Resurrection and Judgment. Many of the manuals sport graphic covers of the one-eyed al-Dajjal or the accursed tree of al-Zaqqum and employ eschatological motifs to suggest that the political struggles of Muslims in the Middle East are part of the larger backdrop of the end of time.

While the eschatological manuals are mostly focused on the state of the individual soul, they do sometimes provide descriptions of the Garden and the Fire. The torments of the grave and the Fire are the most prominent themes within the manuals. Hence, the purpose of the manuals seems to be focused on reform through the development of fear. Those works or sections of works that deal with the Garden focus on two major categories: trees and houris. Trees, such as the Lote Tree of the Boundary, are mentioned to indicate the beneficence of the Garden, while the traditions of the houri are the central focus of the life in the Garden. Interestingly, most mentions of houris are qualified by the term *abkaran*, "virginal," signifying the calcification of a popular belief about their virginity.

MATERIAL CULTURE OF THE AFTERWORLD

More than anything else, the Garden and the Fire have been understood through their materials. Over time, certain materials figure more prominently than others. Rivers, for example, do not predominate in the eschatological manuals from the ninth to twelfth century; however, jewels do. Slave boys are not discussed in later manuals; however, houris were still popular. It is likely that the objects transformed into tropes that epitomized the luxury of the Garden or the punishment of the Fire. By contrast, the twentieth century has offered a more contested approach to the materials of the Garden. Twentieth-century theologians rejected the literal pleasures that materials of the Garden offer in favor of a metaphorical perspective where the goods are symbolic indications of blessedness.

Popular expressions of Islam still draw on the material dimension of the Garden and the Fire. An excellent example is when Iran used children to clear minefields during the Iran-Iraq war of 1980–89.[4] According to the nonprofit foundation Center of War and the Child, a variety of methods were employed to encourage students to volunteer to be human minesweepers. Sound trucks rolled through villages; radio and television messages linked patriotism with religious belief. Government representatives promised parents that if their children were killed, families would be entitled to greater rations and money. During training, children were lectured on the beauties of the hereafter and wore headbands with religious slogans and khaki jackets imprinted with the phrase, "With permission given to enter heaven by the imam." The children were often fed "martyrs' syrup," essentially sugar water, and sent to the front with wooden sticks to detonate mines. When children worked in the minefields, they wore "keys of Paradise" around their necks to guarantee their entry into heaven in case the landmines detonated.[5] The objects that the children wore not only had a didactic purpose; the keys also offered the children a physical intermediary whose purpose was not to preserve the children's lives, but to guarantee speedy entry into Paradise if they were killed.

The image of the Garden also inspires celebrations. Examples include the state-sponsored projects of the Gulf nations. In September 2000, President Sheikh Zayed bin Sultan al-Nahyan was to return to Abu Dhabi from surgery abroad. To celebrate his recovery, a contract was negotiated with a French company to perfume the air of Abu Dhabi and to have perfume sprayed through its fountains for three days.[6] The United Arab Emirates unveiled a plan to build a resort of two hundred private villas and forty luxury hotels in the Persian Gulf. The planned community, called The Palm, is now in the shape of a symmetrical palm tree, and its contour is prominent enough to be visible from the moon.[7] The aesthetic inspirations for these developments derive from Qur'anic images of the Garden.

What does the invocation of material objects in the afterworld reveal about Islamic faith and practice? Medieval Christian theologians suggested that the traditions of the Garden evinced the crude character of Arabs and the fraudulent nature of Muhammad's prophecy, since Christians shunned the corporeal delights of the Garden. It was one thing to taste, hear, see, and feel pleasure; it was quite another to have that heightened sensual celebration in the place where the Christian pilgrim achieves his or her pure state to meet and commune with the Lord. For Christian theologians, Islamic Paradise provided the ultimate example that Islam was a religion that lacked spirituality.[8] Instead, Islam offered materiality: the promise of a physical world where one could live a life filled with sensation and surrounded by things. For Christians, the spiritual and the material were in opposition. If the material was corrupted with original sin, then it was clearly the wrong location for divine blessing. Islam, by contrast, privileged the pleasures by enjoining that if one abstained from them in this life, one would obtain myriad in quality and quantity in the next. Contemporary American representations of the Garden, specifically with a focus on the houri, also evince limited insight into a different kind of afterworld. In many articles and Internet sites, Muslims are charged as being perverted for desiring a sexual paradise. Some articles even question if Muslims are rational and modern for not questioning whether houris are pure females or something radically different, such as white raisins.[9] Just as medieval Christian theologians could not understand the material dimension of the Islamic afterworld due to an inherently antimaterial sensibility, contemporary American media cannot assess the role of female companionship in the Islamic afterworld without projecting perceptions of Islam as driven by sex and violence.

The explanations for a material character of the Islamic afterworld often depend on judgment of a misunderstood phenomenon. Sometimes the explanations are overly deterministic. Rivers do not predominate in the Garden *because* Muhammad lived in a desert locale. Instead, geography may have played a role in early texts, but it is not the sole cause of the compelling image of rivers and foundations. Geography also does not explain why later texts written by authors in different contexts invoke the same images. Houris do not emerge as the central object of the Garden *because* Muslim men are starved for female companionship. Instead, the role of female companions in the afterworld was contingent on complex relationships between Muslims and their servants or slaves, and that relationship had a metaphorical dimension that extended into and transforms in contemporary times. As a warning against resorting to the easy explanation, Aziz al-Azmeh counsels against understanding the sensuality of the Garden as a result of "the desires of impotent men living in desert surroundings."[10]

To return to our question, then, what does the material character imply about the early formation of the Islamic afterworld? This book suggests that material culture is contingent on the correspondence between seen and unseen worlds. Not only are the two worlds temporally linked, but the unseen afterworld can also be experienced only after being rewarded or paying the consequences for the way that Muslims conducted their earthly lives. As realms of existence and meaning, the earthly world and the afterworld are entangled in complicated ways that can be glimpsed through articulations of the future world to come. In this book, I have argued that these visions, whether deemed literal or metaphorical, are not limited to the beatific interactions with cosmic beings. The material character of the Islamic afterworld allowed human longings for and fears of a future life to actualize into visions of a future world.

The range of visions of the future world affected Islamic traditions and practices in several ways. In the case of the formation of the Muslim community in Mecca and Medina, the promise that a future world followed an earthly one provided motivation for community formation and physical defense. Muslims drew on the image of the Garden and the Fire to provide solace in the face of battle with the Meccans and to develop anticipation of a better time and place to come. In the case of ethical impact, the connecting of the world with the afterworld offered a foundation to establish a behavioral code for the early community. The distinction between the believer and the unbeliever was understood through where one chose to enjoy sumptuous goods. Those who venerated God and rid themselves of the love for opulent materials were rewarded the objects of the

Garden. Those who sought goods instead of submission to God were met with the pain of the Fire. Women occupied an intermediary place in the ethics of the afterworld, since they were allowed silk fabrics but also condemned to be the majority of the Fire.

In the case of constructing images of the afterworld, Muslim imaginings created future physical worlds that reflected certain aspirations, such as lush green landscapes, while ignoring other realities, such as the economic place of domesticated animals. The privileging of certain aspects of earthly life over others becomes even clearer when it comes to the realities of social life and relationships. Banquets that depend on servant classes predominate so that believers could enjoy a glorious life, while domestic lives with families became less important over time. In the case of preaching and religious instruction, the developed images of the afterworld became the focus of meditations on the importance of realizing that earthly life had consequences. When the visions of the future world began to formalize into a set rubric of scenes, rewards, and punishments, a distinct aesthetic of the afterworld emerged. The Garden and the Fire not only were mechanisms for offering spiritual and ethical instruction, but they also became metaphors for the very best and worst that life could offer. Within the realm of aesthetics, certain gardens transformed through metaphor into the Garden on earth, while political strife in the Middle East is sometimes understood through metaphor as the prefiguring of the Fire to come.[11]

The Garden and Fire acted as doctrines of faith, promises of future lives, spaces for human imaginings, motivations for ethical behavior, mechanisms for reform, and a vocabulary to express the extremes bounties and horrors of human imagination. Their functions were expansive not just because the concept of the afterworld is an enduring idea in human society, but also because Muslims were able to comprehend and fashion their visions of the afterworld through objects, beings, and social realities. In creating a world, as opposed to just extending life, Muslims developed an Islamic afterworld that had the power to introduce the faith, guide believers to follow appropriate behaviors, and admonish those who needed reform. The Garden and the Fire provided spaces that allowed believers to imagine the consequences of their earthly choices. While reflecting on where their earthly choices would lead, Muslims envisioned, constructed, and developed their future worlds.

NOTES

INTRODUCTION

1. The Fatimid caliph al-Amir coined the term *hashishiyya* in the 1120s. The creation of the myth began with Crusaders' misunderstandings of Islam and Nizari Isma'ilis. See Farhad Daftary, *The Assassin Legends*, 98 and 66.
2. Interestingly, Daftary maintains that while the myth of the Assassins was created and accepted in Europe, Muslims did not consider the account factual until European historical novels became popular in the nineteenth century. See ibid., 123.
3. Teodolinda Barolini, *The Undivine Comedy*, 3–20.
4. Miguel Asin, *Islam and the Divine Comedy*, 246–277.
5. Alan Bernstein, *Formation of Hell*, 21–49.
6. Merlin Swartz translates the terms *al-janna* as "Paradise" and *al-nar* as "Hell." All English translations have been slightly modified to render more faithfully eschatological terms. Ibn al-Jawzi, *Kitab al-qussas wa-l-mudhakkirin*, 171.
7. In his article "The Seven Names of Hell in the Quran," Thomas O'Shaughnessy argues that Muhammad used *jahim,* but in the last half of the Meccan period he switched to the terms *laza, sa'ir,* and *hutama.* In the second Meccan period, *jahim* disappeared and transformed into the term *jahannam.*
8. While all the *sahih* collections were studied, the book draws upon the particularly rich collections of al-Bukhari (d. 870), Muslim (d. 875), al-Tirmidhi (d. 892), and Malik ibn Anas (d. ca. 710).

1. THE GARDEN, THE FIRE, AND ISLAMIC ORIGINS

1. Ibn al-Kalbi, *Book of Idols*, 4–7.
2. Henri Lammens, *Le berceau de l'Islam*, 70–72.
3. D. B. MacDonald, "Djinn."
4. Jane I. Smith and Yvonne Yazbeck Haddad, *The Islamic Understanding of Death and Resurrection*, 5.

5. Ibid., 5.
6. Ibid., 28–29.
7. MacDonald, "Djinn."
8. Ibn Hisham, *Sira al-nabawiyya li-Ibn Hisham*, 1:271; Ibn Ishaq, *The Life of Muhammad*, 93–94.
9. Ibn Hisham, *Sira al-nabawiyya li-Ibn Hisham*, 1:365–366; Ibn Ishaq, *Life of Muhammad*, 134.
10. Ibn Hisham, *Sira al-nabawiyya li-Ibn Hisham*, 1:366; Ibn Ishaq, *Life of Muhammad*, 134.
11. Ibn Hisham, *Sira al-nabawiyya li-Ibn Hisham*, 1:366–367; Ibn Ishaq, *Life of Muhammad*, 134.
12. Ibn Hisham, *Sira al-nabawiyya li-Ibn Hisham*, 2:139–140; Ibn Ishaq, *Life of Muhammad*, 222.
13. Ibn Hisham, *Sira al-nabawiyya li-Ibn Hisham*, 1:367; Ibn Ishaq, *Life of Muhammad*, 140.
14. Ibn Hisham, *Sira al-nabawiyya li-Ibn Hisham*, 1:387; Ibn Ishaq, *Life of Muhammad*, 141.
15. Ibn Hisham, *Sira al-nabawiyya li-Ibn Hisham*, 1:447; Ibn Ishaq, *Life of Muhammad*, 167.
16. Ibn Hisham, *Sira al-nabawiyya li-Ibn Hisham*, 1:446; Ibn Ishaq, *Life of Muhammad*, 167.
17. Ibn Hisham, *Sira al-nabawiyya li-Ibn Hisham*, 1:395: Ibn Ishaq, *Life of Muhammad*, 145.
18. Ibn Hisham, *Sira al-nabawiyya li-Ibn Hisham*, 1:438–439; Ibn Ishaq, *Life of Muhammad*, 162.
19. Ibn Hisham, *Sira al-nabawiyya li-Ibn Hisham*, 1:445; Ibn Ishaq, *Life of Muhammad*, 165.
20. Ibn Hisham, *Sira al-nabawiyya li-Ibn Hisham*, 2:11; Ibn Ishaq, *Life of Muhammad*, 169.
21. Ibn Hisham, *Sira al-nabawiyya li-Ibn Hisham*, 2:100; Ibn Ishaq, *Life of Muhammad*, 205.
22. Ibn Hisham, *Sira al-nabawiyya li-Ibn Hisham*, 2:100; Ibn Ishaq, *Life of Muhammad*, 204–205.
23. In Arabic, *hur* is plural of the singular *hawra'*; the collective noun is *huriyya*. The term entered English through the Persian sing *huri* and plural *huriyyat* in the form of "houri" for the singular and "houris" for plural. A.J. Wensinck and C. Pellat, "Hur."
24. W. Montgomery Watt, *Muhammad*, 125.
25. Ibn Hisham, *Sira al-nabawiyya li-Ibn Hisham*, 3:33; Ibn Ishaq, *Life of Muhammad*, 349–350.
26. Ibn Hisham, *Sira al-nabawiyya li-Ibn Hisham*, 3:480; Ibn Ishaq, *Life of Muhammad*, 519.
27. Maher Jarrar, "The Martyrdom of Passionate Lovers," 94–102.
28. Ibn Hisham, *Sira al-nabawiyya li-Ibn Hisham*, 3:480; Ibn Ishaq, *Life of Muhammad*, 519.
29. Ibn Hisham, *Sira al-nabawiyya li-Ibn Hisham*, 3:128; Ibn Ishaq, *Life of Muhammad*, 383.
30. Reuven Firestone, *Jihad*, 132.

31. Al-Bukhari, *Kitab al-jihad*, bk. 14, no. 64.

32. Ibid., bk. 22, no. 73.

33. Ibid., bk. 52, no. 72.

34. Malik ibn Anas, *al-Muwatta'*, no. 21.13.25.

35. al-Bukhari, *Kitab al-jihad*, bk. 22, no. 73.

36. Ibn Hisham, *Sira al-nabawiyya li-Ibn Hisham*, 3:300; Ibn Ishaq, *Life of Muhammad*, 450.

37. Malik ibn Anas, *al-Muwatta'*, no. 21.1.2.

38. Ibn Hisham, *Sira al-nabawiyya li-Ibn Hisham*, 2:139–140; Ibn Ishaq, *Life of Muhammad*, 222.

2. VISIONS OF THE AFTERWORLD

1. Malik ibn Anas, *al-Muwatta'*, no. 12.1.2.

2. Ibid., no. 12.1.1.

3. Muslim, *Kitab al-salat*, bk. 4, no. 1968.

4. Ibid., no. 1973.

5. Ibid., no. 1968.

6. Ibid., no. 1976.

7. Michael Sells, "Ascension."

8. Ibid.

9. Ibid.

10. Ibid.

11. J. E. Bencheikh, "Mi'radj."

12. Ibn Hisham, *Sira al-nabawiyya li-Ibn Hisham*, 2:42; Ibn Ishaq, *The Life of Muhammad*, 181.

13. Heribert Busse, "Jerusalem in the Story of Muhammad's Night Journey and Ascension," 311.

14. Ibn Hisham, *Sira al-nabawiyya li-Ibn Hisham*, 2:43; Ibn Ishaq, *Life of Muhammad*, 181.

15. Ibn Hisham, *Sira al-nabawiyya li-Ibn Hisham*, 2:43; Ibn Ishaq, *Life of Muhammad*, 182.

16. Ibn Hisham, *Sira al-nabawiyya li-Ibn Hisham*, 2:43; Ibn Ishaq, *Life of Muhammad*, 183.

17. Ibn Hisham, *Sira al-nabawiyya li-Ibn Hisham*, 2:44; Ibn Ishaq, *Life of Muhammad*, 182.

18. Ibn Hisham, *Sira al-nabawiyya li-Ibn Hisham*, 2:44–45; Ibn Ishaq, *Life of Muhammad*, 182.

19. Ibn Hisham, *Sira al-nabawiyya li-Ibn Hisham*, 2:45; Ibn Ishaq, *Life of Muhammad*, 183.

20. Ibn Hisham, *Sira al-nabawiyya li-Ibn Hisham*, 2:46; Ibn Ishaq, *Life of Muhammad*, 183.

21. Ibn Hisham, *Sira al-nabawiyya li-Ibn Hisham*, 2:46–47; Ibn Ishaq, *Life of Muhammad*, 183.

22. Ibn Hisham, *Sira al-nabawiyya li-Ibn Hisham*, 2:51–52; Ibn Ishaq, *Life of Muhammad*, 184.

23. Ibn Hisham, *Sira al-nabawiyya li-Ibn Hisham*, 2:52–53; Ibn Ishaq, *Life of Muhammad*, 185.

24. Ibn Hisham, *Sira al-nabawiyya li-Ibn Hisham*, 2:52–53; Ibn Ishaq, *Life of Muhammad*, 185.
25. Ibn Hisham, *Sira al-nabawiyya li-Ibn Hisham*, 2:54; Ibn Ishaq, *Life of Muhammad*, 185–186.
26. Ibn Hisham, *Sira al-nabawiyya li-Ibn Hisham*, 2:55; Ibn Ishaq, *Life of Muhammad*, 186.
27. Maher Jarrar suggests that the lower heaven bears relation to the earthly heaven. From the lower heaven, God sends down rain or plagues. Jarrar, "Heaven and Sky."
28. Al-Bukhari, *Kitab al-ansar*, bk. 6, no. 27.
29. Ibid., bk. 40, no. 226.
30. Ibid., bk. 48, no. 171.
31. These include the first four caliphs (Abu Bakr, Umar, Uthman, Ali) and other male companions (Talha b. 'Ubayd Allah, al-Zubayr b. al-'Awwam, 'Abd al-Rahman b. 'Awf, Sa'd b. Malik, Sa'id b. Zayd, and Abu 'Ubayda 'Amir b. al-Jarrah). Maya Yazigi, "Hadith al-'ashara or the Political Uses of a Tradition," 159–167.
32. Al-Bukhari, *Kitab al-sahaba*, bk. 6, no. 18.
33. Ibid., bk. 22, no. 97.
34. Al-Bukhari, *Kitab al-sahaba*, bk. 6, no. 23.
35. Al-Bukhari, *Kitab al-ayman wa-l-nudhur*, bk. 31, nos. 150, 151, 152; *Kitab al-sahaba*, bk. 7, no. 29.
36. Al-Bukhari, *Kitab al-ansar*, bk. 21, nos. 164, 165, 167.
37. Ibid., no. 168.
38. Al-Bukhari, *Kitab al-iman*, bk. 88, no. 203.
39. Ibid., bk. 90, no. 209.
40. Ibid., bk. 88, no. 209; Al-Bukhari, *Kitab al-ayman wa-l-nudhur*, bk. 51, no. 566; Al-Tirmidhi, *al-Jami' al-sahih*, no. 2604.
41. Al-Bukhari, *Kitab al-ta'bir*, bk. 55, no. 155.
42. Leah Kinberg, "Interaction Between This World and the Afterworld," 296–297.
43. Al-Bukhari, *Kitab al-ta'bir*, bk. 36, no. 56.

3. MATERIAL CULTURE AND AN ISLAMIC ETHIC

1. In the state of *barzakh*, the time and place between death and resurrection, there is an absolute separation from life. Once one enters *barzakh*, no one can reenter into the realm of life on earth but must instead stay in that place until the next life, whether in *al-janna* or *al-nar*. *Barzakh*, then, acts as an intermediary space, but it does not have the same type of function as the Christian purgatory that is an intermediate place between heaven and hell. Instead, *barzakh* is temporary by nature, and once the believer has been located to *al-janna* and *al-nar*, *barzakh* as a place, space, time, and experience is no longer available.
2. Jane I. Smith and Yvonne Yazbeck Haddad, *The Islamic Understanding of Death and Resurrection*, 38.
3. Ibid., 41.
4. Ibid., 42.
5. Mention of the trumpet is found in Qur'anic verses such as 50.20.
6. Smith and Haddad, *Islamic Understanding of Death and Resurrection*, 42.
7. Muhammad Abdel Haleem, *Understanding the Qur'an*, 162.
8. Ibid., 169–170.

9. Malik ibn Anas, *al-Muwatta'*, no. 15.8.32.

10. Ibid., no. 17.10.22.

11. Al-Bukhari, *Kitab fard al-khumus*, bk. 53, no. 347.

12. Malik ibn Anas, *al-Muwatta'*, no. 36.8.10.

13. Ibid., no. 36.8.11.

14. Ibid., no. 56.7.16.

15. Ibid., no. 56.7.16.

16. Al-Bukhari, *Kitab al-maghazi*, ch. 59, no. 616.

17. Malik ibn Anas, *al-Muwatta'*, no. 56.5.11.

18. Al-Bukhari, *Kitab al-salat*, bk. 4, no. 372. Those who itch when they wear other fibers may wear silk, *Kitab al-jihad*, bk. 52, no. 169, 170, 171, 172.

19. Malik ibn Anas, *al-Muwatta'*, no. 48.7.18.

20. Al-Bukhari, *Kitab manaqib al-ansar*, bk. 58, no. 146.

21. Al-Bukhari, *Kitab al-jihad*, bk. 52, no. 289.

22. Muslim, *Kitab al-libas wa-l-zinah*, bk. 24, no. 5159, 5161, 5162; al-Bukhari, *Kitab al-libas*, bk. 72, no. 731.

23. Malik ibn Anas, *al-Muwatta'*, no. 48.5.9.

24. Ibid., no. 48.4.7.

25. Al-Bukhari, *Kitab al-libas*, bk. 72, no. 722.

26. Ibid., bk. 72, no. 753, 754, 755, 756, 757; *Kitab al-marda*, b. 70, no. 553.

27. Malik ibn Anas, *al-Muwatta'*, no. 49.7.11.

28. Muslim, *Kitab al-libas wa-l-zinah*, ch. 24, no. 5140.

29. Malik ibn Anas, *al-Muwatta'*, no. 49.10.29.

30. N. Steensgaard, "Harir."

31. Muslim, *Kitab al-riqaq*, ch. 36, no. 6596, 6597, 6600.

32. Al-Bukhari, *Kitab al-iman*, ch. 2, no. 28.

33. Muslim, *Kitab al-iman*, bk. 1, no. 142.

34. Al-Bukhari, *Kitab al-salat*, ch. 12, no. 712; *Kitab bad' al-khalq*, bk. 54, no. 535.

35. Al-Bukhari, *Kitab al-jana'iz*, ch. 23, no. 480.

36. Ibid., ch. 23, no. 478.

37. Al-Bukhari, *Kitab al-jihad*, ch. 93, no. 175.

38. Muslim, *Kitab al-iman*, ch. 18, no. 46.

39. Muslim, *Kitab al-jana'iz*, bk. 23, no. 329.

40. Muslim, *Kitab al-'ilm*, bk. 3, no. 131.

41. Malik ibn Anas, *al-Muwatta'*, no. 46.1.2.

42. Al-Bukhari, *Kitab al-jihad*, bk. 52, no. 41.

43. Muslim, *Kitab al-imara*, ch. 20, no. 4690, 4691.

44. Al-Bukhari, *Kitab al-jihad*, bk. 52, no. 59.

45. Ibid., bk. 52, no. 53.

46. Ibid., bk. 52, no. 49.

47. Malik ibn Anas, *al-Muwatta'*, no. 21.14.28.

48. Al-Bukhari, *Kitab al-jihad*, bk. 52, no. 66.

49. Ibid., bk. 52, no. 48.

50. Al-Bukhari, *Kitab al-iman*, bk. 2, no. 21.

51. Al-Bukhari, *Kitab al-raqaq*, bk. 76, no. 565.

52. Muslim, *Kitab al-iman*, bk. 1, no. 165.

53. Al-Bukhari, *Kitab al-raqaq*, bk. 76, no. 575.

4. OTHERWORLDLY LANDSCAPES AND EARTHLY REALITIES

1. Muslim, *Kitab al-janna*, bk. 40, no. 6778; al-Bukhari, *Kitab al-riqaq*, bk. 76, no. 494.
2. Jibrail S. Jabbur, *The Bedouins and the Desert*, 45.
3. Henri Lammens, *Le Berceau de l'Islam*, 27.
4. Ibid., 46.
5. Ibid., 47.
6. Ibid., 27–29.
7. Al-Bukhari, *Kitab al-tawhid*, bk. 93, no. 519.
8. Al-Tirmidhi, *al-Jami' al-sahih*, 4:2530.
9. Al-Tirmidhi, *al-Jami' al-sahih*, 4:2571.
10. Muslim, *Kitab al-janna*, bk. 40, no. 6807.
11. M. Canard, "Djayhan."
12. C. P. Haase, "Sayhan."
13. Jabbur, *The Bedouins and the Desert*, 65.
14. Ibid., 67.
15. Ibid., 68.
16. Ibid., 70.
17. Anthony C. Miller and Miranda Morris, *Plants of Dhofar*, 176–181.
18. Edward William Lane, *Arabic-English Lexicon*, Book 1, Part 3, 1238–1239.
19. Al-Tirmidhi, *al-Jami' al-sahih*, 4:2585.
20. Jabbur, *The Bedouins and the Desert*, 71.
21. Ibid., 77.
22. Ibid., 80.
23. A. Dietrich, "Kafur."
24. Patricia Crone, *Meccan Trade and the Rise of Islam*, 76–77.
25. A. Dietrich, "Kafur."
26. Patricia Crone, *Meccan Trade and the Rise of Islam*, 83.
27. Ibid., 93.
28. Ibid., 88.
29. Ibid., 88–89.
30. A. Dietrich, "Lu'lu'."
31. A. Dietrich, "Mardjan."
32. M. Keene and M. Jenkins, "Djawhar."
33. Al-Biruni, *al-jamahir*, 107–155, 188–275.
34. Al-Tirmidhi, *al-Jami' al-sahih*, 4:2526.
35. Al-Bukhari, *Kitab al-tafsir*, bk. 60, no. 488.
36. Al-Tirmidhi, *al-Jami' al-sahih*, 4:2525.
37. Ibid., 4:2541.
38. Ibid., 4:2528.
39. Ibid., 4:2542.
40. Malik ibn Anas, *al-Muwatta'*, no. 49.10.31.
41. Al-Tirmidhi, *al-Jami' al-sahih*, 4:2543.
42. Muslim, *Kitab al-janna*, bk. 40, no. 6810; Al-Tirmidhi, *al-Jami' al-sahih*, 4:2573.
43. Al-Bukhari, *Kitab bad' al-khalq*, bk. 60, no. 455.
44. Malik ibn Anas, *al-Muwatta'*, no. 57.1.1; Al-Tirmidhi, *al-Jami' al-sahih*, 4:2589, 2590.

45. Malik ibn Anas, *al-Muwatta'*, no. 57.1.2.
46. Al-Tirmidhi, *al-Jami' al-sahih*, 4:2591.
47. Muslim, *Kitab al-janna*, bk. 40, no. 6813–6814; Al-Tirmidhi, *al-Jami' al-sahih*, 4:2575.
48. Muslim, *Kitab al-janna*, bk. 40, no. 6780, 6781, 6782, 6783.
49. Al-Bukhari, *Kitab al-jihad*, bk. 52, no. 51.
50. Al-Tirmidhi, *al-Jami' al-sahih*, 4:2529.
51. Muslim, *Kitab al-janna*, bk. 40, no. 6790, 6788; Al-Bukhari, *Kitab bad' al-khalq*, bk. 54, no. 478.
52. Al-Tirmidhi, *al-Jami' al-sahih*, 4:2530, 2531.
53. Al-Bukhari, *Kitab bad' al-khalq*, bk. 54, no. 474; 6:376; *Kitab tafsir*, bk. 60, no. 403; Al-Tirmidhi, *al-Jami' al-sahih*, 4:2523, 2524.
54. Al-Tirmidhi, *al-Jami' al-sahih*, 4:2548.
55. Muslim, *Kitab al-janna*, bk. 40, no. 6813, 6814; Al-Tirmidhi, *al-Jami' al-sahih*, 4:6.
56. W. Hinz, "Farsakh."
57. W. Hinz, "Dhira."
58. Al-Bukhari, *Kitab bad' al-khalq*, bk. 54, no. 482; al-Tirmidhi, *al-Jami' al-sahih*, 4:2592.
59. Muslim, *Kitab al-janna*, bk. 40, no. 6818.

5. HUMANITY, SERVANTS, AND COMPANIONS

1. Muslim, *Kitab al-janna*, bk. 40, no. 6867.
2. Al-Bukhari, *Kitab al-tafsir*, bk. 60, no. 264.
3. Ibid., no. 441.
4. Muslim, *Kitab al-janna*, bk. 40, no. 6849, 6850.
5. Ibid., *Kitab sifat al-qiyamah wa-l-janna wa-l-nar*, bk. 39, no. 6738.
6. Ibid., *Kitab al-janna*, bk. 40, no. 6840.
7. Al-Tirmidhi, *al-Jami' al-sahih*, 4:2577.
8. Ibid., 4:2580.
9. Ibid., 4:2587.
10. Malik ibn Anas, *al-Muwatta'*, no. 49.6.9.
11. Al-Tirmidhi, *al-Jami' al-sahih*, 4:2581.
12. Ibid., 4:2582.
13. Ibid., 4:2583.
14. Ibid., 4:2584.
15. Ibn Hisham, *Sira al-nabawiyya li-Ibn Hisham*, 2:46–47; Ibn Ishaq, *The Life of Muhammad*, 183.
16. W. Montgomery Watt. "Abu Lahab."
17. Al-Bukhari, *Kitab al-ahkam*, bk. 89, no. 264.
18. Al-Bukhari, *Kitab al-fitan*, bk. 88, no. 218.
19. Muslim, *Kitab al-janna*, bk. 40, no. 6868.
20. Al-Tirmidhi, *al-Jami' al-sahih*, 4:2584.
21. Muslim, *Kitab al-janna*, bk. 40, no. 6809.
22. Ibid., no. 6803.
23. Al-Tirmidhi, *al-Jami' al-sahih*, 4:2545.
24. Muslim, *Kitab al-janna*, bk. 40, no. 6803.

25. Ibid., no. 6809.
26. Ibid., nos. 6793, 6796.
27. Ibid., nos. 6795, 6796.
28. Al-Tirmidhi, *al-Jami' al-sahih*, 4:2536.
29. Muslim, *Kitab al-janna*, bk. 40, no. 6793.
30. Ibid.
31. Ibid., no. 6797.
32. Ibid., no. 6792.
33. Edward Lane, *Arabic-English Lexicon*, 1444–5.
34. Ibid., 192. *Istabraq* is sometimes woven with gold.
35. A. de Biberstein Kazimirski, *Dictionnaire Arabe-Français*.
36. Al-Bukhari, *Kitab bad' al-khalq*, bk. 54, no. 447.
37. Patricia Crone, *Meccan Trade and the Rise of Islam*, 81.
38. Al-Tirmidhi, *al-Jami' al-sahih*, 4:2563.
39. Ibid., no. 2543.
40. Ibid., nos. 2562, 2553.
41. Muslim, *Kitab al-janna*, bk. 40, no. 6804.
42. Al-Bukhari, *Kitab bad' al-khalq*, bk. 54, no. 466.
43. Muslim, *Kitab al-janna*, bk. 40, nos. 6805, 6806; Al-Bukhari, *Kitab bad' al-khalq*, bk. 54, no. 466.
44. Al-Bukhari, *Kitab al-salat*, bk. 8, no. 345.
45. Al-Bukhari, *Kitab al-ansar*, bk. 58, no. 168; *Kitab al-tawhid*, bk. 93, no. 588; *Kitab al-adab*, bk. 73, no. 33.
46. Ibn Hisham, *Sira al-nabawiyya li-Ibn Hisham*, 1:366–367; Ibn Ishaq, *Life of Muhammad*, 134.
47. Al-Tirmidhi, *al-Jami' al-sahih*, 4:2549.
48. Ibid.
49. Ibid., no. 2550.
50. R. Brunschvig, "'Abd."
51. Ibid.
52. Ibid.
53. Crone, *Meccan Trade*, 106.
54. Suzanne Pinckney Stetkevych, "Intoxication and Immortality," 223, 227.
55. A. J. Wensinck, "Khamr."
56. Crone, *Meccan Trade*, 105
57. Wensinck, "Khamr."
58. Crone, *Meccan Trade*, 105.
59. Ralph Hattox, *Coffee and Coffeehouses*, 46–60.
60. Kathryn Kueny, *The Rhetoric of Sobriety*, 15.
61. Jane I. Smith and Yvonne Yazbeck Haddad, "Women in the Afterlife," 41; Lenn Goodman, "Islamic Humanism," 60; Charles Wendell, "The Denizens of Paradise," 49.
62. Smith and Haddad, "Women in the Afterlife," 41.
63. Al-Tirmidhi, *al-Jami' al-sahih*, 4:2533.
64. Ibid., no. 2564.
65. Smith and Haddad, "Women in the Afterlife," 48.
66. Ze'ev Maghen, "Virtues of the Flesh," 15–16.
67. Wendell, "The Denizens of Paradise," 56–57; Stetkevych, "Intoxication and Immortality," 225.

6. INDIVIDUALIZED GARDENS AND EXPANDING FIRES

1. Fred Donner has developed a list of the earliest historical works; see *Narratives of Islamic Origins*, 299.
2. Ibn Abi al-Dunya, *Kitab al-mawt (Book of Death) and kitab al-qubur (Book of Graves)*.
3. Al-Samarqandi, *Kitab al-haqa'iq wa-l-daqa'iq*; al-Qadi, *Daqa'iq al-akhbar fi dhikr al-janna wa-l-nar*; Ibn Kathir, *Ahwal yawm al-qiyama*; Suyuti, *Sharh al-sudur*; Ghazali, *al-Durra al-fakhira*.
4. Jane I. Smith, "Introduction," 8.
5. Richard W. Bulliet, *View from the Edge*, 13–22.
6. Ibid., 89.
7. Merlin Swartz, "Introduction," 13–92.
8. Ibn al-Jawzi, *Kitab al-qussas wa-l-mudhakkirin*, no. 23.
9. Ibid., 118.
10. Anne-Marie Schimmel, *The Mystery of Numbers*, 263–264.
11. Ibn al-Jawzi, *Kitab al-qussas wa-l-mudhakkirin*, no. 197.
12. Ibid., nos. 216, 217.
13. Ibid., no. 232.
14. Ibid., no. 234.
15. Ibid., no. 236.
16. Smith, "Introduction," 8.
17. R. Arnaldez. "al-Muhasibi."
18. Al-Muhasibi, *Une vision humaine des fins dernières*, no. 104.
19. Ibid., no. 127.
20. Arnaldez, "al-Muhasibi."
21. Al-Ghazali, *The Precious Pearl*, 62.
22. Al-Ghazali, *The Remembrance of Death and Afterlife*, 13.
23. Ibid.
24. Ibid., 130.
25. Ibn Habib, *Wasf al-firdaws*, no. 208.
26. Ibid., no. 221.
27. Ibid., no. 209.
28. Ibid., no. 223.
29. Ibid., nos. 203, 205.
30. Ibid., no. 204.
31. Rosenthal, "Reflections of Love in Paradise," 250–254.
32. Smith and Haddad, "Women in the Afterlife," 46.
33. Ibn Habib, *Wasf al-firdaws*, no. 202.
34. Al-Muhasibi, *Une vision humaine des fins dernières*, no. 135.
35. Ibid., no. 139.
36. Ibid., no. 140.
37. Al-Muhasibi, *Une vision humaine des fins dernières*, no. 143.
38. Ibid., no. 149.
39. Ibid., no. 160.
40. Ibid., no. 163.
41. Al-Ghazali, *The Remembrance of Death and Afterlife*, 245.
42. Al-Ghazali, *The Precious Pearl*, 55.

43. Al-Ghazali, *The Remembrance of Death and Afterlife*, 79.
44. Ibid., 80.
45. Ibid., 132.
46. Al-Qadi, *Daqa'iq al-akhbar fi dhikr al-janna wa-l-nar*, 80–81.
47. Ibid., 80.
48. Ibid., 75–76; al-Samarqandi, *Kitab al-haqa'iq wa-l-daqa'iq*, D3.
49. Al-Samarqandi, *Kitab al-haqa'iq wa-l-daqa'iq*, D4; al-Qadi, *Daqa'iq al-akhbar fi dhikr al-janna wa-l-nar*, 76.
51. Ibid., 77.
52. Ibid.
53. Ibid., 78.
54. Ibid.
55. Ibid.; see also al-Samarqandi, *Kitab al-haqa'iq wa-l-daqa'iq*, D8; Ibn Habib, *Wasf al-firdaws*, nos. 90 and 93.
56. Al-Ghazali, *The Precious Pearl*, 87.
57. Ibid.
58. Ibid., 61.
59. Ibid., 62.
60. Ibid., 61.
61. Ibid.
62. Ibid., 60.
63. Ibid.
64. Ibid.
65. Ibid., 63.
66. Al-Qadi, *Daqa'iq al-akhbar fi dhikr al-janna wa-l-nar*, 64.
67. Ibid., 64–65.
68. Ibid., 65.
69. Ibid., 70.
70. Ibid., 72.
71. Ibid.
72. Ibid., 81.
73. Ibid., 73.

7. LEGACY OF GARDENS

1. Al-Bukhari, *Kitab al-ahadith al-anbiya'*, bk. 55, no. 554.
2. Ebrahim Moosa, *Ghazali and the Poetics of Imagination*, 32–63.
3. Khaled Moaz. Tombstones from the eleventh and thirteenth century in the Bab al-Sagir cemetery in Damascus contain inscriptions; many allude to death and resurrection through Qur'anic verses or wish for Allah's favor during the Last Judgment. Inscriptions deal with the idea of intercession or mention the delights of the Garden, starting from the twelfth century to the fifteenth century. Those that invoke God's favor often quote: "Who is there that can intercede in his presence except as he permitteth" (2.555). Other inscriptions mention the actual Garden: "and of Garden for them, wherein are delights that endure" (9.22). These include no. 78 as well as variations in no. 53, 4m, 2.
4. Ibid., nos. 16, 36, 37, 41.

5. Finbarr Barry Flood suggests that the focus on light is misplaced in the verse. The light is not the light of God as much as it is the light of prophecy. He suggests that instead of a lamp, pearls or other luminescent devices were represented in the *mihrab*, including a black stone in the *mihrab* in the Dome of the Rock, representing the presence of prophet Muhammad. Finbarr Barry Flood, "Light in Stone," 311–360.

6. Al-Ghazali, *The Niche of Lights*, 10–11.

7. Ibid., 11.

8. Ibid., 22.

9. Oleg Grabar, "From Dome of Heaven to Pleasure Dome," 17.

10. William C. Chittick, "Death and the World of Imagination: Ibn al-'Arabi's Eschatology," 53.

11. Ibid., 14.

12. Ibid., 30.

13. Josef M. Meri, *The Cult of Saints Among Muslims and Jews in Medieval Syria*, 12.

14. Ibid., 12.

15. Ibid., 30.

16. Sheila Blair "What is the Date of the Dome of the Rock?" 59–87; Amikam Elad, "Why Did 'Abd al-Malik Build the Dome of the Rock," 33–58; Josef van Ess "'Abd al-Malik and Dome of the Rock," 1:89–103.

17. Oleg Grabar and Said Nuseibeh, *The Dome of the Rock*, 47.

18. Grabar notes that the inscription is placed on the side of the building that faces a valley said to contain the entrances to both Hell and the Garden, which Christians already identified as the place of Christ's return at the end of time. Ibid., 49–51. Quotation from Grabar, *The Shape of the Holy*, 61.

19. Grabar, *The Shape of the Holy*, 126.

20. Ibid., 130–131. Later it was associated with the *mihrab* of Dawud, the place of judgment.

21. Grabar and Nuseibeh, *The Dome of the Rock*, 51.

22. Ibid.

23. Myriam Rosen-Ayalon, *The Early Islamic Monuments of al-Haram al-Sharif*, 49, 68–69.

24. Priscilla Soucek, "The Temple of Solomon in Islamic Legend and Art," 73–123.

25. Nasser Rabbat, "The Meaning of the Umayyad Dome of the Rock," 18.

26. Rosen-Ayalon, *The Early Islamic Monuments of al-Haram al-Sharif*, 60.

27. Ibid.

28. Ibid., 60–63.

29. Ibid., 63.

30. Afif Bahnassi, *La Grande Mosquée Omeyyad à Damas*, 115.

31. Ibid., 114.

32. Ibid., 116.

33. Brigid Keenan, *Damascus: Hidden Treasures of the Old City*, 27.

34. Ibid., 116.

35. Ibid., 27.

36. Finbarr Barry Flood, *Great Mosque of Damascus*, 25.

37. Ibid., 55.

38. Ibid., 47–50.

39. Nasser Rabbat, "The Dome of the Rock Revisited: Some Remarks on al-Wasiti's Accounts," 67–75.
40. Flood, *Great Mosque of Damascus*, 112.
41. Bahnassi, *Grande Mosquée*, 118.
42. Marie-Rose Séguy, *The Miraculous Journey of Mahomet*, plate 30.
43. al-Qazwini, *Kitab 'aja'ib al-makhluqat wa ghara'ib al-mawjudat*. Versions listed in bibliography.
44. J. E. Bencheick, "Mi'radj," 97–105.
45. Séguy, *The Miraculous Journey of Mahomet*, plate 53.
46. Julie Scott Meisami, "Allegorical Gardens in the Persian Poetic Tradition," 229–260.
47. Ibid., 238.
48. Ibid., 106.
49. Nizami, *Haft Paykar: A Medieval Persian Romance*, 115.
50. W. Montgomery Watt, "Iram."
51. Michel Conan, "Introduction," 3.
52. William L. Hanaway Jr., "Paradise on Earth," 43–67.
53. Ibid., 48.
54. Ibid., 47.
55. Julie Scott Meisami, "Palaces and Paradises," 24.
56. Hanaway, "Paradise on Earth," 49.
57. Daniel Schlumberger, "Le Palais Ghaznévide de Lashkari Bazar," 251–270.
58. Mahvesh Alemi, "Princely Safavid Gardens: Stage for Rituals of Imperial Display and Political Legitimacy," 113–137.
59. D. Fairchild Ruggles, *Gardens, Landscape and Vision in the Palaces of Islamic Spain*, 218.
60. Ibid.
61. Ibid., 219.
62. Yasser Tabbaa, "The Medieval Islamic Garden," 303–329.
63. Yasser Tabbaa, "Towards an Interpretation of the Use of Water in Islamic Courtyards and Courtyard Gardens," 197.
64. Ibid., 218.
65. Cynthia Robinson, "Seeing Paradise," 153.
66. Deniz Çaliş, "Gardens at the Kağithane Commons During the Tulip Period (1718–1730)," 250.
67. Ibid, 257.
68. Abdul Rehman and Shama Abrine, "Unity and Diversity of Mughal Garden Experiences," 225–226.
69. Ibid., 226.
70. Ibid., 228.
71. Ebba Koch, *The Complete Taj Mahal and the Riverfront Gardens of Agra*, 6.
72. Ibid., 114.
73. In Hanaway, "Paradise on Earth," 47.
74. Mahvash Alemi, "The Royal Gardens of the Safavid Period," 72–95; Ebba Koch, "The Mughal Waterfront Garden," 140–159; 'Abdul Rehman, "Garden Types in Mughal Lahore According to Early Seventeenth Century Written and Visual Sources," 161–167.

EPILOGUE

1. "The Emptiness of Hell."
2. Jeffrey L. Sheler, "Hell Hath No Fury."
3. Nancy Gibbs, "Angels Among Us"; Jeffrey L. Sheler, "Heaven in the Age of Reason"; Leslie Alan Horovitz, "More Americans Than Ever Embrace the Hereafter Now"; David Klinghoffer, "Hell, Yes; Even if You're Not Going to Hell, You Should Believe in It."
4. James Wallace et al., "Iran-Iraq War," 11.
5. John Hughes, "Children at War," 14.
6. Agence France-Presse, "French Perfumes to Fill the Air for President's Return to Emirates."
7. "Fantasy Island."
8. Norman Daniel, *Islam and the West*, 149–151.
9. Nerina Rustomji, "American Visions of the Houri," 92.
10. Aziz al-Azmeh, "Rhetoric of the Senses," 220.
11. David Cook, *Contemporary Muslim Apocalyptic Literature*, 150–171.

GLOSSARY

barzakh	intermediate time and space between life and death that acts as a barrier between this world and the afterworld.
Buraq	a fantastic composite animal upon whom Muhammad rides during his Night Journey and Ascension.
al-Dajjal	one-eyed figure whose appearance at the end of time prefigures the coming of Christ.
dari'	bitter fruit from the tree of Zaqqum in the Fire.
firdaws	often translated as "Paradise," signifies the highest level of heaven.
ghilman	a servant boy of the Garden.
hadith	a saying of the prophet Muhammad or report of one of his deeds, composed of a chain of transmission (*isnad*) and content matter (*matn*). Compilers of hadiths classified them as sound (*sahih*) or weak (*gharib*).
houri	pure female companions promised to male believers in the Garden.
al-isra' wa-l-mi'raj (Night Journey and Ascension)	refers to the narrative when Gabriel awoke the prophet Muhammad and traveled with him on Buraq to Jerusalem, where Muhammad acted as the leader of prayer for Moses, Abraham, and Jesus, and then ascended a fine ladder to see the fires of hell and the levels of heaven.
al-jahannam	one of the terms for the Fire, often translated as hell.
al-jahim	one of the terms for the Fire, often translated as hellfire.
al-janna (the Garden)	the most common term for heaven in Islamic texts; other terms include *al-firdaws* and *samawat* (heavens).
jihad	literally, "striving" or "struggle," referring either to the inner struggle to reform one's self or the militaristic struggle in the name of God.
al-Kawthar	a fountain or pool in the Garden.

Muhammad the founder of Islam, believed by Muslims to be the final prophet of
(ca. 510–632 CE) God.

al-nar (the Fire) the most common term for hell in Islamic texts; other terms include
al-jahannam and *al-jahim.*

Qasab the palace promised to prophet Muhammad's first wife, Khadija, in
the Garden.

Quraysh the leading tribe of Mecca, which opposed Muhammad's claims of
revelation.

Qur'an the collection of revelations that Muhammad received from God
via the angel Gabriel, consisting of 114 suras.

Salsabil a fountain in the Garden.

Shi'a refers to Shi'a 'Ali (the partisans of 'Ali), Muslims who contest succession after Muhammad's death and believe that 'Ali, Muham-
mad's cousin and son-in-law, and thereafter 'Ali's patrilineal descendants should have led the Muslim community.

Sidrat al-Muntaha Lote Tree of the Boundary, a tree in the Garden whose shade extends
for years and is located near the throne of God.

Sirat bridge over which Muslims must cross before entering the Garden
or the Fire. For those destined for the Garden, the bridge widens;
for those destined for the Fire, the bridge narrows to the width of
edge of a blade.

Sufi literally "wearer of wool," those Muslims who practice mysticism to
reach the oneness of God.

Sunni refers to *Ahl al-Sunna* (people of tradition), Muslims who accept
the first four caliphs after Muhammad's death.

wildan a servant boy of the Garden.

yaqut a gem of the Garden, often qualified by color to signify specific
gems.

al-Zaqqum a tree of the Fire on whose branches are demon heads and from
which one drop of pus could contaminate the entire earthly
world.

BIBLIOGRAPHY

MANUSCRIPTS

Higher Regions of Paradise and Hell. Freer Gallery of Art, Smithsonian Institution. F1968.3. Ca. 1800s.

Manuscrit supplément turc 190. Bibliothèque nationale, Paris. Ca. 1500.

Mi'raj-name, Ibrahim Hakki. *Ma'rifetname.* British Library. Or. 12964. Ca. 1756–1757.

Nizami Ganjawi (d. 1209). *Khamsa* of Nizami. British Library. Or. 122208. Ca. 1595.

———. Manuscrit supplément persan 1111. Bibliothèque Nationale. Ca. 1750.

———. Manuscrit supplément persan 1956. Bibliothèque Nationale. ca. 1561.

Al-Qazwini, Zakariyya b. Muhammad (d. 1283). *Kitab 'aja'ib al-makhluqat wa ghara'ib al-mawjudat.* Manuscrit supplément persan 330. Bibliothèque Nationale. 1648–1687.

———. Manuscrit supplément persan 1080. Bibliothèque Nationale. ca. 1785.

———. Manuscrit supplément persan 1180. Bibliothèque Nationale. 1788.

———. Persian 178. British Library. ca. 1475.

———. Or. 1621. British Library. Bijapur. 1640.

———. Add. 7706. British Library. Mughal, ca. 1700.

EDITIONS AND TRANSLATIONS

Abu Dawud, Muhammad b. Ahmad (d. 888). *Sunan Abi Dawud.* Ed. Muhammad Muhyi al-Din 'Abd al-Hamid. 4 vols. n.p.: Dar al-Fikr, n.d.

Arda Wiraz Namag: The Iranian Divina Commedia. Trans. Fereydun Vahman. London: Curzon Press, 1986.

Babur (d. 1530). *Baburnama: Chaghatay Turkish Text with Abdul-Rahim Khankhanan's Persian Translation. Zahiruddin Muhammad Babur Mirza; Turkish Transcription, Persian Edition and English Translation by W. M. Thackston.* Cambridge, Mass.: Department of Near Eastern Languages and Civilizations, Harvard University, 1993.

Al-Biruni, Abu al-Rayhan Muhammad (d. 1048). *Al-jamahir*. Ed. Yusof al-Hadi. Tehran: Sharikat Intishar 'Almi va Farhangi, 1995.

Al-Bukhari, Muhammad b. Isma'il (d. 870). *The Translation of the Meanings of Sahih al-Bukhari: Arabic–English*. 4 vols. Trans. Muhammad Muhsin Khan. Chicago: Kazi Publications, 1976.

Al-Ghazali, Abu Hamid Muhammad al-Tusi (d. 1111). *The Niche of Lights (Mishkat al-anwar)*. Trans. David Buchman. Provo, Utah: Brigham Young University Press, 1998.

———. *The Precious Pearl (Al-durra al-fakhira)*. Trans. Jane Idelman Smith. Missoula: Scholar's Press, 1979.

———. *The Remembrance of Death and Afterlife* (selections from *Ihya 'ulum al-din*). Trans. T. J. Winter. Cambridge: Islamic Texts Society, 1989.

Al-Hakim, Muhammad Abu 'Abdallah Muammad b. 'Abdallah al-Naysaburi (d. 1014). *An Introduction to the Science of Tradition (al-Madkhal ila ma'rifat al-iklil)*. Trans. James Robson. London: Luzac and Co., 1953.

Ibn Abi al-Dunya, Abu Bakr 'Abd Allah b. Muammad b. 'Ubayd b. Sufyan al-Qurasshi al-Baghdadi (d. 894). *Kitab al-mawt (Book of Death) and kitab al-qubur (Book of Graves)*. Ed. Leah Kinberg. Acre: University of Haifa Department of Languages and Literature, 2003.

Ibn al-'Arabi, Muhyi al-Din (d. 1240). *Kitab al-futuhat al-makkiyya*. 5 vols. Ed. 'Uthman Yahya. Cairo: Maktaba al-'Arabiyya, 1972.

Ibn Habib (d. 852 or 853). *Wasf al-firdaws*. Beirut: Dar al-Kutub al-'Ilmiyya, 1987.

Ibn Hanbal, Ahmad (d. 855). *Musnad*. 6 vols. Beirut: Dar al-Kutub al-'Ilmiyya, 1985.

Ibn Hisham, Ahmad b. Hasan (d. 834). *Sira al-nabawiyya li-Ibn Hisham*. 4 vols. Al-Zarqa', Jordan: Maktabat al-Manar, 1988.

Ibn Ishaq (d. 768). *The Life of Muhammad: A Translation of Ishaq's Sirat Rasul Allah*. Trans. A. Guillaume. London: Oxford University Press, 1955.

Ibn al-Jawzi, Abu al-Faraj (d. 1200). *Kitab al-qussas wa-l-mudhakkirin*. Ed. and trans. Merlin Swartz. Beirut: Dar El-Machreq, 1986.

Ibn al-Kalbi (d. 819). *Book of Idols, Being a Translation from the Arabic of the Kitab al-Asnam*. Trans. Nabih Amin Faris. Princeton: Princeton University Press, 1952.

Ibn Kathir (d. 1373). *Ahwal yawm al-qiyama*. 2nd ed. Damascus: al-Yamama, 2001.

Ibn Maja (d. 887). *Sunan Ibn Maja*. 2 vols. Ed. Muhammad Fu'ad 'Abd al-Baqi. Beirut: al-'Ilmiyya, 1980.

Ibn Qayyim al-Jawziyah, Muhammad ibn Abi Bakr (d. 1350). *Kitab al-Ruh*. Hyderabad: Matba'at Majlis Ma'arif al-'Uthmaniyya, 1906.

Malik ibn Anas (d. 708–716). *al-Muwatta' of Imam Malik ibn Anas: The First Formulation of Islamic Law*. Trans. Aisha Abdurrahman Bewley. London and New York: Kegan Paul International, 1989.

Al-Muhasibi (d. 857). *Une vision humaine des fins dernières: Le kitab al-tawahhum d'al-Muhasibi*. Trans. André Roman. Paris: Librairie Klincksieck, 1978.

Muslim b. Hajjaj (d. 875). *Sahih Muslim, Arabic English*. 8 vols. Trans. Abdul Hameed Siddiqui. Delhi: Adam Publishers, 1999.

Al-Nasa'i, Abu 'Abd al-Rahman (d. 915). *Sunan al-Nasa'i*. 8 vols. Cairo: Mustafa al-Babi al-Halabi, 1964.

Nizam al-Mulk (d. 1092). *The Book of Government of Rules for Kings (Siyasat-nameh)*. Trans. Hubert Darke. London: Routledge and Kegan Paul, 1978.

Nizami Ganjawi (d. 1209). *Haft Paykar: A Medieval Persian Romance*. Trans. Julie Scott Meisami. Oxford: Oxford University Press, 1995.

Al-Qadi. *Daqa'iq al-akhbar fi dhikr al-janna wa-l-nar.* Cairo: Maktaba al-Sa'idiyya, n.d.
——. *Islamic Book of the Dead: A Collection of Hadiths on the Fire and the Garden.* Trans. Aisha Abdurrahman Bewley. Norwich, England: Diwan Press, 1977.
Al-Qazwini, Zakariyya b. Muhammad (d. 1283). *Kitab 'aja'ib al-makhluqat wa ghara'ib al-mawjudat.* Ed. Faruq Sa'd. Beirut: Dar al-Afaq al-Jadida, 1981.
Qur'an. Trans. 'Abdullah Yusuf Ali. *The Meaning of the Holy Qur'an.* Beltsville, Md.: Amana Publications, 1989.
Al-Qurtubi (d. 1273). *al-Tadhkira fi ahwal al-mawta wa-umur al-akhira.* Cairo: Maktaba al-Kulliyat al-Azhariyya, 1980.
Al-Samarqandi (d. 1002). "Paradise" (Selections from *Kitab al-haqa'iq wa-l-daqa'iq*). Trans. J. Macdonald. *Islamic Studies* 5 (1966): 331–383.
Séguy, Marie-Rose. *The Miraculous Journey of Mahomet.* Trans. Richard Pevear. New York: G. Braziller, 1977.
Al-Suyuti, Jalal al-Din (d. 1505). *Bushra al-ka'ib bi-liqa' al-habib.* 2nd ed. Cairo: Mustafa al-Babi al-Halabi, 1969.
——. *Sharh al-sudur: bi-sharh hal al-mawta wa-l-qubur.* Ed. Yusuf 'Ali Badwi. Damascus: Dar Ibn Kathir, 1989.
Al-Tabari, Abu Ja'far Muhammad (d. 923). *Jami' al-bayan 'an ta'wil al-Qur'an.* 12 vols. Eds. M. Shakir and A. Shakir. Cairo: Dar al-Ma'arif, 1986–87.
——. *Chronicle of Prophets and Kings (Tarikh al-rusul wa-al-muluk).* Trans. Franz Rosenthal. Albany: State University of New York Press, 1985.
Al-Tirmidhi, Abu 'Isa Muhammad (d. 892). *al-Jami' al-sahih.* 4 vols. Ed. Ibrahim 'Atwa 'Aud. Cairo: Dar Ihya' al-Turath al-'Arabi, n.d.

SECONDARY SOURCES

Abrahamov, Binyamin. "The Creation and Duration of Paradise and Hell in Islamic Theology." *Der Islam* 79 (2002): 87–102.
Agence France-Presse. "French Perfumes to Fill the Air for President's Return to Emirates." 20 September 2000.
Alemi, Mahvesh. "Princely Safavid Gardens: Stage for Rituals of Imperial Display and Political Legitimacy." In *Middle East Garden Traditions: Unity and Diversity: Questions, Methods and Resources in a Multicultural Perspective,* ed. Michel Conan, 113–137. Cambridge, Mass.: Harvard University Press, 2007.
——. "The Royal Gardens of the Safavid Period: Types and Models." In *Gardens in the Time of the Great Muslim Empires,* ed. Attilio Petruccioli, 72–96. Leiden: Brill, 1997.
Almond, Philip C. *Heretic and Hero: Muhammad and the Victorians.* Wiesbaden: Harrassowitz, 1989.
Andrae, Tor. *Muhammad: The Man and His Faith.* Trans. Theophil Menzel. New York: Harper, 1960.
Apostolos-Cappadona, Diane, ed. *Art, Creativity, and the Sacred: An Anthology in Religion and Art.* New York: Continuum, 1986.
Arkoun, Mohamed, Jacques le Goff, Toufic Fahd, and Maxime Rodinson. *L'étrange et le merveilleux dans l'Islam médiéval.* Paris: Editions J. A., 1978.
Ariès, Phillipe. *Western Attitudes Towards Death: From the Middle Ages to the Present.* Baltimore: John Hopkins University Press, 1974.
——. *The Hour of Our Death.* New York: Knopf, 1981.

Armstrong, Karen. *Muhammad: A Biography of the Prophet*. San Francisco: Harper San Francisco, 1992.

Arnaldez, R. "al-Muhasibi, Abu 'Abd Allah al-Harith." In *Encyclopaedia of Islam*, online edition, ed. P. Bearman, T. Bianquis, C. E. Bosworth, E. van Donzel, and W. P. Heinrichs. Brill, 2007.

Arnold, Sir Thomas W. *Painting in Islam: A Study of the Place of Pictorial Art in Muslim Culture*. New York: Dover, 1965.

Asin, Miguel. *Islam and the Divine Comedy*. Ed. and trans. Harold Sunderland. London: John Murray, 1926.

Al-Azmeh, Aziz. "Rhetoric of the Senses: A Consideration of Muslim Paradise Narratives." *Journal of Arabic Literature* 26 (1995): 215–231.

Bagot, Jean, et al. *L'ABCdaire des Cinq Sens*. Paris: Flammarion, 1998.

Bahnassi, Afif. *La Grande Mosquée Omeyyad à Damas: Le Premier Chef D'oeuvre de L'art Musalman*. Damascus: Tlass, 1990.

Barolini, Theodolinda. *The Undivine Comedy: Detheologizing Dante*. Princeton: Princeton University Press, 1992.

Bashier, Salman H. *Ibn al-'Arabi's Barzakh: The Concept of the Limit and the Relationship Between God and the World*. Albany: State University of New York Press, 2004.

Belting, Hans. *Likeness and Presence: A History of the Image Before the Era of Art*. Trans. Edmund Jephcott. Chicago: University of Chicago Press, 1994.

Bencheick, J. E. *Le Voyage Nocturne de Mahomet*. Paris: Imprimerie Nationale, 1988.

———. "Mi'radj: In Arabic Literature In *Encyclopaedia of Islam*, online edition, ed. P. Bearman, T. Bianquis, C. E. Bosworth, E. van Donzel, and W. P. Heinrichs. Brill, 2007.

Berkey, Jonathan P. *Popular Preaching and Religious Authority in the Medieval Near East*. Seattle: University of Washington Press, 2001.

Bernstein, Alan. *The Formation of Hell: Death and Retribution in the Ancient and Early Christian Worlds*. Ithaca, N.Y.: Cornell University, Press, 1993.

Blair, Sheila S. "What Is the Date of the Dome of the Rock?" In *Bayt al-Maqdis: Jerusalem and Early Islam*, ed. Jeremy Jones, 1:59–87. Oxford: Oxford University Press, 1999.

Blair, Sheila S., and Jonathan M. Bloom. *Images of Paradise in Islamic Art*. Austin: University of Texas Press, 1991.

Bloom, Harold. *Omens of Millennium: The Gnosis of Angels, Dreams, and Resurrection*. New York: Riverhead, 1996.

Brend, Barbara. *The Emperor Akbar's Khamsa of Nizami*. London: British Library, 1995.

Brown, Peter. *The World of Late Antiquity, AD 150–750*. New York: Harcourt Brace Jovanovich, 1971.

Browne, Sir Thomas. *Collected Works*. New York: Penguin Books, 1995.

Brunschvig, R. "*Abd*." In *Encyclopaedia of Islam*, online edition, ed. P. Bearman, T. Bianquis, C. E. Bosworth, E. van Donzel, and W.P. Heinrichs. Leiden: Brill, 2007.

Bulliet, Richard. *Islam: A View from the Edge*. New York: Columbia University, 1994.

Burckhardt, Titus. *Mirror of the Intellect: Essays on Traditional Science and Sacred Art*. Trans. William Stoddart. Albany: State University of New York Press, 1987.

Busse, Heribert. "Jerusalem in the Story of Muhammad's Night Journey and Ascension," In Uri Rubin, ed., *The Life of Muhammad*, 279–318. New York: Routledge and Kegan Paul, 1998.

Bynum, Caroline Walker. *Resurrection of the Body in Western Christianity, 200–1336*. New York: Columbia University Press, 1995.

Bynum, Caroline Walker, and Paul Freedman, eds. *Last Things: Death and the Apocalypse in the Middle Ages*. Philadelphia: University of Pennsylvania Press, 2000.

Çaliş, Deniz. "Gardens at the Kağithane Commons During the Tulip Period (1718–1730)." In *Middle East Garden Traditions: Unity and Diversity: Questions, Methods and Resources in a Multicultural Perspective*, ed. Michel Conan, 239–266. Cambridge, Mass.: Harvard University Press, 2007.

Canard, M. "Djayhan." In *Encyclopaedia of Islam*, online edition, ed. P. Bearman, T. Bianquis, C. E. Bosworth, E. van Donzel, and W. P. Heinrichs. Leiden: Brill, 2007.

Cantwell Smith, Wilfred. *The Meaning and End of Religion*. New York: Harper & Row, 1978.

Chittick, William C. "Death and the World of Imagination: Ibn al-'Arabi's Eschatology." *The Muslim World* 78 (1988): 51–82.

———. "Eschatology." In *Islamic Spirituality: Foundations*, ed. Seyyed Hossein Nasr. 378–409. New York: Crossroad, 1987.

———. *The Self-Disclosure of God: Principles of Ibn al-'Arabi's Cosmology*. Albany: State University of New York Press, 1998.

Conan, Michel. "Learning from Middle Eastern Garden Traditions." In *Middle East Garden Traditions: Unity and Diversity: Questions, Methods and Resources in a Multicultural Perspective*, ed. Michel Conan, 3–19. Cambridge, Mass.: Harvard University Press, 2007.

Cook, David. *Contemporary Muslim Apocalyptic Literature*. Syracuse, N.Y.: Syracuse University Press, 2005.

———. *Studies in Muslim Apocalyptic*. Princeton: Darwin Press, 2003.

Cook, Michael A. *Muhammad*. New York: Oxford University Press, 1983.

Corbin, Henry. *Creative Imagination in the Sufism of Ibn 'Arabi*. Trans. Ralph Manheim. Princeton: Princeton University Press, 1969.

———. *Temple and Contemplation*. Trans. Philip Sherrard. London: Islamic Publications, 1986.

Crone, Patricia. *Meccan Trade and the Rise of Islam*. Princeton: Princeton University Press, 1987.

Crone, Patricia, and Michael Cook. *Hagarism: The Making of the Islamic World*. Cambridge: Cambridge University Press, 1977.

Daftary, Farhad. *The Assassin Legends: Myths of the Isma'ilis*. London: IB Tauris, 1994.

Daniel, Norman. *Islam and the West: The Making of an Image*. Edinburgh: Edinburgh University Press, 1960.

Décobert, Christian. *Le mendiant et le combatant*. Paris: Seuil, 1991.

Delumeau, Jean. *Une histoire du paradis: Le jardin des délices*. Paris: Fayard, 1992.

———. *Mille ans de bonheur*. Paris: Fayard, 1995.

———. *Que reste-t-il du paradis?* Paris: Fayard, 2000.

Denny, Walter. "Saff and Sejjadeh." *Oriental Carpet and Textile Studies* 3 (1990): 93–104.

Dietrich, A. "Kafur" "Lu'lu'," and "Mardjan." In *Encyclopaedia of Islam*, online edition, ed. P. Bearman, T. Bianquis, C. E. Bosworth, E. van Donzel, and W. P. Heinrichs. Leiden: Brill, 2007.

Donner, Fred. "The Death of Abu Talib." In *Love and Death in the Ancient Near East: Essays in Honor of Marvin H. Pope*, ed. John H. Marks and Robert M. Good, 237–245. Gilford, Conn.: Four Quarters, 1987.

———. *Early Islamic Conquests*. Princeton: Princeton University Press, 1981.

———. *Narratives of Islamic Origins: The Beginnings of Islamic Historical Writing*. Princeton: Darwin Press, 1998.

Dunlop, D. M. "Sources of Gold and Silver According to al-Hamdani." In *Production of the Exploitation of Resources*, ed. Michael G. Morony, 3–23. Aldershot: Ashgate, 2002.

Eklund, Ragnar. *Life Between Death and Resurrection According to Islam.* Uppsala: Wiksells Boktryckeri-A-B, 1941.

Elad, Amikam. "Why Did 'Abd al-Malik Build the Dome of the Rock: A Re-examination of the Muslim Sources." In *Bayt al-Maqdis: Jerusalem and Early Islam*, ed. Jeremy Jones, 1:33–58. Oxford: Oxford University Press, 1999.

El-Zein, Amira. "Water of Paradise." In *Encyclopaedia of the Qur'an*, ed. Jane Dammen McAuliffe. Leiden: Brill, 2006.

Emerson, Jan Swango, and Hugh Feiss. *Imagining Heaven in the Middle Ages: A Book of Essays.* New York: Garland, 2000.

"The Emptiness of Hell." *Maclean's*, September 9, 1999. 35.

Ettinghausen, Richard. "Persian Ascension Miniatures of the Fourteenth Century." In *Islamic Art and Archaeology: Collected Papers*, ed. Myriam Rosen-Ayalon, 360–383. Berlin: Gebr. Mann Verlag, 1984.

Fahd, T. "Nar." In *Encyclopaedia of Islam*, online edition, ed. P. Bearman, T. Bianquis, C. E. Bosworth, E. van Donzel, and W. P. Heinrichs. Leiden: Brill, 2007

"Fantasy Island." *New York Times.* May 6, 2001.

Firestone, Reuven. *Jihad: The Origin of Holy War in Islam.* New York: Oxford University Press, 1999.

Flood, Finbarr Barry. *Great Mosque of Damascus: Studies on the Makings of an Umayyad Visual Culture.* Leiden: Brill, 2001

——. "Light in Stone. The Commemoration of the Prophet in Umayyad Architecture." In *Bayt al-Maqdis: Jerusalem and Early Islam*, ed. Jeremy Jones, 2:311–360. Oxford: Oxford University Press, 1999.

Fouchécour, C.–H de. *La description de la nature dans la poésie lyrique persane du Xie siècle.* Paris: 1969.

Gardet, L. "Djanna" and "Djahannam." In *Encyclopaedia of Islam*, online edition, ed. P. Bearman, T. Bianquis, C. E. Bosworth, E. van Donzel, and W. P. Heinrichs. Leiden: Brill, 2007.

Gardiner, Eileen, ed. *Visions of Heaven and Hell Before Dante.* New York: Italica Press, 1989.

Gibbs, Nancy. "Angels Among Us." *Time*, December 27, 1993.

Goldziher, Ignaz. *Muslim Studies.* Trans. C. R. Barber and S. M. Stern. 2 vols. London: George Allen and Unwin, 1966.

Goodman, Lenn. *Islamic Humanism.* Oxford: Oxford University Press, 2003.

Grabar, Oleg, and Said Nuseibeh, eds. *The Dome of the Rock.* New York: Rizzoli, 1996.

——. *The Formation of Islamic Art.* New Haven: Yale University Press, 1973.

——. "From Dome of Heaven to Pleasure Dome." *Journal of the Society of Architectural Historians* 49, no. 1 (March 1990): 17.

——. *The Mediation of Ornament.* Princeton: Princeton University Press, 1992.

——. *The Shape of the Holy: Early Islamic Jerusalem.* Princeton: Princeton University Press, 1996.

Haleem, Muhammad Abdel. *Understanding the Qur'an.* London: IB Tauris, 1999.

Halevi, Leor. *Muhammad's Grave: Death Rites and the Making of Islamic Society.* New York: Columbia University Press, 2007.

Hanaway, W. L., Jr. "Bag: in Persian Literature." In *Encyclopaedia Iranica*, ed. Ehsan Yarshater, 3:395–396. London: Routledge and Kegan Paul, 1989.

——. "Paradise on Earth." In *The Islamic Garden.* Ed. Elisabeth B. MacDougall and Richard Ettinghausen, 3–67. Washington, D.C.: Dumbarton Oaks, 1976.

Al-Haritani, D. Sulayman. *al-Mawaqif min al-khamra*. Damascus: Dar al-Husad lil-Nashr wa-l-Tawzi', 1996.

Hattox, Ralph. *Coffee and Coffeehouses: The Origins of a Social Beverage in the Medieval Near East*. Seattle: University of Washington Press, 1995.

Haase, C. P. "Sayhan." In *Encyclopaedia of Islam*, online edition, ed. P. Bearman, T. Bianquis, C. E. Bosworth, E. van Donzel, and W. P. Heinrichs. Leiden: Brill, 2007.

Haykal, Muhammad Husayn. *The Life of Muhammmad*. Trans. Ismail Ragi al-Faruqi. London: Shorouk, 1983.

Hawting, Gerald. *The Idea of Idolatry and the Rise of Islam: From Polemic to History*. New York: Cambridge University Press, 1999.

Himmelfarb, Martha. *Ascent to Heaven in Jewish and Christian Apocalypses*. New York: Oxford University Press, 1993.

——. *Tours of Hell: An Apocalyptic Form in Jewish and Christian Literature*. Philadelphia: University of Pennsylvania Press, 1983.

Hinds, Martin. "'Maghazi' and 'Sira' in Early Islamic Scholarship." In *Life of Muhammad*, ed. Uri Rubin, 1–10. Aldershot: Ashgate, 1988.

Hinz, W. "Dhira" and "Farsakh." In *Encyclopaedia of Islam*, online edition, ed. P. Bearman, T. Bianquis, C. E. Bosworth, E. van Donzel, and W. P. Heinrichs. Leiden: Brill, 2007.

Homerin, T. Emil. "Echoes of a Thirsty Owl: Death and Afterlife in Pre-Islamic Arabic Poetry." *Journal of Near Eastern Studies* 44, no. 3 (June 1985): 165–184.

Horovitz, Leslie Alan. "More Americans Than Ever Embrace the Hereafter Now." *Insight*, October 22, 1997.

Hughes, John. "Children at War." *Christian Science Monitor*, October 28, 1987.

Hunt, John Dixon. *Gardens and the Picturesque: Studies in the History of Landscape Architecture*. Cambridge, Mass.: MIT Press, 1992.

Ivanow, W. "An Ismaili Poem in Praise of Fidawis." *Journal of the Bombay Branch of the Royal Asiatic Society* 14 (1938): 66–72.

Izutsu, Toshihiko. *Ethico-Religious Concepts in the Qur'an*. Montreal: McGill University Press, 1966.

Jabbur, Jibrail S. *The Bedouins and the Desert: Aspects of Nomadic Life in the Arab East*. Ed. Suhayl J. Jabbur and Lawrence I. Conrad. Albany: State University of New York Press, 1995.

Jarrar, Maher. "Djinn," "Fire," and "Houris." In *Encyclopaedia of the Qur'an*, ed. Jane Dammen McAuliffe. Leiden: Brill, 2006.

——. "The Martyrdom of Passionate Lovers: Holy War as a Sacred Wedding." In *Myths, Historical Archetypes, and Symbolic Figures in Arabic Literature: Towards a New Hermeneutic Approach: Proceedings of the International Symposium in Beirut, June 25th–June 30th, 1996*, ed. Angelika Neuwirth et al., 88–107. Stuttgart: Franz Steiner Verlag, 1999.

——. *"Masari' al-'ushshaq": dirasa fi ahadith fadl al-jihad wa "al-hur al-'ain." al-Abhath*. Ed. Ramzi Baalbaki. Beirut: American University of Beirut, 1993.

Juynboll, G. H. A. "Muslim b. al-Hadjdjadj" and "al-Tirmidhi." In *Encyclopaedia of Islam*, online edition, ed. P. Bearman, T. Bianquis, C. E. Bosworth, E. van Donzel, and W.P. Heinrichs. Leiden: Brill, 2007.

Kazimirski, A. de Biberstein. *Dictionnaire Arabe-Français*. Beirut: Librarie de Liban, 1860.

Keenan, Brigid. *Damascus Hidden Treasures of the Old City*. New York: Thames & Hudson, 2000, 27.

Keene, M. "Djawhar." In *Encyclopaedia of Islam*, online edition, ed. P. Bearman, T. Bianquis, C. E. Bosworth, E. van Donzel, and W. P. Heinrichs. Leiden: Brill, 2007.

Kinberg, Leah. "Compromise of Commerce: A Study of Early Traditions Concerning Poverty and Wealth." *Der Islam* (1989): 193–212.

——. "Interaction Between This World and the Afterworld in Early Islamic Tradition." *Oriens* 29–30 (1996): 285–308.

——. "Paradise." In *Encyclopaedia of the Qur'an*, ed. Jane Dammen McAuliffe. Leiden: Brill, 2006.

Klinghoffer, David. "Hell, Yes; Even if You're Not Going to Hell, You Should Believe in It." *National Review*, November 11, 1998.

Koch, Ebba. *The Complete Taj Mahal and the Riverfront Gardens of Agra*. London: Thames & Hudson, 2006.

——. "The Mughal Waterfront Garden." In *Gardens in the Time of the Great Muslim Empires*, ed. Attilio Petruccioli, 140–159. Leiden: Brill, 1997.

Kubler, George. *The Shape of Time: Remarks on the History of Things*. New Haven: Yale University Press, 1962.

Kueny, Kathryn. *The Rhetoric of Sobriety: Wine in Early Islam*. Albany: State University of New York Press, 2001.

LaHaye, Tim F., and Jerry B. Jenkins. *Left Behind: A Novel of the Earth's Last Days*. Wheaton, Ill.: Tyndale, 1996.

Lammens, Henri. *Le berceau de l'Islam: L'arabie occidentale à la veille de l'hégire*. Rome: Pontifical Institute, 1914.

Lane, Edward William. *Arabic-English Lexicon*. 2 vols. Cambridge: Islamic Texts Society, 1984.

Le Goff, Jacques. *The Birth of Purgatory*. Trans. Arthur Goldhammer. Chicago: University of Chicago Press, 1984.

Lehmann, Karl. "The Dome of Heaven." In *Modern Perspectives in Western Art History: An Anthology of Twentieth Century Writings on the Visual Arts*, 227–270. Toronto: University of Toronto Press, 1989.

Lehrman, Jonas. *Earthly Paradise: Garden and Courtyard in Islam*. Berkeley: University of California Press, 1980.

Le Strange, G. *The Lands of the Eastern Caliphate: Mesopotamia, Persia, Central Asia from the Muslim Conquest to the Time of Timur*. New York: Barnes and Noble, 1905.

Lev, Yaacov, ed. *Towns and Material Culture in the Medieval Middle East*. Leiden: Brill, 2002.

Lings, Martin. *Muhammad: His Life Based on the Earliest Sources*. London: Islamic Texts Society, 1991.

MacDonald, D. B. "Djinn." In *Encyclopaedia of Islam*, online edition. Leiden: Brill, 2006.

——. *Religious Attitude and Life in Islam: Being the Haskell Lectures on Comparative Religion Delivered Before the University of Chicago in 1906*. Beirut: Khayats, 1965.

Maghen, Ze'ev. *Virtues of the Flesh: Passion and Purity in Early Islamic Jurisprudence*. Brill: Leiden, 2005.

Al-Mahami, Muhammad Kamil Hasan. *Al-Janna fi al-Qur'an al-Karim*. Beirut: al-Maktab al-'Ilmiyya al-Taba'at wa-l-nashar, 1988.

Mahmoud, Ibrahim. *Jugrafiya al-maladhdhat al-jins bi al-janna*. Beirut: Riyad al-Rayyis, 1998.

Masquelier, Adeline. *Prayer Has Spoiled Everything: Possession, Power, and Identity in an Islamic Town of Niger*. Durham, N.C.: Duke University Press, 2001.

McDannell, Colleen, and Bernhard Lang. *Heaven: A History*. New Haven: Yale University Press, 1988.

Meisami, Julie Scott. "Allegorical Gardens in the Persian Poetic Tradition: Nezami, Rumi, and Hafez." *International Journal of Middle Eastern Studies* 17 (1985): 229–260.

——. "Palaces and Paradises: Palace Descriptions in Medieval Persian Poetry." In *Islamic Art and Literature*, ed. Oleg Grabar and Cynthia Robinson, 21–54. Princeton: Markus Wiener, 2001.

Meri, Josef. M. *The Cult of Saints Among Muslims and Jews in Medieval Syria*. Oxford: Oxford University Press, 2002.

Mernissi, Fatima. *Women in Moslem Paradise*. New Delhi: Kali for Women, 1986.

Metlitzki, Dorothee. *The Matter of Araby in Medieval England*. New Haven: Yale University Press, 1977.

Miller, Anthony C., and Miranda Morris. *Plants of Dhofar, The Southern Region of Oman: Traditional, Economic, and Medicinal Uses*. Oman: Sultan of Oman, 1988.

Moaz, Khaled, and Solange Ory. *Inscriptions Arabes de Damas: Les Stèles Funéraires I, Cimetière d'al Bab al-Sagir*. Damascus: Institut Francais de Damas, 1977.

Monés, H. "'Isa b. Dinar." In *Encyclopaedia of Islam*, online edition, ed. P. Bearman, T. Bianquis, C. E. Bosworth, E. van Donzel, and W. P. Heinrichs. Leiden: Brill, 2007.

Moore, Charles, William J. Mitchell, and William Turnbull Jr. *The Poetics of Gardens*. Cambridge, Mass.: MIT Press, 1993.

Moosa, Ebrahim. *Ghazali and the Poetics of Imagination*. Chapel Hill: University of North Carolina Press, 2005.

Mort, John. *Christian Fiction: A Guide to the Genre*. Greenwood Village, Colo.: Libraries Unlimited, 2002.

Nasr, Seyyid Hossein. *Islamic Art and Spirituality*. Albany: State University of New York Press, 1987.

Newby, Gordon Darnell. *The Making of the Last Prophet: A Reconstruction of the Earliest Biography of Muhammad*. Columbia: University of South Carolina Press, 1989.

O'Shaughnessy, Thomas. *Muhammad's Thoughts on Death*. Leiden: Brill, 1969.

——. "The Seven Names for Hell in the Qur'an." *Bulletin of the School of Oriental and African Studies* 24 (1961): 444–469.

Pedersen, Johannes. "The Islamic Preacher: wa'iz, mudhakkir, qass." In *Ignace Goldziher Memorial Volume*, ed. S. Löwinger and J. Somogyi, 226–251. Budapest: n.p., 1948.

Petrosyan, Yuri A., et al. *Pages of Perfection: Islamic Paintings and Calligraphy from the Russian Academy of Sciences St Petersburg*. Lugano: Electa and ARCH Foundation, 1995.

Rabbat, Nasser. "The Dome of the Rock Revisited: Some Remarks on al-Wasiti's Accounts." *Muqarnas* 10 (1993): 67–75.

——. "The Meaning of the Umayyad Dome of the Rock." *Muqarnas* 6 (1989): 18.

Rehman, 'Abdul. "Garden Types in Mughal Lahore according to Early Seventeenth Century Written and Visual Sources." In *Gardens in the Time of the Great Muslim Empires*, ed. Attilio Petruccioli, 161–167. Leiden: Brill, 1997.

Rehman, Abdul, and Shama Anbrine. "Unity and Diversity of Mughal Garden Experiences." In *Middle East Garden Traditions: Unity and Diversity: Questions, Methods and Resources in a Multicultural Perspective*, ed. Michel Conan, 221–236. Cambridge, Mass.: Harvard University Press, 2007.

Reinhart, A. Kevin. "The Here and the Hereafter in Islamic Religious Thought." In *Images of Paradise in Islamic Art*, ed. Sheila S. Blair and Jonathan M. Bloom, 15–23. Austin: University of Texas Press, 1991.

Rippin, Andrew. "Literary Analysis of Qur'an, Tafsir, and Sira: The Methodologies of John Wansbrough." In *The Qur'an and Its Interpretive Tradition*. Aldershot: Ashgate, 2001.
——. "Quran 7.40 'Until the Camel Passes through the eye of the Needle.'" In *The Qur'an and its Interpretive Tradition*. Ashgate: Valorium, 2001.
Roberts, Allen F., and Mary Nooter Roberts. *A Saint in the City: Sufi Arts of Urban Senegal*. Los Angeles: UCLA Fowler Museum of Cultural History, 2003.
Robinson, Cynthia. "Seeing Paradise: Metaphor and Vision in Taifa Palace Architecture." *Gesta* 36, no. 2 (1988): 145–155.
Robson, J. "Abu Da'ud al-Sidjistani, Sulayman b. al-Ash'ath," "Al-Bukhari, Muhammad b. Isma'il," and "Hadith." In *Encyclopaedia of Islam*, online edition, ed. P. Bearman, T. Bianquis, C. E. Bosworth, E. van Donzel, and W. P. Heinrichs. Leiden: Brill, 2007.
Rodinson, Maxime. *Muhammad*. Trans. Anne Carter. New York: Pantheon, 1971.
Rosen-Ayalon, Myriam. *The Early Islamic Monuments of al-Haram al-Sharif: An Iconographic Study*. Jerusalem: Institute of Archaeology, 1989.
Rosenthal, Franz. "Reflections on Love in Paradise." In *Love and Death in the Ancient Near East: Essays in Honor of Marvin H. Pope*, ed. John H. Marks and Robert M. Good, 247–254. Gilford, Conn.: Four Quarters, 1987.
Rubin, Uri. "Abu Lahab on Sura CXI." *Bulletin of the School of Oriental and African Studies* 42 (1978): 13–28.
——, ed. *The Life of Muhammad*. New York: Routledge and Kegan Paul, 1998.
Ruggles, D. Fairchild. *Gardens, Landscape and Vision in the Palaces of Islamic Spain*. University Park: Pennsylvania State University Press, 2003.
Russell, Jeffrey Burton. *A History of Heaven: The Singing Silence*. Princeton: Princeton University Press, 1997.
Rustomji, Nerina. "American Visions of the Houri." *Muslim World* 97, no. 1 (January 2007): 79–92.
Said, Edward. *Orientalism*. New York: Pantheon, 1978.
Saleh, Soubhi el-. "Les délices et les tourments de l'au-delà dans le Coran." PhD dissertation, Sorbonne, 1954.
——. *La Vie Future Selon le Coran*. Paris: Vrin, 1971.
Schacht, Joseph. *The Origins of Muhammadan Jurisprudence*. Oxford: Oxford University Press, 1950.
Schimmel, Annemarie. *Deciphering the Signs of God: A Phenomenological Approach to Islam*. Albany: State University of New York Press, 1994.
——. *The Mystery of Numbers*. New York: Oxford University Press, 1993.
Schindler, Amy. "Angels and the AIDS Epidemic: The Resurgent Popularity of Angel Imagery in the United States of America." *Journal of American Culture* 22, no. 3 (1999): 49–62.
Sells, Michael. "Ascension." In *Encyclopaedia of the Qur'an*, ed. Jane Dammen McAuliffe. Leiden: Brill, 2006.
Schlumberger, Daniel. "Le Palais Ghaznévide de Lashkari Bazar." *Syria: Revue d'art Oriental et d'archéologie* 29 (1952): 251–270.
Sheler, Jeffrey L. "Heaven in the Age of Reason." *U.S. News and World Report*, March 31, 1997.
——. "Hell Hath No Fury." *U.S. News and World Report*, January 31, 2000.
Smith, Jane. "Concourse Between the Living and the Dead in Islamic Eschatological Literature." *History of Religions* 19 (1980): 224–236.
——. "Eschatology." In *Encyclopaedia of the Qur'an*, ed. Jane Dammen McAuliffe. Leiden: Brill, 2006.

———. "Introduction." In Abu Hamid Muhammad al-Tusi al-Ghazali, *Durra al-fakhira.* Trans. as *The Precious Pearl.* Trans. Jane Idelman Smith. Missoula: Scholar's Press, 1979.

Smith, Jane Idelman, and Yvonne Haddad. *Islamic Understanding of the Afterlife.* Albany: State University of New York Press, 1981.

———. "Women in the Afterlife: The Islamic View as Seen from the Qur'an and Tradition." *Journal of the American Academy of Religion* 43 (1975): 39–50.

Soucek, Priscilla. "The Temple of Solomon in Islamic Legend and Art." In *Temple of Solomon: Archaeological Fact and Medieval Tradition in Christian, Islamic, and Jewish Art,* ed. Joseph Gutmann, 73–123. Missoula: Scholar's Press, 1976.

Spellberg, D. A. *Politics, Gender, and the Islamic Past: The Legacy of 'A'isha bint Abi Bakr.* New York: Columbia University Press, 1994.

Steensgaard, N. "Harir" and "Khamr." In *Encyclopaedia of Islam,* online edition, ed. P. Bearman, T. Bianquis, C. E. Bosworth, E. van Donzel, and W. P. Heinrichs. Leiden: Brill, 2007.

———. *Muhammad and the Golden Bough: Reconstructing Arabian Myth.* Bloomington: Indiana University Press, 1996.

Stetkevych, Suzanne Pinckney. "Intoxication and Immortality: Wine and Associated Imagery in al-Ma'arri's Garden." In *Homoeroticism in Classical Arabic Literature,* ed. J. W. Wright and Everett Rowson, 210–232. New York: Columbia University Press, 1997.

Stowasser, Barbara Freyer. "The End Is Near: Minor and Major Signs of the Hour in Islamic Texts and Contexts." Working Paper, Yale Center for International and Area Studies.

Swartz, Merlin. "Introduction." In Ibn al-Jawzi, *Kitab al-qussas wa-l mudhakkirin,* ed. and trans. Merlin Swartz, 13–92. Beirut: Dar El-Mashreq, 1986.

Tabbaa, Yasser. "The Medieval Islamic Garden: Typology and Hydraulics." In *Garden History: Issues, Approaches, Methods: Dumbarton Oaks Colloquium on the History of Landscape Architecture,* ed. John Dixon Hunt, 13:303–329. Washington, D.C.: Dumbarton Oaks Research Library and Collection, 1992.

———. "Towards an Interpretation of the Use of Water in Islamic Courtyards and Courtyard Gardens." *Journal of Garden History* 7, no. 3 (1987): 197–220.

Tamari, Shmuel. *Iconotextual Studies in the Muslim Vision of Paradise.* Wiesbaden: Harrassowitz, 1999.

Taylor, Christopher D. *In the Vicinity of the Righteous: Ziyara and the Veneration of Muslim Saints in Late Medieval Egypt.* Leiden: Brill, 1999.

Toelle, Heidi. *Le Coran Revisité: Le Feu, L'Eau, L'Air, et La Terre.* Damascus: Institut Français de Damas, 1999.

Tolan, John Victor. *Saracens: Islam in the Medieval European Imagination.* New York: Columbia University Press, 2002.

van Ess, Josef. "'Abd al-Malik and Dome of the Rock." In *Bayt al-Maqdis: Jerusalem and Early Islam,* ed. Jeremy Jones, 1:89–103. Oxford: Oxford University Press, 1999.

van Gelder, Geert Jan. *God's Banquet: Food in Classical Arabic Literature.* New York: Columbia University Press, 2000.

Waines, David. "Abu Zayd al-Balkhi on the Nature of Forbidden Drink: A Medieval Islamic Controversy." In *Patterns of Everyday Life,* ed. David Waines, 329–344. Aldershot: Ashgate, 2002.

Wallace, James, et al. "Iran-Iraq War: New Horrors in a Long-Running Horror Show." *U.S. News and World Report,* April 4, 1988.

Wansbrough, John. *Qur'anic Studies: Sources and Methods of Scriptural Interpretation.* London: Oxford University Press, 1977.

———. *The Sectarian Milieu: Content and Composition of Islamic Salvation History.* London: Oxford University Press, 1978.

Watson, Andrew M. *Agricultural Innovation in the Early Islamic World.* Cambridge: Cambridge University Press, 1993.

Watt, W. Montgomery. "Abu Lahab" and "Iram." In *Encyclopaedia of Islam,* online edition, ed. P. Bearman, T. Bianquis, C. E. Bosworth, E. van Donzel, and W. P. Heinrichs. Leiden: Brill, 2007.

———. *Muhammad: Prophet and Statesman.* London: Oxford University Press, 1974.

———. *Muhammad at Mecca.* Oxford: Clarendon, 1953.

———. *Muhammad at Medina.* New York: Oxford University Press, 1981.

———. *Muhammad's Mecca: History in the Qur'an.* Edinburgh: Edinburgh University Press, 1988.

Wendell, Charles. "The Denizens of Paradise." In *Humaniora Islamica,* ed. Herbert W. Mason et al., 2:29–59. The Hague: Mouton, 1974.

Wensinck, A. J., and C. Pellat. "Hur," "Khamr," "Mi'radj," and "al-Nasa'i." In *Encyclopaedia of Islam,* online edition, ed. P. Bearman, T. Bianquis, C. E. Bosworth, E. van Donzel, and W. P. Heinrichs. Leiden: Brill, 2007.

Widengren, G. *Muhammad, The Apostle of God, and His Ascension.* Uppsala: Almqvist and Wiksells, 1955.

Yazigi, Maya. "Hadith al-'ashara, or the Political Uses of a Tradition." *Studia Islamica* 86 (1977): 159–167.

Zaki, Mona M. "Barzakh." In *Encyclopaedia of the Qur'an,* ed. Jane Dammen McAuliffe. Leiden: Brill, 2006.

Zaleski, Carol. *Otherworldly Journeys: Accounts of Near-Death Experience in Medieval and Modern Times.* New York: Oxford University Press, 1987.

Zaleski, Carol, and Philip Zaleski, eds. *The Book of Heaven: An Anthology of Writings from Ancient to Modern Times.* Oxford: Oxford University Press, 2000.

INDEX

Al-, el-, and other initial articles in all languages are ignored in alphabetization. Figures are indicated by "f" following page number.

LaVergne, TN USA
11 August 2010
192931LV00001B/3/P